TWAYNE'S WORLD AUTHORS SERIES
A Survey of the World's Literature

AUSTRALIA

Joseph Jones, University of Texas

EDITOR

Frank Dalby Davison

TWAS 514

Frank Dalby Davison

FRANK DALBY DAVISON

By LOUISE E. RORABACHER

TWAYNE PUBLISHERS
A DIVISION OF G. K. HALL & CO., BOSTON

(Street)
PR9619
.3
.D35Z8

Library of Congress Cataloging in Publication Data

Rorabacher, Louise Elizabeth, 1906 -
Frank Dalby Davison.

(Twayne's world authors series ; TWAS 514 : Australia)
Bibliography: p. 210 - 15
Includes index.
1.   Davison, Frank Dalby, 1893 - 1970—Criticism and
interpretation.
PR9619.3.D35Z8   823   78-15794
ISBN 0-8057-6355-4

To Mrs. Paula Fanning,
Chief Librarian, Australian Studies,
National Library, Canberra,
with admiration and gratitude

Contents

About the Author

Since Dr. Louise E. Rorabacher first reached Australia as a tourist in 1959, she has returned a number of times for periods of travel and research, particularly since her early retirement from her position as a professor of English, first from Purdue University, later from Western Carolina University.

Her interest in Australian literature has resulted in three previous books. Two of these are anthologies of Australian short stories that she edited for F. W. Cheshire in Melbourne: *Two Ways Meet* (1963), stories of the immigrant influx following World War II, a book still widely used in Australian schools; and *Aliens in Their Land* (1966), stories of the aborigines and their growing problems. Also, previous to this study of Frank Dalby Davison, she wrote one about two of his close friends in Sydney, Marjorie Barnard and Flora Eldershaw (*Marjorie Barnard and M. Barnard Eldershaw*, Twayne, 1973).

She has held several postwar educational assignments in the Far East: Korea with the Fifth Army Air Force at Kimpo; Taiwan with the Purdue Team at Cheng Kung University; and Japan, first with the Eighth Army in Yokohama, later as a Fulbright Lecturer at Tokyo Women's University. She also served on the staff of the Washington, D.C., headquarters of the American Association of University Professors. Her several college textbooks on writing have gone into numerous editions.

Preface

The writing career of Australia's Frank Dalby Davison, who lived from 1893 to 1970, falls into two parts. The first covers some fifteen years, extending from his sudden appearance on the literary scene in 1931 through his first eight published books, the last of which appeared in 1946. Had this present study been made in the middle of the century, it would have recorded his success as a writer of novels and short stories, mostly of Australia's back country, fiction that accurately and sensitively portrayed the lives of animals and men alike. These books are mostly small in size, but several of them are acknowledged Australian classics.

Frank lived on for another quarter of a century, however, most of which he spent developing the last thing his earlier readers would have expected of him—an enormous novel of urban life consisting of an in-depth study of a single aspect of that life, sex. This book, *The White Thorntree*, and the necessity of bringing it to terms with his earlier work will certainly occupy—even preoccupy—the minds of his serious readers for a long time to come. The present volume is only one of the attempts, large and small, sure to be forthcoming.

A writer's work cannot be fully understood without some knowledge of his life. Frank left no autobiography save for a brief unfinished manuscript concerning his later years, but fortunately for scholars, an abundance of personal information about him may be found in several sources. One is his long correspondence with fellow-writers Vance and Nettie Palmer, well over a hundred letters which, dating from 1932 to 1964, cover almost the whole of his life as a serious writer. Another source is a group of three long, analytical letters he wrote in 1942 in generous response to D. C. Meacham, a University of Melbourne student who had written him for information about his life and work to be used in a thesis toward a B.A. degree.

Other sources date from the 1960s, two of them being interviews with him at his home, Folding Hills, near Arthur's Creek, Victoria, in 1967. One was conducted by John Barnes in February for an Australian Broadcasting Commission schools' program in Western

Australia; extracts from a transcript of this appeared, with pictures of Frank, his wife Marie, and their farm, in the quarterly *Westerly* later in the year. The other, a longer interview, was conducted by Owen Webster during two days in March, also for A.B.C.; an archival transcript of the resulting tapes is now available in the library of the University of Melbourne. A more formal source is an address made by Frank in November, 1968, at a dinner at Union House, University of Melbourne, on the occasion of the first and private publication of *The White Thorntree;* this was printed in the quarterly *Southerly* the following year as the fifth of its Australian Writers in Profile series. Finally there is in the hands of Marie Davison an invaluable typescript of material that Frank wrote and dictated during 1968-1970, which was to have become a book entitled "The Folding Hills," had Frank lived to complete it. I have gratefully made use of them all.

Acknowledgments

I am obligated both to Australia and to Australians innumerable for insights and materials and for other assistance in preparing this book on a dedicated native son, especially to the gracious staffs and invaluable resources of three great libraries: the Mitchell Library in Sydney for general information; the library of the University of Melbourne for the use of letters from Frank Dalby Davison to D. C. Meacham and of the archival transcripts of Owen Webster's two-day interview with the author for the Australian Broadcasting Commission; and to the National Library in Canberra, which holds both Frank's and Marjorie Barnard's many letters to Vance and Nettie Palmer and, of special importance to the early part of this study, the copies of Fred Davison's periodicals, donated by Frank and bearing his notations, as well as his father's, as to the authorship of individual pieces. But I am most deeply indebted to Marie Davison for permission to use her husband's writings, both published and unpublished, and for the opportunity to spend a couple of days in their rural home in Victoria, Folding Hills, and absorb a little of its spirit.

Chronology

1893	Frank Dalby Davison born in Glenferrie, Victoria, on June 23, and named Frederick Douglas, Junior.
1897	His printer father, Fred, becomes the first editor of *The Advance Australia* in Melbourne for two years.
1899	Frank goes to school at Jolimont, later at Caulfield State School, for six years.
1905	Leaves school to work on rural properties in Victoria for three years.
1908	Goes with his family to the United States, becomes an apprentice printer, and distributes his first literary work.
1913	Goes to New York, works on a farm upstate, and makes three trips to the Caribbean as printer on a passenger-cargo ship.
1914	Sails from Halifax to Liverpool with a shipload of horses, joins the British cavalry, and sees extensive action throughout the war with it and later with the infantry.
1915	Marries English Kay Ede at Aldershot.
1918	Daughter Doris born.
1919	Demobilized, returns with his family to Australia, where they spend four years in a soldier settlement in Queensland.
1920	Contributes verses and prose to his father's *Australian Post*.
1922	Son Peter born.
1923	Takes his family back to Sydney; works for two years as advertising manager and contributor for father's publication, *Australia;* later works with him in real estate.
1929	Depression wipes out real estate business; Frank and his brother peddle books door to door.
1931	Rewrites some of his *Australia* material into two novels, *Man-Shy* and *Forever Morning*, published by the family firm.
1932	*Man-Shy* awarded the Australian Literary Society's gold medal for the best novel of 1931. Meets Vance and Nettie Palmer.

1933   *The Wells of Beersheba* published. From now on uses the name "Frank Dalby" Davison.

1934   Meets Marjorie Barnard. Begins to write short stories regularly. Makes camping trip through northeastern ustralia with Dr. Brooke Nicholls and his wife.

1935   *Blue Coast Caravan* published.

1936   *Caribbean Interlude* and *The Children of the Dark People* published. Begins three years of critical writing for the Red Page of the Sydney *Bulletin*. President of the Fellowship of Australian Writers for two years.

1938   Is made M.B.E. for contributions to literature. Publishes polemic pamphlet *While Freedom Lives*.

1939   On a fellowship from the Commonwealth Literary Fund, collects a volume of his short stories.

1940   *The Woman at the Mill* published.

1941   Works as a clerk at the Mascot Plant, Commonwealth Aircraft Corporation, later with the Department of Labour and National Service.

1942   Frank and Kay separate. Father dies.

1944   Edits short story anthology *Coast to Coast 1943*. Marriage dissolved. Marries Edna Marie McNab of Sydney; they move to Melbourne.

1946   *Dusty* appears, winning the *Argus* prize of £500.

1949   Gradually moves to a farm, Folding Hills; gives up government job.

1950   Writes daily feature "Bush Diary" for the *Argus* for several months. Farming and working on his huge final novel.

1964   Publishes second collection of short stories, *The Road to Yesterday*, including a reprint of *The Wells of Beersheba*.

1968   *The White Thorntree* privately published in Melbourne.

1970   *Thorntree* republished, commercially, in Sydney, in two large volumes, appearing in April and October. Dies on May 24, a month short of seventy-seven. Ashes scattered at Folding Hills.

CHAPTER 1

Background

I *Father*

F RANK Dalby Davison was born on June 23, 1893, and died
on May 24, 1970, after a life span of over three quarters of a
century. During this period Australian literature rose from obscurity
and neglect to a firm and recognized place in the culture of its nation and beyond. Davison was one of its guides, as important,
perhaps, for his influence as for his own writing, much of which is in
itself notable.

One of Australia's prominent journals has long carried the slogan
"Temper democratic, bias Australian." This might well have been
Frank's. He was an Australian by birth, as were his parents before
him. His father, Frederick (better known as Fred), like most of his
compatriots in the nineteenth century, was of English ancestry; his
mother, Amelia (née Watterson), was of Manx descent. The boy,
oldest of a family of four, was named Frederick Douglas, Junior, but
in the midst of his first great success as a writer, he took instead the
names Frank Dalby, by which he has ever since been known.

Frank's father is customarily dismissed as having been "a
Melbourne printer" at the time of his first child's birth, but to understand something of the son's energy and ambition, his ability
and its direction, we need to look more attentively at the father.
Fred Davison was a printer, true, but he was also, at intervals
throughout his own life, a publisher, an editor, an inventor, a
soldier, an author (of both fiction and nonfiction), and an ardent
proponent of causes.

Frank was four years old when his father became the first
proprietor (serving as both business manager and editor) of a small
Melbourne-based monthly called *The Advance Australia*. This was
the voice of an organization that had begun a quarter of a century
earlier as the "Victorian Natives' Association," a society for mutual

15

benefit (in sickness and death) and for mutual improvement (in moral, social, and intellectual matters). To indicate a broadened aim and constituency, the name was shortly changed to the "Australian Natives' Association" ("the members of which it may be mentioned for the benefit of readers outside Australia, were not black-skinned"[1]). This group had had early literary leanings, and as the result of a competition held in connection with its National Fete, published in 1893 an anthology of prize poems, essays, and even a novelette—this, in the year of Frank's birth. The organization had grown more and more politically minded in the turmoil of the late 1880s, and became a strong force in the encouragement of federation for the scattered Australian colonies, an end finally achieved with the formation of the Commonwealth in 1901. Frank was then an impressionable eight-year-old.

Although the interests of the A.N.A. became increasingly national, its strength remained in Victoria, and its house organ, *The Advance Australia*, in Melbourne, the capital city to which Victorian Fred Davison had come as a youth. It is easy to understand what attracted the A.N.A. to this able and literate young printer, and what appealed to him about the job, which gave him early experience of both causes and letters. It was he who got out the first issue of *The Advance Australia*, a monthly, on January 26, 1897, and who saw it through more than two years—critical years in the fight for federation.

While much of the little paper's space was necessarily devoted to routine reports of the many A.N.A. branches, the young editor had a chance to dabble in a wide variety of material. In that first issue, an editorial by "Ourselves" (later, in one of Fred's own magazines, *Australia*, it was to be "Himself") proposed that the publication be a national newspaper with no specific geographical or political or economic lines but devoted to the advancement of all that would tend to promote the welfare of Australia as a whole. Happily, that included fostering the growth of an Australian literature, although that aim did not have much popular support in the 1890s outside of Sydney's recently founded *Bulletin*. "Australian literature has not yet become Australian; it is still in its youthful and imitative stage,"[2] Fred Davison announced—a theme that his elder son was to continue to echo through several decades. For his part, the father promised to print "original tales, essays, poems etc.," and the A.N.A. offered two £50 prizes for the best essays submitted, one of which was to be an "Essay upon Australian Literature"—this, a whole quarter of a century before Nettie Palmer's prize-winning Lothian essay on the subject. A larger amount was being offered as a cycle prize, it was conceded (in a tone that came naturally to the Davisons, father and son), but "the 'bike' is booming, and brains never have boomed very much."[3] When a month later an editorial offered further small prizes for two-thousand-word short stories, it specified that their subjects be "distinctly Australian," and the poetry column hopefully asked for contributions "from Australians by preference."

The chief literary star in *The Advance Australia's* crown appeared, like numerous other contributors, under a pseudonym. "Ulimoroa" signified scholar and poet Bernard O'Dowd, whose passionate interest in the "Young Democracy" made him a valuable addition to the magazine as well as a valuable literary acquaintance of its young editor. O'Dowd's frequent columns dealt with a wide variety of subjects, from politics to poetry, one of them on a pair as diverse as Persia's poet Omar Khayyam and Australia's historic Eureka Stockade. For the most part, however, his concern was with the arts. His first contribution, in the initial issue, dealt with "An Unfashionable Poet," Francis Adams. So did the editor, for in that first poetry column, Davison's request for contributions set the tone with this stanza from a highly patriotic poem by Adams, who had himself been in his short life (as O'Dowd was to be in his long one) a strong supporter of Australian democracy:

> Fling out the flag and let friend or foe
> Behold, for gain or loss,
> The sign of our faith and the fight we fight—
> The stars of the Southern Cross.[4]

That this remained a measure of Davison's patriotism and literary taste alike is indicated by his using it regularly, in Sydney a quarter-century later, to head the editorial column of one of his later and greater publishing ventures, the monthly magazine *Australia*, in which he was assisted by his son Frank.

The Advance Australia appears to have prospered, for it could soon boast that contributors from all over the continent were appearing in its pages. Besides strictly A.N.A. business matters, it carried more and more material written specifically for it: more poetry, more short stories, more book reviews, more articles on literature. But although it survived into 1910, the April 7, 1899, number carried the announcement that "with this issue, the original proprietor and editor, Fred. Davison, concludes his connection with it . . . having launched and successfully conducted it for two years."[5] Why he left is not mentioned. Perhaps because he wearied of the routine—he was not one to stick to the same thing for long. Perhaps because the initial excitement was over—although federation was still a couple of years away, its advent was now assured. The A.N.A. had done its share toward the project throughout the preceding quarter of a century, and its conference in Bendigo in 1898 had voted to support the Draft Federal Constitution adopted by the Federal Convention of States. Fred Davidson, dark and mustached, appears in a group picture of this decisive gathering. The important consideration for us, however, is that he emerged from *The Advance Australia* with a considerable political and literary experience that was to be reflected in various enterprises later, some of which were to affect the future of his eldest son, at this time just attaining school age.

II *Childhood*

In his later years Frank was to remember his childhood as a happy one. His father believed in "Liberty Hall" for his children (a rare idea in that period, surely) as long as they didn't hurt others; he even proved sympathetic rather than minatory when he once had to reclaim his ten-year-old son from the police who had taken into custody Frank and two companions (obvious and well-equipped runaways) to await their fathers' arrivals. The four Davison children (Frank had a brother, Douglas, and two sisters, Dulcie and Doris, all younger) were born in the family home on Glenferrie Road, from which Frank went for a while to Jolimont School; after the family moved to Elsternick, he attended Caulfield State School. He later remembered his schooling as having been enjoyable, on the whole, but by what would seem to be a great misfortune for a promising boy, it ended as soon as he reached the "leaving age" of twelve. His sixth-class teacher, as short of temper as he was tall of form, was strong on caning, and the boy rebelled sharply at encountering punishment such as he had never known.

This early departure is understandable on Frank's part as one comes to know his independent nature, but it is difficult to comprehend how a literate, even literary, urban father, and a mother who was a book lover too, could permit a likely son to end all formal

education at such an early age. Frank's explanation, years later, was
that "this took place at the juncture in my father's life when he was
a bit mixed up too."[6] Frank also admitted to having sometimes
wondered what would have been his destiny had he had a formal
education instead of having to train himself by reading, study, and
association with educated people. He wisely recognized that this
alternative would have meant the exchange of the identity he knew
for that of a different man. He might have added, however, that it
would probably have shortened his long, painful years of apprenticeship to his trade.

At twelve the boy would not have appeared to be a very likely
candidate for a writing career. But already, in his brief schooling as
well as at home, he had encountered important shaping influences.
As a child he had been precocious enough to be ·disturbed by the
fact that the "Old Royal Reader" of his school days was definitely
"bias British," not only printed in England but wholly English in
content. Surely the life around him, he felt (and here one clearly
discerns the influence of his father's strongly patriotic bent), should
be written about too.

Others were beginning to share this feeling, early in the century
that had opened with the formation of the Australian Commonwealth. The Education Department in Victoria began to issue
for school use a sixteen-page monthly devoted to the Australian
scene. Frank paid his penny and consumed the publication on the
spot, devouring everything from an account of growing maize in
Gippsland to poetry by the nation's early greats, Adam Lindsay
Gordon and Henry Kendall. He was later to recall the appearance
of Kendall's "The Song of the Shingle Splitters," which led to
"three or four of us lads chanting it together as we marched home
from school with our bags on our backs."[7] The little monthly, he
always felt, had been a great service to all Australian children and a
particular stimulus to him because it "supported me in my idea that
you look at the life around you and write about that."[8] All his life he
looked and wrote. The "life around him" was later to include areas
far from his homeland, but of them he wrote relatively little, and he
always saw them through Australian eyes. As a child he had been
busy storing in his memory the sights and sounds, the animals, people, and ways of life of his own country which would be drawn on
for his later writing.

For three years after he left school, Frank worked in the Victorian
bush, happy enough in this sudden shift from town boy to country

man. At first he went to the Kingslake region (not far from where he would live during his last quarter-century) to a piece of land belonging to his enterprising father, still a Melbourne printer. With a great-uncle who had recently returned from making—and losing—money in America, the boy set out to subdue the bush, his father coming out from the nearby city on weekends to join in their labors. But the soil proved to be poor, and the great-uncle, wearying of the job, went to live more comfortably with a sister in Sydney. Fred Davison subsequently gave up the land, getting Frank a job as a "wood and water" boy on a developed farm in the picturesque mountains north of Bairnsdale. Here the boy also got his hand in at some bigger jobs such as gardening, stock-riding, pig-killing, meat-curing. Thus he not only developed a variety of agricultural skills that were to serve him well in his maturity but also got the material for one of his last, longest, and best short stories, "The Road to Yesterday."

III   The Years Abroad

During these three impressionable years of his early teens, Frank saw little of his Melbourne-based family. But in 1908 (the boy was now fifteen) Fred Davison dreamed a new dream, one that required uprooting the entire family and replanting them in the United States. Frank was to say in later years, not altogether facetiously, that his father went to America as an inventor but found they already had plenty there. At least Fred's hopes of a fortune from patents failed, and he went back to his former work, printing, first in St. Louis, then Chicago. His son Frank, fresh from rural Australia, was apprenticed to his father's trade.

More important, it was in the United States that Frank first set-tled down seriously, while still in his teens, to teach himself the more difficult trade of writing. He had always been a voracious reader, encouraged by his mother (except when she found him settl-ing down to a book before breakfast). In addition, he later reflected, "I think I had some innate feeling for prose,"[9] and with it a driving desire that led him this early to spend a whole evening trying to get a single paragraph just right. It was in Chicago that he wrote a set of narrative verses that he himself printed and distributed among a group of Australians there—his first literary work set before his first reading public. The subject was, quite properly, drawn from his ex-perience of the Australian bush, and the material was to be incorporated long after into one of his finest novels, *Dusty*. This is an early example of what was to become a habit of his—finding more than one use for a piece of his creative writing.

His printer's apprenticeship completed, Frank was once more to be separated from his family, this time (to use that peculiar English idiom in both its senses) "for good." The rest of the Davisons ultimately left Chicago for California, from which in 1917, after an absence of some nine years, they went back to Australia and settled in Sydney. As for Frank, now armed with a trade and man's estate (he was twenty), he went to New York to seek his fortune but found only unemployment. With nothing to hold him in the city and with a young man's natural eagerness to see more of the country, he soon set out through upstate New York, hobnobbing with hobos and sleeping in haystacks. In Albany he was picked up, with others, for riding the rails, which earned him the new experience of ten days in jail. There he "studied at close quarters some of the most depraved specimens of humanity I have ever encountered," until "freedom was like Paradise regained."[10] It has been suggested that his jail mates then may have supplied some of the material for the study of sex deviants in his last novel, *The White Thorntree*, a half century later; if so, it appears, strangely, to be the only literary use he made of his several impressionable years in the United States.

Luckily for him at the time, richer pastures lay just ahead. Going "back to the land," he helped a Dutch farmer with his haying long enough to earn the money to return to New York City not only within the law but in some luxury as a paying passenger on a Hudson River packet. On his arrival he redeemed the suitcase that his former landlord had been holding for back rent. Then he knocked around the waterfront until he found a job on a tourist-and-freight ship bound for the West Indies and beyond. He once remarked that he had tried personal service and did not like it—not to be wondered at, with his passion for independence. But his newly acquired trade spared him any obsequious drudgery, as he was taken on as ship's printer (menus and such). His three subsequent voyages lingered in his memory and his diary to emerge at book length nearly two decades later as *Caribbean Interlude*.

What direction Frank's life might have taken, what destinations arrived at, had he been left to chart its course in normal times, remain conjecture. But in 1914, Europe was ignited by war. At first Frank did not plan to enlist, but soon, along with other young men of British origins, compulsion overcame reluctance. After a last

Caribbean trip (one that he remembered later for the fear engendered at night by a darkened ship), he decided to join up. "I was a Kiplingesque romantic,"[11] he later remarked of this period, but as a realist, too, he saw little possibility of getting back to Australia to be with his own countrymen. British officials in New York were not allowed to accept recruits, but they sent Frank and a number of other prospective fighting men to Halifax, Nova Scotia, ostensibly as escorts for a load of several hundred horses en route to Liverpool. On that journey Frank's boyhood experience in Victoria paid off. "I think I was the only man on board," he recalled later, "who knew which end of a horse you put the feed in."[12] This modest beginning landed him in the British cavalry for his first military service, an experience that contributed later to his remarkable little volume *The Wells of Beersheba*.

Other than that small book and the short story "Fathers and Sons," written of World War I from the vantage of World War II, scarcely a hint of battle appears in his later writing, although Davison endured the whole course. He saw extensive service in those next four years: first, mounted action with the cavalry at the Somme and at Arras; later, trench warfare when the cavalry was dismounted to relieve the infantry. He was not at all averse in later years to reminding people that he had been in the service, but he never laid claim to any heroic actions, turning off all inquiries with a joke. An enlisted man, he attained a corporal's stripes ("for saluting under shellfire,"[13] he would explain facetiously). Later he was sent to train for a commission, but attained the rank of lieutenant only as the war ended.

In the meantime, Frank had achieved another distinction that he did not hesitate to boast of later: of the many troopers stationed at Aldershot early in the war, he was one of the few to win a wife! His marriage to Kay Ede in 1915 endured for almost thirty years, providing him with his only children, a daughter Doris and a son Peter. Also while he was in the service Frank met his father again, in Europe. Although past fifty, Fred Davison was not a man to miss out on 'new experiences, especially those that would promote Australia. Restless in Sydney after his return from America in 1917, he dyed his hair and persuaded the A.I.F. (Australian Imperial Force) to accept him for military duty. But he did not reach Europe until almost the end of the fighting and was back in Australia long before the British had mustered out his son.

Neither his early years in America nor his English marriage seem to have given Frank any thought for the future other than returning to the land of his birth. This consummation was delayed until 1919, however, for he was among the newly commissioned sent to relieve in peace those who had been involved most steadily in war. Frank drew a stint in Belgium from which he was demobilized a year after the war ended. Then came the trip to Australia on a military vessel, accompanied by his young English wife and the daughter born the previous year. Home again at twenty-six, Frank had been away eleven years.

CHAPTER 2

Queensland

E VEN before Frank and his family embarked for his homeland, he had pretty well made up his mind about the future.
From Australia House in London's Strand he had picked up information about the Queensland properties being offered in blocks for
settlement by returned servicemen. Later he was to call this
"government propaganda," but at the time it intrigued him. Shortly after they had disembarked he left his wife and child with his
family in Sydney and, with his brother Douglas, went up to
Queensland to look things over. For Douglas, a look was apparently
enough, but Frank was more favorably impressed. He could have
had eighty acres in the far north, in the area of the coastal town of
Cairns, but as space appealed to him in his youthful vigor, he went
from Brisbane some three hundred miles inland into southern
Queensland. In the Maranoa district there, he finally chose a couple
of square miles (more than twelve hundred acres) of what was
known as "open forest" country in the general vicinity of Roma (not
the "Wilgatown" of most of his later short stories, Frank said, but
admittedly the same sort of place). Within six weeks he had completed an extensive hut of the bark and galvanized iron customary
in the area, and was shortly joined by Kay and little Doris.

I *The* Australian Post

The nearest we have to a sustained factual account of choosing
and moving onto a "selection" (a chosen piece of available land) is
to be found in a series of articles that Frank sent down from
Queensland to his father's latest publishing venture, the *Australian
Post*. This is worth a close look by anyone interested in the Davison
contribution to Australian letters. The *Post* was no organizational
outlet such as Fred had managed for the A.N.A. in Melbourne more
than twenty years earlier, but a private undertaking obviously in-

24

spired by his years in the United States, for the *Australian Post*, "An Illustrated Magazine of Fact & Fiction," bore more than a casual resemblance to America's popular *Saturday Evening Post*, in title, size, and appearance, even to the shaded lettering of the headings (although Fred's was achieved with dots instead of diagonals). It was not a weekly, however, but a monthly.

The cover of the new journal was of a piece with Fred's earlier somewhat jingoistic publishing, bearing the slogan "Australia First." The first issue (September 1, 1920) opened with many of the same declarations of objective that were to appear in its more important successor, the *Australian*, three years later. The *Post* was a family affair, written mostly by Fred Davison himself (who in Australia was better qualified to do an article on "Americans at Home"?), with a story by daughter Dulcie (her start on a journalistic career) and a poem by "Fred Davison Junr.," who had not yet emerged from his father's shadow, by his own later choice, as Frank Dalby Davison. From him, too, is the issue's only letter, "from a man who is fighting to get established on the land out somewhere near where the Australian sun sets." Signed "Bush Settler," it contained a statement interesting as a returned soldier's viewpoint on the homeland that he had left as a boy: "If Australians would drop politics they would make more money. Make our motto: 'Business First' and we will all be more prosperous." The maturer man would some day repudiate this sentiment; but there was no argument, only despair mixed with fortitude, in the postscript: "I can see the bottom of my tank, and water is giving out everywhere, but I guess we will manage somehow."[1] This statement dates from Frank's beginnings on the land, but in content and spirit it continued to be true of all too much of his settlement experience.

The *Australian Post* remained a family affair throughout its short life (six monthly issues, September 1, 1920, to February 7, 1921). Father Fred continued to supply the editorials, most of the articles, some of the stories (one, under the pen name "Holt Gibbons," he later developed into his novel *Duck Williams and His Cobbers*, 1939). Daughter Dulcie wrote stories and articles under her own name and as "Janet Farghar." And even Mother Davison, as "Eunice Moore," contributed articles such as "The Home of My Dreams" and "The Gospel of Fun," as well as helping Dulcie with a later department, "For Australian Women." Frank (whose first contributions to literature had been those narrative verses written and printed back in Chicago) continued to contribute long poems under his given name, Fred Junr., and short ones under the pseudonyms "John Sandes" and "T. Bone." Frank's verse is worth examining as a stage in his development as a writer, although these examples appear to be among his last published efforts. The first is by "John Sandes":

My Sweetheart

No lass with mine can well compare,
None half so dear, none half so fair.
She has two merry dark brown eyes,
Full innocent, yet quaintly wise;
In her soft cheeks wild roses blow;
The sweetness of her lips, I know.
Her dimpled smile, her spun-gold hair,
Earth has no fairer things I swear;
Nor sweeter bliss holds heav'n above
Than when she says to me "I love."
But if by this you have been led
To think we two shall some day wed,
Then I'm afraid that you've been had—
She's two years old, and I'm her dad.[2]

No one, not even the author, would try to call this poetry, but the *Australian Post* has no literary pretensions. Another piece, published a little later, was typical of Frank's work in its concentration on description (usually of nature) and a little more venturesome in its metrics. It is signed "T. Bone."

My Camp

I've built my camp on a low hilltop,
Where the sandalwood and native hop
    And the purple lupines grow;
Where brigalows wave aloft their plumes
Where the air drifts sweet from wild bush blooms,
    And the blue bells nod and blow.
Afar I can see the low range lie
A dark blue smudge on a turquoise sky
    And the green vale down below.[3]

In these and others of his verses one finds traces of the very un-Australian affectations that Frank was to speak out strongly against later: poetic contractions like "heav'n," "o'er," "afar," and "'neath," and here, the use of the English "vale" to describe the view from an Australian outback camp. If his poems are such as neither writer nor reader wished later to recall, however, the discipline of experimenting with rhythm and rhyme was probably salutary for an aspiring writer with little educational background and a not altogether reliable ear.

The second issue of the *Post* asked for short stories; the terms, which were to be repeated in yet another Davison publication later, were unfortunately to restrict Frank in his first fiction. Earlier *The Advance Australia*, limited in space, specified two thousand words; now the length had been extended to between five and six thousand. Australianism was again stressed: "Those [stories] of Australian interest will be given preference. It is not absolutely necessary that they deal with Australia, or that the plot should be laid here, but they must be Australian in sentiment." And what was that sentiment? Up till now, the editor explained, most writers had dealt with life out back—usually with its hard side. Does it lack romance, he asked, that they have to tell of drought, heat, rabbits, beer, "in terms of real life?" (No realists, it would appear, need apply!) And why limit to the outback (this city editor continued)—how about stories of business and its opportunities, shipping, factories, etc.?[4]

Frank succeeded in meeting his father's standards with two stories published under the pseudonym "Scott McGarvie." In "The Paint Ladder"[5] one can almost hear him saying, "All right, Dad, here's the one you asked for on business." Certainly his heart was not in this conventional story of "man has job, man loses job, man gets job"—a much better job. The most notable thing about this effort is its curious connection with yet another conventional business story in yet another of his father's magazines that we shall examine later (p. 39).

Frank's other *Post* story, "Ted Allen's 'Spud,'"[6] was surely closer to the heart of a man battling for a living in the outback. Ted, alone on a grazing selection eight miles from the nearest neighbor, where a good dog is worth two men, finds companionship as well as help in Spud, for "A man can like cattle, he can like a horse, but he can love only something which can return love." Comes a riding accident, and Spud's loyalty and intelligence save his owner's life. This is a second story with a happy ending but with a more genuine ring—and is of some importance as another of the forerunners of

Frank's moving novel *Dusty,* published a quarter of a century later.

Frank's most notable contributions to his father's *Post* were neither poetry nor fiction but articles written, like the poem "My Camp," under the unprepossessing pseudonym "T. Bone." Each of the last five of the monthly's six issues carries an installment of a series relating the problems of a new settler (told in the first person) in selecting and starting to subdue a block of land. Together these carry us only to the beginnings of the bark hut and the fencing, and obviously some "fabrication" has been added to personal experience, as the author was to admit later of his *Caribbean Interlude;* this selector's family, for instance, becomes "Mary and the little one"—no great sea change from Kay and young Doris. These installments not only ring true to the spirit of the time and the place, however, but contain much that is clearly autobiographical. At one point the selector says, "Of course I write in retrospect," but it was a retrospect of months, not years, over an important period in Frank's life that survives for us otherwise only in much later fiction and a few chance remarks drawn from memory.

Early in the first of the series ("A Bit of Australia,"[7] an account of his trip into Queensland to look for property), Frank concludes a fascinating description of an all-night train ride to "Aulahlah," a "ten-pub" town, with the reflection: "It was strange to be in a bush town again, after much tramping in foreign lands. The years of absence—some of them boyhood's years—have turned me, a native-born Australian, into a new chum."[8] He was disappointed to find that he had grown critical: the old romantic glamour was gone, and the tipsy men leaning against the pub verandah's posts were no longer bushmen on a glorious spree but a nuisance and an eyesore. "This home-coming was a delusion." He worried about its effect on his wife ("fresh from the English countryside"), but he himself recognized the Australian ugliness as transient, and was eager to join these new settlers who were working not only for themselves but for the "destiny of a proud young nation." Despite the considerable discomforts of his journey, he reported, "It was great to be getting back in the bush again. A new enterprise, new hopes, and new possibilities." The smell of the gum trees awakened memories that had slept through his years of wandering in strange cities, and filled him with "eagerness to pick up the thread of life where I had dropped it years ago. It is good to feel eager." The cattle and sheep reminded him that "I was glad to be back in Australia's bush. The homesickness I had forgotten years ago came back to me in retrospect, and I regretted the years spent beneath foreign skies." A little of this eagerness disappeared at the close of the first install- ment when he discussed at length the area's soil and water problems; he recognized that finding a solution to these would determine "how much of this continent is going to belong to Australia and how much to the lizard and the crow."

Later installments suggest an increasing mixture of fiction with fact, as if the author had come to recognize the possibility of a long series and was trying to make more and more of his actual ex- perience. But revealing flashes of Frank's own personality remain, as when he returns from his prospecting "full of enthusiasm" to a companion (Douglas?) who was interested but unmoved. "As to myself, I am afraid I go to the other extreme." His companion's stolidity caused Frank to reflect that "A fair scene will cause me to catch my breath."[9] A flash of his later-expressed belief in "the fellowship of all flesh" appeared in his conclusion as the reason he didn't anticipate a kangaroo steak: "Perhaps it is because one hard- ly fancies eating the flesh of a fellow countryman."[10]

This early series is important for style as well as subject, as it reveals Frank to be a remarkably fine writer of expository prose some years before he matured as a writer of fiction. His style here is vividly pictorial, perceptive, humorous, clear-cut—in fact, still altogether readable for its own sake. One could wish that the *Australian Post* had survived long enough for a full coverage of Frank's experiences as a Queensland selector, right down to his ul- timate admission of failure and his consequent departure. Gathered into book form, this material would now have not only a literary value but a historical one that is necessarily lacking in his two later nonfiction books, *Caribbean Interlude*, based on a youthful ex- perience abroad, and *Blue Coast Caravan*, in which he views Australia as a spectator. But if these early articles have not become readily available to the reader, the experience on which they are based remained with the writer and served him well in years to come. It was his prolonged participation in Queensland life that gave his later writing about it both accuracy and depth.

The *Post* failed in Sydney long before Frank did in Queensland; its sixth monthly issue (February 7, 1921) was announced as the last. The reason given was the failure of the editor to find an efficient advertising man, leading him to quit while he could still pay his debts. To anyone who wished to carry on, Fred offered a small

printing plant and some unexpired advertising contracts. As for
himself, he was leaving, he explained, a wiser but "By no means a
sadder man. There is still corn in Egypt."[11] Two years later he was
ready to try again, this time with more than a contributor's help
from his eldest son.

II   *Failure on the Land*

In the meantime, Frank continued the battle to establish himself
on his selection. Since his *Post* series covered only the beginnings of
the struggle, we could wish for other reports on its later stages. One
source might have been Jack Cumming, Queensland's crown lands
ranger in the area of Frank's selection, who, according to Owen
Webster, knew the Davisons well as the couple with the two babies
(son Peter having been born during the Queensland years) in the
two-room humpy in belah and brigalow scrub, a home that became
an oasis to Cumming. He could have reported in detail on Frank,
"whose daily life and battle against nature he must have known,
during those rugged, vital years, better than any man or woman."[12]
But the ranger died shortly after Frank did and before Webster,
seeking information about Frank's Queensland years, had a chance
to interview him. Our best source consequently remains the
numerous Queensland short stories in Frank's two later collections,
from which we can deduce with considerable accuracy what the
author's own experience as a settler was like.
    With the other soldier-selectors, Frank had back pay from the
army and loans from the government for stock and fences. He
planned to run a dairy herd, saving his calves until he had about a
hundred and twenty head on his twelve hundred acres; but he
never got that far. It was not from lack of trying, but because
everything needed doing at once; the building, the clearing, the
ring-barking, the fencing, the dam-building, the tank-sinking. Not
but that he enjoyed it. He was not yet thirty, and as he remarked
long afterward, "I can get drunk on work—never thought of grog in
those days."[13] But the days were not long enough, from dawn till
dark, nor were there enough of them, even with seven to the week.
Frank laid his ultimate failure to a combination of "sheer ignorance,
bad luck, bad season."[14] Admitting that others in the settlement
survived the droughts that ruined him, he later concluded that "it's
possible that I wasn't a farmer to begin with, I was only a crazy
writer from the very start."[15] Still more thought-provoking was his

recognition that had he succeeded as a farmer, he would have lived his life within the boundary of his selection and would never have made a name as a writer.

It is fortunate for Australian literature, then, that he failed, but it is equally fortunate that he made the effort, for three of his four novels and most of his short stories are rooted in his Queensland experience. Not that he was consciously looking to it for material, he once explained, but that he lived it so intensely. "This was one of the most colourful periods of a not uncolourful existence," he wrote twenty years later, "and one to which my thoughts often return, so that I am given to sowing there the seeds of stories often gathered far from there."[16] In none of his available later recollections, however, does he mention having done any writing while he was in Queensland, though his contributions to his father's *Australian Post* prove that he did.

It took four years of "hard graft" (the Australian term for strenuous manual labor) in Queensland to make Frank admit defeat. When he did, he surrendered his title and moved his growing family back to Sydney, where the rest of the Davisons had been living since their return from the United States a half dozen years before. There his father had gone into real estate as a vocation, joined by son Douglas, who had only "looked and left" when he accompanied Frank on that first trip to Queensland. Now Frank joined both, not just in the real estate business but also in the publishing ventures that his father continued to dabble in. With Frank's return, Fred embarked upon his third and most ambitious periodical venture, one that was to lead, through a long chain of events, to the arrival of Frank Dalby Davison on the Australian literary scene.

CHAPTER 3

Apprenticeship

I Australia

*T*HE *Advance Australia*—then the *Australian Post*—now the
Australian, which started life in March, 1923, as a glossy
monthly magazine of about a hundred pages, featuring "Illustrated
articles and short stories" and declaring itself to stand "For Liberty
of the Individual." This declaration remained unchanged, but the
magazine experienced some other alterations during its two years of
existence: in paper, from gloss to cheap newsprint; in price, from a
shilling down to ninepence; and in title, with the fifth issue, from
the *Australian* to *Australia.* But in essentials it remained the same:
in type of content, in political outlook, and in management. The
editor and manager was Fred Davison; the assistant editor and
advertising manager was his son Frank.

As to its outlook, its rather militant Australianism was sounded
monthly in the quatrain (p. 17) by Francis Adams that the editor
had first used a quarter of a century earlier in *The Advance
Australia.* Now it was never missing from the head of the editorial
column. And regularly, in a one-column box somewhere in the
issue, appeared this statement, which grows in interest by comparison with the assistant editor's later convictions:

"Australia" is a short story magazine and something more. Besides giving
its readers the best fiction obtainable—Australian for preference—it
publishes articles of Australian interest calculated to advance the interests
of the Commonwealth. "Australia" will support individual independence
and freedom from unnecessary Government interference—and most
Government interference is unnecessary. It will do its part toward killing
the "What is the Government going to do?" spirit too common in our country.

The present-day Australian is cheating himself out of the big things that
enter into the life of men in other lands. For this, he alone is to blame. To

"the Government" he has turned over nearly everything of a worthwhile nature—retaining for himself in his private capacity little but the "corner groceries" of life.

That "the Government" has failed, and because of the nature of all Governments must continue to fail, in any enterprise that requires business management, is becoming very obvious. The time is not far distant when Australians will reverse their policy and open their continent to development by private enterprise.

"Australia" is out to preach the gospel of individual self-help. Reasonable Governmental regulations—Yes! Life under the Government Job—No!

Despite this continual declaration, the amount of space devoted in the magazine to political and economic issues was negligible, going little beyond the monthly editorials and an occasional biographical article under the inclusive heading of "Leaders, Subleaders—and Mis-leaders." In keeping with the taste of its day, *Australia* carried mostly fiction. Although even this was to be "Australian for preference," the early issues depended heavily on reprints from such popular American writers as Fanny Heaslip Lea, Richard Washburn Child, and Rex Beach. As time went on, however, the notation "written for *Australia*" appeared more and more frequently, applied to the work of such still well-known native authors as S. Elliott Napier, who contributed an essay; Daisy Bates, who furnished a couple of articles on the aborigines among whom she had spent the better part of her life; and established fiction-writer J. H. M. Abbott, who supplied a number of historical short stories from the Macquarie period. Two other still more famous names appeared above selections from novels: A. B. ("Banjo") Paterson with *An Outback Marriage* and Vance Palmer, later to be Frank's close friend and admired literary mentor but now just becoming known, with *Cronulla, A Story of Australian Station Life*.

Of greater interest here, however, is the extent to which the contents as well as the management of *Australia* remained a Davison family affair. The magazine was as exclusively "home-grown" as the *Australian Post* had been. Fred not only managed and edited, he wrote the editorials and an occasional article in his own name as well as ghosting others. Journalist daughter Dulcie contributed a number of light stories under the pseudonym "Una Dea." And son Frank managed, in addition to his editorial and advertising duties, to contribute heavily. By this time he had been encouraged by getting a few bits—"pars"—accepted by the *Bulletin* (for years the open sesame to Australian letters); and he now undertook to supply so many words a month to his father's new venture. These consisted of some literary criticism, a few other articles, and a great deal of fiction. Neither long-lived nor important enough to get so much as a mention in the *Australian Encyclopaedia's* discussion of the periodicals of its era, *Australia* will nonetheless go down in literary history as the birthplace of three of Frank Dalby Davison's later novels.

II   *Pseudonyms*

For well over a year the name of their author-to-be appeared only on the masthead. Dulcie, a relatively minor contributor, might choose to hide her identity under only one pseudonym; her brother concealed himself in the early issues (presumably to pretend to a more varied list of contributors than *Australia* had yet attracted) under three. Of the dozen pieces in the first number alone, four were his: one by "Frederick Douglas" (his own two given names), one by "Francis Daly," two by "Frank Daniels." (History does not record whether any readers of the new magazine noticed a similarity of initials—and style.)   Frank Daniels wrote no more; Francis Daly lasted only a few months; but Frederick Douglas missed scarcely an issue until, in the August, 1924, number, in the midst of installments that were later to become the bulk of the novel *Forever Morning*, he became a mere parenthetical after Frank's own name, "F. D. Davison," and two months later disappeared altogether, leaving Frank an acknowledged author henceforward.

What an opportunity *Australia* provided for an aspiring young writer! (Frank was now thirty but still virtually unpublished.) First, he got to flex his incipient critical muscles, not only in an occasional article of his own but in the continual need, as assistant editor, to help choose the best from among the contributions of others. His choices of fiction, however, must have been somewhat circumscribed by the limitations of *Australia's* policy as stated in a notice in the July, 1924, number:

To Short Story Writers

This magazine is in the market for short stories—from 5000 to 10,000 words for preference—but it wants them of a cheerful nature. Very many of the stories we decline are turned down because of their morbid or doleful tone. It is not alone because readers prefer the cheerful stories that we refuse them, but because such a country as Australia is worthy of something better than tales of failure and misery. That failure and misery exist here is true—but so do success and happiness. No helpful end is served by dwelling on the former, whereas much good is done by preaching the worthwhileness of effort and hopefulness. Writers who wish to have their stories accepted, please take notice.

Was this Fred's dictum, one wonders? Probably, since it enlarges on the policy of the earlier *Australian Post*. And did it reflect personal conviction or only an effort to attract readers? If Frank agreed with it at the time, he fortunately outgrew such limitations in his own later work, even before his final monument to "failure and misery," his novel *The White Thorntree*.

But he was loyal to it then. The last three issues of *Australia* (it ended, after two years, with the February, 1925, issue) each carry a page of capsule comments directed to short story contributors identified by initial. It seems possible that these were the work of Frank, since he was the fiction man of the organization; at least he presumably concurred in them at the time. Some of them are very cutting; all toe the "party line" enunciated above. For example,

"S.E.P.D.: Good story. Accepted. But we had to cut out the drought and pay off the mortgage."
"G.G.: It's well written—but too ghastly. Let's have some of the joy of life."
"P.X.: Again—Again—Again! We don't want stories of failure."
"D.P.L.: Held for consideration. It's a good story, but too sorrowful. Full of blasted hopes and wrong turnings. Of course there are such things, but why bother about them?"
"A.S.: What's the matter with you. Don't waste your time scratching your (metaphorical) sores. Take a dose of the medicine of common sense. Success is not the dust and ashes business you make it out to be. It is something worth while striving for and achieving."

Against such explicit—and narrow—standards, it is irresistible to measure the works of Frank Daniels, Francis Daly, Frederick Douglas, and ultimately F. D. Davison. "Frank Daniels" was a writer obviously familiar with outback life, and he made a couple of rather good ironic passes at it before his early demise. His "Shifting Sands"[1] in the first issue of the magazine is particularly worth looking at, since it is one of the pieces that Frank would later exhume, renovate, retitle—and republish in a book. It deals with a Melbourne printer (presumably a familiar figure to the "editor and

manager") who so yearned to maintain a new life in the
Queensland bush in spite of many early disappointments and a dis-
approving wife who "continued to say a great deal by saying
nothing" that he worked unceasingly, to the limits of his ingenuity
and strength, to secure the water supply on his new selection with a
diversionary dam, after the tank-sinkers (pond makers) had
failed—only to find, with additional rain, that he had failed too.
When he discovered the fact, "a jackass overhead sent hoot after
hoot of derisive laughter pealing through the bush." Life can be
like that—but such a portrayal would fail to meet the *Australian*'s
standards. So, after the settler has had to admit defeat and is
preparing to return to city life, "the monotonous dead level of a
weekly wage," and an everlasting ache for the might-have-beens of
the bush—comes a rain so hard that it packs down and builds up his
faulty dam and saves his water supply! Whereupon the jackass,
"after a preliminary chuckle or two, sent peal after peal of honest
mirth ringing through the bush"—a much more suitable sound for
these pages than the earlier "derisive laughter."

A second piece—same issue, same pseudonym— is far briefer but
equally ironic. In "Making an Easy Day of It,"[2] two men laboring
to fence a selection stopped to do some needed burning off, for an
"easy day." But the fire got away from them, and the day was
anything but easy. Still, as in "Shifting Sands," they finally got it
under control, thus meeting with enough success to satisfy the
Australian's prescription.

Now for a look at "Francis Daly," who started out in that first
issue on a lighter note in "Monkeying with Ernest."[3] Told in the
first person by a typical "new chum" from England, it is the typical
horse yarn of the critter that can't be ridden or driven, so is sold to a
series of innocent buyers, starting here with the narrator. Slight but
humorous, it "gets by," even if it will not make literary history. In
the third issue (May) Daly turns to the essay, a humorous one called
"Distant Fields Look Green,"[4] in which he analyzes a current
Australian epidemic: "Land Crazy is now a recognized disease" to
which no son of Adam is immune. But "If he is a native Australian
he thinks he is qualified for farming by virtue of his nationality.
[There is no greater mistake than this. Ed.]" In June, Daly combines exposition and narration in "Just Between Neighbors,"[5] starting off with an essay on the unscrupulousness of "dealing," then
dropping into the second person for an example of how you, the
newcomer on the land, escape being tricked by refusing to buy a

bull, after prolonged negotiations, only to buy a bull calf and get tricked anyway. Failure? Well, all in good fun; it was *somebody's* success!

Daly's last appearance, in August, was his longest. Though narrative in form, "Joe Takes It On"[6] is less a short story than an animated account of the trials endured by a new settler from an English factory as he tries to subdue his land and his family. Ultimately he fails, but not finally, for we leave him on his way to an area nearer to the coast and predictable rainfall (the area that Frank had first been offered and had refused, preferring to go farther inland for more space) where he will work for wages until he can try the land again. This was the end of Francis Daly; perhaps his expository leanings did not satisfy *Australia*'s requirements.

We come now to "Frederick Douglas," who had not only the support of the author's given names but the most prolific fictional pen. He too is a man familiar with the outback. His "Boss of Bongawarra"[7] is a story that fits *Australia*'s stated requirements perfectly. The hero Bob battles to win back Bongawarra, the station that his grandfather founded, that his father lost to drought, and that he himself now manages for its present owner, a wholesale butcher. Enter Dorothy the butcher's daughter. Love at first sight, but unfortunately she is engaged to her father's general manager, the villain Ferry, a childhood enemy of Bob's, who gets him fired for the misjudgments of others. Then—comes the STAMPEDE! Ferry saves himself (thus proving to be both the coward and the cad we had suspected all along), while Bob heroically rescues Dorothy. The pair are now scheduled to live happily ever after—in Bob's ancestral home, now that it's back in the family. No failure here.

This story "reads" well, having a rich background and convincing characters as well as a conventional plot. "An Interrupted Idyll"[8] does not; rather, it confirms what "The Boss of Bongawarra" had strongly suggested: that at this time Frank had more to contribute when he stuck to the problems of the land than when he turned to those of the human heart. The mounted policeman who tries to barter Barbara's brother's freedom from a charge of cattle-stealing for her hand is as black a villain as ever held mortgage in melodrama. The only refreshing angle to the story is the girl's saving herself (and her brother) by a clever stratagem, leaving nothing for her belatedly returning fiancé to do but mop up the street with the policeman, just for good measure.

Away from the overworked theme of love, however, Frederick

Douglas could do better. In "The Regeneration of Jimmy,"[9] the protagonist is a likeable chap, but the curse of an amiable though characterless father causes him to turn the other cheek to bruiser Carson: first, when he is personally insulted, and later when the brute steals his girl on the dance floor for all to see. But when Carson goes so far as to kick his dog—Jimmy fights! Jimmy wins!! Jimmy is, in fact, such a new man that he breaks his engagement to the simpleton cousin his mother had thrust upon him and defies the old termagant face to face. This regeneration is convincing, if not particularly original. More, it shows the place that some of Frank's later short stories and a still later novel accord to man's best friend.

By far the best of these early "Douglas" stories is one that forgoes the popular portrayal of a period of devastating work and dessicating drought for the new settler, to present instead a single life-and-death struggle with the elements. "Many Miles from Surrey"[10] pictures an English "new chum" and his wife leaving their selection for a Sunday walk in the bush where as newcomers they are soon hopelessly lost. The physical hardships of their subsequent three days and two nights of tramping, ending in the wife's complete collapse and the husband's carrying her, are realistically and grippingly related; as vividly described is the man's mental collapse and hallucinations before they finally arrive—by luck—back on their own property and into the kindly hands of concerned neighbors. We may observe, however, that the editor felt it necessary to "forego the element of suspense" by stating, in an introductory note, that the people concerned were still alive—presumably to keep the magazine's readers, secure in the promise of happy endings, from crying "Foul!" along the way.

III   Urban Stories

Besides their authorship, all of these "F. D." contributions have in common an authentic bush background. In *Australia*, as in his earlier *Australian Post*, however, editor Fred Davison, urging writers to contribute stories of Australian life as lived, reminded them that "That doesn't mean in the Bush only. Our cities are as truly Australian as is the country." It was probably under such editorial urging that "Frederick Douglas" twice ventured from the Queensland setting that Frank himself had known so recently and so intimately to an urban background with which he was only now becoming familiar and in which he was still ill at ease. One result was "Burned Fingers,"[11] an account of an affair between a married man and a young woman with whom he becomes infatuated while his wife and children are away on a vacation. At the inevitable end of their brief intimacy, he passes it off to himself with " 'Well, it was over now—and Never Again!' The Everlasting Man of It." She, for her part, sobs into her pillow with grief: "The Everlasting Woman of It." No great story, and notable chiefly for the implication of those last lines, a popular distinction between the emotional reactions of the sexes which Frank examines at much greater length and with much more discernment many years later in his final novel, *The White Thorntree.*

Frank's other venture off the Queensland reservation was a story of business called "Getting under the Fence."[12] Here he set to fiction a national injustice that his father editorialized about as "the greatest tragedy in Australian industrial life," the fault not of the unions but of the law, which prevented those beyond boyhood from learning trades, thus consigning them to a lifetime of hand-to -mouth odd jobs. The story is, curiously, more than reminiscent of "The Paint Ladder" (p. 27) that had appeared in the *Australian Post* only two years earlier—it is to a large extent identical! "The Paint Ladder" is about Tom, unemployed after a paint firm, which had never paid properly for his extraordinary self-taught skill, closed; "Getting under the Fence" is about Hugh, unskilled, who lost his temporary job through a similar shutdown. Ultimately Tom got a job with another paint firm where his knowledge was properly rewarded; ultimately Hugh got his own construction business, thanks to a Russian builder who was kind enough to train him by means of a two-year "break-law" apprenticeship. The startling thing is that the central portion of the first story (a detailed account of about two thousand words of the effect of Tom's long unemployment) reappears in the second with no changes save that "Tom" becomes "Hugh," and wife "Elsie," "Betty." There is presumably no legal reason why an author cannot reuse his own material, if his publisher is willing, nor is this by any means the only occasion on which Frank made a piece of writing do double duty. One suspects, however, that this time, at least, he was prompted by pressure of work and perhaps boredom with his subject rather than by a conviction that here was something he could not willingly let die. Apparently neither he nor his editor had any fear of reader recognition, even though the two appearances of the section were in magazines published in the same city only a couple of years apart.

IV *Dog Stories*

An older Frank was to look back on these early years in Sydney as
a time when he was immature and still innocent about human
relationships despite his thirty years. Certainly he did better with
animals. "One of the Dinkums"[13] concerns the Irish terrier
"Digger," of a breed useless to the stockman but of interest for his
character. The story consists of his repeated encounters with Black
Bear, a large and ferocious cattle dog—encounters that always
meant a fight, and these fights always meant defeat for Digger
though he never attempted to avoid them. Because his spirit continued to be undefeated, the bigger dog finally made friends. Those
who were to find symbolism in Frank's later animal novels could
discern here a celebration of the indomitable Australian character.

A second dog story is still more worthy of a backward look. In
"The Killer,"[14] a winning sheep dog is discovered—and later discovers himself—to be a half-breed dingo, and thus the
"battleground of forces as old as the human race." When he turns
from protector of sheep to killer, men pursue him, but he escapes
them—only to fall victim to a female dingo who, "after the manner
of her kind when they have mated with a tame dog," turned on him
and tore his throat open. "Fearful of the dilution of pure dingo
blood by the tame dog, Nature demanded his death as the penalty
of his mingled strain." Here in embryo is the moving and again
symbolic *Dusty*, the excellent short novel that Frank wrote twenty
years later. But in it there was no question of reusing chunks of
prose, only ideas.

Just why Frank finally decided to abandon the last of his
pseudonyms and write under his own name we do not know, we
only know when. In both the August and September, 1924, issues
(*Australia* was now a year and a half old), pieces attributed to "F.D.
Davison (Frederick Douglas)" appeared as a transition; from then
on, only an unabashed "F. D. Davison." It was not that he had experienced a sudden access to excellence and wanted the credit; "A
Losing Game,"[15] the September contribution, was a very long,
tedious, clumsily handled cattle-stealing yarn, inferior to several
that had preceded it. With only one exception, none of these
Australia stories was found worthy to be included in his later
collected volumes, and that ("Shifting Sands") only after considerable rewriting.

All of these contributions to his father's magazines, however, served a purpose. Whether or not journalism can be rightly acclaimed as the best training for a young creative writer, it has the virtue of forcing him to put paper into typewriter regularly. Frank admitted twenty years later that he wrote a lot of rotten short stories for *Australia*, but concluded: "I got a lot of experience writing for it, all over the shop."[16] He also remarked that some of his work at that time contained good ore, badly handled—material that he was able to draw on later. This was putting it mildly, for the magazine carried not only the substance of *Dusty*, as we have noted, but the bones and much of the flesh of his first two novels, which by a kind of delayed Caesarian appeared a half dozen years after the journal died. These were *Forever Morning* and *Man-Shy*, very different in content and quality, but both appearing in book form in 1931. That, however, is another story.

CHAPTER 4

Man-Shy

W HEN in 1921 the *Australian Post* was abandoned after only six issues, editor Fred Davison gave as the reason his lack of an efficient advertising man. When Frank settled in Sydney after giving up his Queensland selection, he took over this office for his father's new venture, *Australia*, but he was to admit later that he had been "its somewhat unsuccessful advertising manager."[1] This magazine lasted through twenty-four issues (March, 1923 - February, 1925), at which point, having incurred an indebtedness of some £2000 (much to Frank's mother's annoyance), it was allowed to expire. Probably much of the original interest in the venture had drained away, too, as was likely to happen with the volatile Fred.

I *The Depression*

Besides, *Australia* had been only a side interest at best, and the Davison clan now turned its full attention to its booming real estate business. Douglas had been working with his father in this all along (and continued to do so until Fred's death in 1942); now Frank began to work seriously with them as a salesman, admittedly "good at the game," as one might guess from the widespread reports of his personal charm. He later opened a branch for his father, still later bought it from him. It could be said, as Frank himself remarked of his Queensland venture, that if he had continued to be successful in this endeavor, he might never have gained fame as a writer. But again he was spared by failure, this time owing to the onset of the Depression, that worldwide phenomenon that struck Australia with extraordinary severity. It caught Frank in 1929 with his funds spread so thin that he was among the first to go under.

But the family drew together in adversity. "Dad was ever fertile of ideas," Frank later reflected, and he led the way to the book business as a possibility for making a living now that real estate had failed them. "It was," his elder son reported, "the old man being inventive again."[2] At his suggestion they bought up a printing of *Flight Across the Pacific* by Australia's famed early aviator, Kingsford Smith, for a shilling a copy, to sell for two. This book and others the brothers hawked from door to door, leaving packages of assorted books overnight for people to choose from. Nearly half a century later, Frank (for whom the Depression was to become personally devastating) was to recall people in good-class Sydney suburbs opening their doors a crack only to say, "There's unemployment in this house," and closing them again.

Douglas, apparently, was responsible for the Davisons' move from book selling to book publishing. Feeling that sixpence would be a more attractive price than two shillings, he suggested (with some inherited ingenuity, surely) that they resurrect some of Frank's material from the files of *Australia*, making it into a volume slim enough to be manufactured for twopence. Frank, concurring, settled down to a process that we shall look at in some detail later, collecting and adding to certain related contributions to *Australia* to make a small novel. Understandably failing to interest Sydney's leading publisher, Angus & Robertson, in the manuscript, the brothers had some two hundred copies of the material printed on good quality woven paper, taking the sheets home to fold and bind between red boards for reviewers and book shops. Eight hundred more, printed on newsprint, they bound with wallpaper. These they set about peddling for sixpence. When the time came that they could no longer afford repairs on their little Rover car, they sold the remaining couple of hundred copies of this larger printing for threepence each to the N.S.W. Bookstall Co. Now they are collectors' items.

Thus was born in 1931, through the medium of the Davisons' Australian Authors Publishing Co., what many of his readers still feel to be Frank's greatest book, *Man-Shy*. Douglas's reward was to have the book dedicated to him; Frank's was to find the world of serious literature suddenly open to him—but not immediately. *Man-Shy* in its home-grown book form might have attracted little more attention than it had in the pages of *Australia* where the bulk of it had long lain dormant. Again, however, "Dad was fertile of ideas." Without consulting Frank, whom he knew to be too modest for such aspirations, Fred entered the book in competition for the A.L.S. medal.

II *The A.L.S. Medal Winner*

This award had recently been instituted by the Australian
Literature Society of Melbourne. Founded in 1899, the A.L.S. announced itself as the only society in the entire Commonwealth that
sought to provide a public for Australian authors; its membership
was open to all who wanted to foster an appreciation of Australian
literature. Through the generosity of Colonel R. H. Crouch, it had
begun in 1928 to offer annually a gold medal for the best Australian
novel of the year, an award acclaimed by critic M. Barnard
Eldershaw as the highest honor available to the fiction writer in
Australia. Its judges had certainly got it off to a distinguished start:
the first award went to "Martin Mills" (Martin Boyd) for his splen-
did historical novel *The Montforts;* the second (1929) to "Henry
Handel Richardson" (Ethel Lindesay) for *Ultima Thule,* the concluding volume of her remarkable trilogy *The Fortunes of Richard
Mahoney;* the third (1930) to Vance Palmer, already well on his way
to becoming "the dean of Australian literature," for *The Passage.*
And now, to this distinguished company was added, for 1931, a
fourth, an unknown, more than justifying Fred Davison's paternal
confidence and initiative—Frank Dalby Davison for *Man-Shy.*

If Frank did not wake up the next morning to find himself
famous, he was at least well on the way. Everyone wanted to know
the identity of this new writer who had won Australia's most distinguished literary recognition. An interesting reflection on Frank's
previous obscurity and the early impact of *Man-Shy* is to be found
in a letter to critic Nettie Palmer, Vance's wife, in mid-1932 from
novelist Marjorie Barnard, herself a recent newcomer to the literary
scene through a share with her collaborator, Flora Eldershaw, in a
Bulletin prize for their novel *A House Is Built* (1929). Concerning
A.L.S.'s recently announced award for the preceding year, she
wrote: "It went to J. B. Davidson [*sic*] of Sydney for his novel 'Man-
Shy.' . . . I have not read Man-Shy but must at once. I did not
know it existed until just before the announcement, when I heard
Lady MacCullum praise it very highly. . . . I wonder what you
think of [it]. . . . I'll buy a copy forthwith. With you, I most
sincerely hope that it is a first class novel so that the prize may keep
its value and continue to be an honour."[3]

Two months later she had read the book and was able to write of
it, "I thought it a very beautiful, restrained and tragic book. . . . I
realize acutely—almost as if I had tried it—the difficulty of creating

a poetic tragedy out of so tenuous and simple a theme. It requires a spontaneity and artistic sincerity that are generally associated only with genius."⁴ A half dozen years later, when Marjorie and Flora included a long study of Frank's work in their volume *Essays in Australian Fiction* (1938), they were to say of *Man-Shy* that "It is not, perhaps, in the conventional sense a novel at all," but they added, memorably, "It is something between a long short story and a universe."⁵

Man-Shy is small but not slight. Its fourteen chapters run to less than forty thousand words, and it is so deceptively simple that it is often considered to be a book for children, which it is—but no more exclusively than Swift's *Gulliver's Travels*. It opens with a sentence now familiar to every Australian with any knowledge of his nation's literature and to many readers abroad: "The mustering for drafting and branding was a distressing time for the cattle."⁶ That sentence establishes the tone of a story that was to find cattle more important than men, and to succeed in the very difficult job of seeing the world largely from the animals' point of view, without nature-faking or sentimentality.

The reader's chief concern is for the cattle, whose natural enemies are men and dogs. The first chapter, "Telling of the Herd," describes the annual muster on an Australian outback station, a time of brief terror and pain for the cattle but followed, for most of them, by relief and forgetfulness, for "There was no looking back to musterings past, and no looking forward to musterings to come. Within a week the routine of cattle-life was established again, to remain undisturbed for another year."⁷

But *Man-Shy* is not about this contented majority who had made a kind of reciprocal if uneasy peace with man and his dogs; it is about the fewer bold ones, the "scrubbers," who, preferring the dangers of liberty, had broken away from man's domination to seek refuge in the "scrub" of the farther ranges. Sometimes "famine was the penalty of freedom,"⁸ and individuals fell to drought or raids by stockmen or the bullets of kangaroo shooters; but as a mob they lived on.

Theirs was a life for the slave brutes of man to dream of. Their hides had never known the searing whip or the sting of the branding iron; nor did the shadow of the slaughter-house fall across their years. Companions of the creatures of the wilderness—the emu, the dingo, and the kangaroo—their life was the life of the dumb brutes as it was on earth in the beginning. They were free as the winds that played about their mountains; free as the

rains that swept up the gorges; and free as the range itself, hoisting its
timber-crested palisades into the blue. They lived secure and content in the
simple wisdom the Creator has given to dumb things.[9]

The next section (chapters 2 and 3, there being only a half dozen
headings for the fourteen numbers) is entitled "One in Ten
Thousand." Here the story narrows from the herd to the individual,
as John Steinbeck in *The Grapes of Wrath* moved from the Okies to
the Joads, the more intimately to engage our interest and sympathy.
These chapters center on what is now only a four-day-old heifer calf
of an old red cow "on the verge of bovine senility."[10] Individuals,
yes, but we do not lose sight of the universal. Left alone on the top
of the bank above the creek to which her mother was going for
water, the calf uttered a cry that was "thin and quavering and
plaintive—the baby cry, the world over,"[11] and was answered by "a
reassuring croon—the mother croon the world over."[12] But the old
cow, literally on her last legs, got bogged down in the mud of the
much-used water hole and drowned. Too young to feel loss, the
orphaned calf at first scampered gaily in her new freedom. By the
next day, however, she was desperately hungry and discouraged by
the sharp rebuffs given to her advances by potential foster mothers
in the herd. Her destiny?

Such orphans wander for a day or so and lie down, then get up and wander
again, and lie down for a longer time. Then they get up and wander for a
short while, after which they lie down for a long while, until, at last, they
cannot get up at all. Then they stretch out and slowly pant their little lives
away.[13]

The infant red heifer, however, won a thousand-to-one chance,
finding just in time that rare creature, a cow with one calf but willing to adopt another.

The heifer is the "one in ten thousand," however, in the
spiritedness she develops. "The Outlaw" (chapters 4 through 6)
details her early experiences with men and dogs. From her first
muster she was exempted by a stockman's decision that a cow with
two young calves would fare poorly in the moving mob. During the
second muster her spirit rebelled, and twice she broke away from
the mob, only to learn the pain from a dog's teeth on her heels. In
the branding yard she was branded—but not broken. Back at the
rails she made an incredible standing jump and regained—for the
time—her freedom.

But she found her old stamping ground empty, and as "All cow-brutes abhor solitude,"[14] she was only too glad to join a small band of scrubbers that had come into her area to drink; she followed them to the far ranges. There, "the quiet and the isolation they enjoyed appealed to her. Their secrecy and caution struck within her a responsive chord. The fear and wildness that her adventures in the stockyard had awakened in her found a calming environment in the haunts of the scrubbers."[15] Yet homesickness brought her back to her old semi-domesticated mates shortly (feed was plentiful down there and water abundant besides); and for two years she went back and forth between the two groups, divided between love of liberty and old ties. She missed the next muster—her third—by being off with the scrubbers, but was caught in the fourth. A stockman who recognized her by both appearance and manner decided that this was a good time to take her to market. For "The stockman was not concerned with the fate of a calf from the calf's viewpoint. He was interested in beef for profit—beef in a slaughter-pen—beef on the hook!"[16]

With this switch to man's point of view come a few paragraphs of contrast:

Beef on the hoof is live-stock—living on the waterholes of the western creeks and rivers foraging through the clumpy brigalow, wading knee-deep in blue and Mitchell grasses, camped at night on the lee of the ridges under the dry and starry skies of the west. But beef on the hoof is not profit.

The day comes when the bullocks and cows, as fat as seals, are hustled away from the peace and contentment of their wide-flung ranges, and pushed and prodded and yelped up the loading shute into the trucks. Then, for a couple of days, bewildered and moaning among themselves, they are bumped and banged and shunted about on their way to the city.

In the city sale-yards they come under the hammer of the auctioneers. The butchers and the buyers for the big meat-works are grouped around the pens. They are not concerned with the deep-shadowed waterholes of the western creeks; the sweeping miles of blue grass rolling away under Queensland skies are not in their thoughts; neither are the quiet, contented camps, when a hundred head lie drowsing in the tepid starlit night. These fellows are out to realize beef for profit. They can see it, too—see it right under the hide. . . .

It matters little to the beast, scrubber or purebred, when the sale is over. Bedeviled and bewildered and aching for the lost freedom of the western country, they are driven to the slaughter-house. The smell of the blood strikes terror into them, and their bellowing voices their fear.

The finish comes quickly. A blow that crashes consciousness into darkness; a body still quivering with life, that falls on the blood-slippery floor of the killing-pen! In a short while, beef-on-the-hoof, gone for ever from the wide runs of the back country, is beef-on-the-hook—beef for profit. And that is the destiny of every beast that roams the cattle country—with occasional exceptions.[17]

The red heifer, of course, is one of those—a notable one. Moving unhappily with the driven herd, she was inspired by the distant trumpeting of a scrubber bull to make a break for freedom. A dog that fastened his teeth in her snout, "his body curled under her jaws like an enormous grub,"[18] was left behind with a broken leg. Then came the horseman and his whip, running her until she fell. "Blown, panic-stricken and bewildered, she sought refuge in passivity"[19] while man and horse waited for her to rise and be driven tamely back to the herd. But she rose only to gallop into the safety of some nearby scrub.

Although chapters 7 through 10 are called "The Scrubbers," the first two are devoted principally to Man the Enemy. Chapter 7 pays a genuine if reluctant tribute to the shrewdness with which Joe, the lone stockman sent by the station manager, who has decided to bring the scrubbers in from the range, finally succeeds in locating them without alarming them. Man's point of view is made explicit:

Joe had been too long in the cattle business to have any sentiment to spare for the scrubbers. He felt no regret at the prospect of bursting into their contented solitude; of stampeding them away from their beloved ranges; of desolating the waterhole with the loss of its people who would never come again; of sending them at last on the rattling, bumping railway trucks, bewildered and forlorn, on their way to the markets and the shambles. It was just work, for which he received three pounds a week and his tucker. Dangerous work it would be, too; the sort of danger that a man looks forward to with nervous eagerness and back upon with joy. Joe's feelings were those of the big-game hunter who has caught up with his quarry.[20]

The next chapter (8) is the exciting—even breath-taking—account of the roundup of the scrubbers by Joe and five other trained stockmen, a tribute to men, horses, and dogs alike. Of the twenty-three scrubbers only three were lost—two calves unable to keep up with the mad chase, and a bull who fell into the bottom of a washout. Of the twenty safely yarded, four were bullocks who had "gone bush" since branding and so were already on the station books. The red heifer, too, bore her early brand. But the remainder were "clean-skins," wild cattle from birth, and the manager, in strengthening the paddock fence to hold them all securely, found himself studying "with calculating eye the meat-works' value of the scrubber mob"[21]—upwards of a hundred windfall pounds.

It proved to be premature chicken-counting: true, the four branded bullocks settled down, finding the grass of the paddock more inviting than the freedom of the ranges, and they were followed by a few of the younger scrubbers, who also "accepted the bondage of domestication."[22] As for the red heifer, the day after arrival she walked up to the rails, successfully repeated her earlier leap, and headed back to the range. Her scrubber companions remained inconsolable, endlessly pacing along the unfamiliar confining fence, drinking little, eating not at all. The manager assured himself and his men that as soon as the cattle got properly hungry, they would eat. But as we learn from the dramatic concluding paragraph of chapter 9: "He was wrong in that. The scrubbers were dying."[23]

They were close to death, certainly—they grew so hopelessly thin that the men finally persuaded the manager to give up his dreams of the meat-works and shoot them at once for the lesser value of their hides. His only satisfaction lay in the fact that that very day his expectations were enlarged by one big hide with the arrival of the old roan bull who had fallen into a washout during the roundup and had only now caught up with his dwindling mob. The relief of the old fellow upon arrival was short-lived, however, for he realized that he was smelling death. "It was the offensive odour that the bodies of beasts who are poverty-stricken to the point of death give off."[24] In his terrified effort to jump the rails, he broke them down—and off he went, followed by a straggling file of shaky scrubbers "wending its way toward the safety and seclusion of the ranges."[25]

This was to be their last triumph—the beginning of the end for them. In the magazine version, the story ended at this point for a full year, but in the book the author takes time out from their tragedy only to insert "Bulls in Battle" (chapter 11), newly written, in which he describes at some length the epic encounter between a young bull grown eager for mastery and the old one who has long been the established male of the herd. In "a slow motion battle," the old bull finally wins, but "some day defeat must overtake him."[26]

Similarly it is in the nature of man's conquest of Australian space that the scrubbers must ultimately yield—their freedom or their lives. *Man-Shy* is, among other things, a history of the development of the Australian outback, from its beginnings in the huge unfenced cattle stations where herds ran freely from muster to muster, to the period of enclosure, when these vast areas were cut up into selections for the small individual farmer (Frank himself had been a part of this transition in Queensland after World War I), with consequent fencing. The first phase had seen the origin of the scrubbers as they escaped from the station's herds to run freely in the scrub or other inaccessible areas; the final phase, as man progressively fenced in the old water holes, saw their end.

"The Tides of Change" is appropriately the title of the final three chapters in the book (12 - 14). Of the scrubbers this section begins, "The herd life of cattle is a thing most pleasing to observe,"[27] a sharp contrast to the mood of the opening sentence of *Man-Shy* (p. 45), where men and dogs had intruded. But the life of the scrubbers soon ceased to be an idyll. First there was the professional shooter, out for beef and hides, who not only picked off a few but terrified the rest into going still deeper into the scrub. The red heifer, with whom the story had begun and who had since become a "blood-red cow," now came into her own. We learned at the time of the bull fight that "in spite of the romantic tale-tellers, it is the females among the wild horses and cattle herds who provide the leaders, the males being occupied with duels among themselves and with the propagation of the species."[28] The middle-aged cow who had formerly led the scrubbers had been picked off by a shot, and

With the death of their leader that office fell upon the blood-red cow. She possessed in the fullest degree to which animals are given, the power of taking the initiative against untoward circumstances. When the others clung together, suffering thirst and hunger in passive misery, she, with her calf trotting at her heels, started away toward some place of feed and water as yet unvisited by the terror that pursued them. The rest followed her. She would have gone her way even had they not. That, probably, is why they chose to follow. And that, very likely, is the essence of all leadership.[29]

It was she, then, who saw the first "row of patches of raw yellow clay twice her own length apart. In the centre of each stood a post."[30] But the wires had not yet been run, and the cattle went through and drank.

Later, an ambush by armed men at the water hole took half their remaining number, whereupon their leader guided the survivors to the last unfenced water in a remote area. When its new owner arrived, he proved to be a humane man who let the scrubbers drink as long as he could. But when the last wire had to be run, he was forced to choose between fencing in the wild herd (now down to ten), in which event he was warned by his men that "they'll stand in one place and starve to death," or fencing them out to "die of thirst in the ranges."[31] He chose the kindest course for the cattle: to complete the fence while they drank at night and yard the full-grown next morning to be shot, hoping that the calves would settle down with his mob. The plan worked, save for the red cow: she saw the rails of the yard in time to bolt, trample a dog, escape a horseman, and return with her calf—to freedom.

But freedom is no unmixed blessing. The two scoured the ranges only to find them empty of other cattle, as of water, and they suffered increasingly and unceasingly from loneliness and thirst. The red cow had no milk for her calf, no hope for herself. Our last view of her comes in this moving passage with which the book closes:

> She had reached the last and highest of the camps. The reedy pool from which she and her mates used to drink when camped high on the mountain was now dry—its bed criss-crossed with a thousand cracks. Fenced out from all other water, the end was not far off.
>
> From the plateau where she stood the range fell away, fold on fold of green, to the level lands below. Behind her the ironstone cliffs rose sheer to the blue. Over her head the scant leaves of the box-trees turned in the faint air, with dry rustlings.
>
> The sun rose higher and beat more hotly down as the hours passed, but the red cow did not move.
>
> Gaunt and solitary, she stood, waiting to join the shadowy company of her kind—the wild herd that had passed from the ranges forever.[32]

Man-Shy is short enough to be read as Edgar Allan Poe recommended—at a single sitting in order to produce a strong emotional effect—and it is likely that few readers have come to the end unmoved. For rising critic Marjorie Barnard, "That last picture of the red cow with her liberty and nothing else fitted down on my mind like a black cap and made me sharply unhappy for days."[33]

Asked years later about his use of symbolism, Frank confessed: "It is never deliberate with me, but I have a theory that if you are sufficiently penetrating in your treatment of the Particular, you come upon the pattern of the General underlying it."[34] And of

Man-Shy specifically, he wrote (admitting that he might sound portentous), "The red heifer is the Heroic Will, Man pitted against the Infinite."[35]

III   *Genesis and Development*

The genesis of *Man-Shy* is now almost as familiar, to Australian readers at least, as the story itself. Frank has frequently explained how, under pressure of his promised quota for the next issue of his father's *Australia,* he thought back into the past (always, apparently, the recent Queensland past) for a story, and there came to mind a day when he had been riding through the scrub looking for lost cattle. He stopped to roll a cigarette, and as he looked up to light it, saw the head and shoulders of "a magnificent blood-red beast, with grey branching white horns with ebony tips, and great big eyes looking at me"—a cow three or four years old, in "the very peak of life." With his movement, she bolted, leaving him with only the sound of crashing in the undergrowth. He recalled then that he had seen tracks of "scrubbers" (the wild range cattle) at his dam, and as he turned the incident over in his mind, he also remembered hearing about roundups at outstations, where these cattle refused to settle down. Now in Sydney two or three years later, the picture still vividly before him, he decided to go back to the beginnings of such a beast, as a calf, and carry her story through: "the story of an animal who learnt early to value freedom above everything else and like all creatures must, animal or human, die possessed of nothing else."[36]

Not that the whole story came to him at once. He started with only a vague idea for a little story about a calf, and as a stockman he approached it somewhat facetiously. Early in the first installment in the magazine, he wrote of the red heifer's mother, "There was something rather funny about that skinny old cow lurching and grunting across the mud." In book form, the "rather funny" was changed, happily, to "grotesque." In the same installment, a report that the white cow, with both her own and the adopted red calf nursing, was "ruminative and contented," was followed by this unfortunately anthropomorphic subject of her ruminations: "A calf for nix!—which proves that merit does get its deserts, sometimes in this old world, after all!" This the book version wisely omits entirely. It also drops a final four paragraphs of the installment that had included the calves' expressions, after the cow had bedded them down and gone off for a drink, as being "that of those who would say, 'Not a bad old sort, is she, cobber?' "[37]

Further installments needed no such changes, as Frank had quickly begun to realize the possibilities of his subject and to treat it with due respect. In fact, putting the story together was an increasing joy; this writer who usually had to sweat over his composition was now working under the impetus of inspiration. "*Man-Shy* flowed like sap in spring," he admitted later; "I did as many as 4000 words at a sitting with almost no alterations or corrections." Again, "*Man-Shy* unravelled like a well-knit chemise."[38] Certainly the fluency of its style reflects this ease of writing; it did not stay with him when he faced workaday jobs.

But in the *Australia* version the author was still a long way from recognizing the full potential of his material. He later remembered its having appeared in the magazine in "about five slabs—say five weekends of work."[39] Actually, it was four. The bulk of the story was printed as three consecutive installments (November and December, 1923, and January, 1924) with the titles "One in Ten Thousand," "Man-Shy," and "The Scrubbers." Not until a year later (suggesting an afterthought) and only one issue before *Australia* ceased publication did "The Lesser Brethren," much of which was to become most of the novel's introduction, appear. As chapter 1 this became "Telling of the Herd," three paragraphs being dropped to allow for opening with the now familiar sentence about the mustering of the cattle (p. 45), and several pages of new material on the life of the cattle being added. Beyond this, the process of turning magazine installments into book went roughly like this: *Australia's* first installment became chapters 2 and 3; its second, 4 through 6; its third (minus the first fourteen paragraphs), 7 through 10. The only notable addition was the whole of chapter 11, the moving new "Bulls in Battle." The final chapters, 12 - 14, came largely from the conclusion of the belated last installment (January, 1925), which had already provided the opening of the book.

Thus the bulk of *Man-Shy* had lain quietly in the pages of the defunct *Australia* like a bank account waiting to be drawn upon until, with a new chapter, a few new paragraphs, a few changes in diction, and a little reordering, its unsung author turned it into a gold-medal-winning novel and an undeniable Australian classic.

How great the circulation of *Australia* was is not known, save that it can hardly have lived up to the optimistic monthly comments of its editor or it would not have failed. Certainly the appearance of the *Man-Shy* installments in its pages created little stir; someone in Sydney's literary circles might well have recognized their promise, but the magazine was not one likely to be read by the literati. Only one person is known to have laid later claim to having seen the material before book publication and recognized its promise. This was poet Mary Gilmore, to whom Frank's sister Dulcie had given the original magazine pieces. Mrs. Gilmore was tremendously enthusiastic about both the language and the subject matter, and wrote the author a highly laudatory letter in which she suggested working the four installments into a book. She had other suggestions, too, and invited him to visit her to discuss them. She later took credit, in a letter to the Palmers, not only for having encouraged him and helped him to revise but also for having talked to literary people and written to publishers in his behalf. It is curious that in all his reminiscences, Frank, who later was to know Mrs. (now Dame[40]) Gilmore well through working with her in the Fellowship of Australian Authors has left no record of help offered or received from this prestigious quarter. It was his brother Douglas who got the credit and the dedication.

The book *Man-Shy* left little to take exception to, in content, purpose, or style. It met with only one conspicuously adverse opinion, and that a belated one, worthy of being remembered along with the *Edinburgh Review's* famous dictum "This won't do!" of Wordsworth's and Coleridge's epoch-making *Lyrical Ballads*. It was uttered by John Reed in " 'Man-Shy,' a Criticism—Mainly Destructive," in Melbourne's literary quarterly *Angry Penguins* of 1945. Here, fourteen years after the book appeared, Reed found the inevitable tinge of anthropomorphism in it to be "false sentimentality," and went so far as to conclude that *Man-Shy's* publication was "basically harmful and damaging to our cultural reputation."[41]

Fortunately for Frank, the book was much admired elsewhere. Once the original Davison edition (The Australian Authors Publishing Co., Sydney, 1931) had won the A.L.S. medal, Angus & Robertson, who had refused the book before it became famous, picked it up for publication of a second edition in 1932 and a third in 1933, just for a beginning. It has never been out of print since. There have been English editions and American editions (some issued under the less meaningful title *Red Heifer*), junior library editions, editions illustrated and plain, hard-cover and paperback. A German translation, *Peitsche und Brandeisen*, appeared in 1973.

It is a fair guess that *Man-Shy* has been Australia's most frequently and numerously reprinted novel. In an interview in 1967, three years before his death, Frank was able to claim that in thirty-six years it had reached its twenty-sixth edition with close to a quarter of a million copies—a rare record, surely, for an Australian book. At the time of his death in 1970, it was reported that thirty editions had appeared, at home and abroad, with copies running well over a quarter million. The 1976 Angus & Robertson edition lists some thirty-three editions and reprints for their house alone. And the end is not yet.

As its author was to recall, its being "about a cow" had been a strong argument against it among publishers at first, but later became a talking point. *Man-Shy* is not the only book Frank was to write about animals (horses were to appear prominently in *The Wells of Beersheba*, and a dog as the hero of *Dusty*), but it is the best. Nor is Frank the only Australian to write about animals (he had a contemporary competitor in Henry G. Lamond, a later one in Erle Wilson), but he is the greatest.

From 1931 on (he was nearing forty), Frank was to live and write and be reviewed and introduced and referred to as, above all, the author of *Man-Shy*. When his father published a novel of his own, *Storm Bradley*, in 1932, its reviewers felt it necessary to remind their readers that "Mr. Davison is *not* the author of *Man-Shy*" or "Mr. Davison's son is the author of *Man-Shy*." When Frank himself died, shortly after the publication of a far longer novel about people, it was still his authorship of *Man-Shy*, not of that controversial later work, that was stressed in his obituaries. The reputation of *Man-Shy* opened publishers' doors and readers' purses to Frank's later works.

CHAPTER 5

Forever Morning

F ROM *Man-Shy* we now turn to a briefer examination of a
lesser novel, *Forever Morning*. The two books have in common
a rural setting, an origin in the magazine *Australia*, and an
appearance in book form in 1931. But how they differ: one a short
but brilliantly conceived and executed story of cattle; the other a
considerably longer but all too conventional narrative of people.
Frank himself said of the two, toward the end of his life, that *Man-
Shy* "was a most fortunate book for a young writer such as myself,
in that it gave scope for all I possessed while challenging nothing I
didn't possess. I also wrote *Forever Morning*, a much less successful
novel dealing with people."[1]

Novelist-critic Marjorie Barnard, entranced by *Man-Shy*, was inevitably disenchanted by *Forever Morning*, which she hoped had
been written first: a "first novel" to clear the way for greater rather
than a retrogression from one already great, but the evidence
appears to dash such hopes. Frank himself could not recall, years
later, which of the two narratives he had started first, but since he
was under agreement to fill so much space in *Australia* each month,
it is reasonable to assume that his work was published shortly after
its composition. While the bulk of both books appeared first in the
magazine, most of what was to constitute *Man-Shy* had been concluded there some months before more than a single piece of what
went into *Forever Morning* had appeared. And while both were
published as books in the same year, *Man-Shy* appears to have been
printed first by both the Davisons' and Angus & Robertson's
presses; in fact, it is a fair guess that *Forever Morning* would not
have attained to A&R standing without the prestige of *Man-Shy*.
Further, whereas *Man-Shy* continues to be reprinted to this day,
Forever Morning died with a third edition in 1932, with few,
presumably, to mourn its demise.

Forever Morning is the longer novel by far, containing a substantial hundred thousand words or so, and remained its author's longest piece of fiction for nearly forty years. It is a tale of men and women, creatures with whom Frank was at this time admittedly ill at ease as a writer. Specifically, it is a mill-run story of love between the hired hand and the boss's daughter, who are kept apart by a succession of melodramatic woes for the requisite number of pages before a happy ending. The setting is principally a homestead in a settled area of northern New South Wales, with a sally up into relatively wild Queensland and several down to urban Sydney.

In the story motherless Doris Brunton has spent five adolescent years with an aunt and uncle in Sydney, attaining to the accomplishments of a lady. But her heart has remained all this while in the bush of northern New South Wales with her father, Jim, on his prosperous selection, Ridgelands, though her mind is increasingly on the orphaned Andy—tall, dark, and handsome, background unknown—who has grown up at Ridgelands to be Jim's right-hand man. Now, at twenty, the girl is at last permitted to return home permanently, where she settles down in comfort (there is a resident housekeeper) with the conviction that Andy loves her, even though she doesn't love him—yet.

By coincidence (of which there is considerable in this novel), Andy has only just opened his heart to Doris on the subject of his unknown parentage when a disreputable, drunken female put off the train at Laffin's Creek, the town near Ridgelands, claims to be his long-lost mother. By further coincidence, the woman is killed by a motorcycle a few weeks later, just as it has become apparent that Andy's reluctant but devoted care is not going to change her ways. In the interim, however, he has proved the stuff of which we are glad to find him made by manfully rising to meet his apparent filial responsibility in spite of the pain and shame it costs him.

The result is that just as pity has at last awakened love in Doris's heart (it had lain near the surface all along), Andy packs his gear and rides up to Queensland "to cleanse himself and find his pride anew."[2] He gets a job with a mustering group and distinguishes himself as rider and as man, but remains victim of an inner struggle between his love for Doris and his sense of unworthiness. Fortunately, love wins, he quits his job (now a fencing contract) and, giving up the easier alternative of a Queensland selection and the eager daughter of a Queensland selector, returns to Ridgelands, arriving as the answer to Doris's prayers, for her father has recently been stricken with serious heart trouble. Andy further finds himself

rehabilitated as the result of a private inquiry that Jim had instituted into the boy's past, which revealed that the old sot was an
imposter, his real mother, now deceased, having been a far superior
sort. The cloud of illegitimacy, still present, could not obscure the
bright rays of hope with which Andy is now surrounded.

Here the book might have ended, but it drags on, through Jim's
death leaving a shockingly encumbered Ridgelands (bad judgment
plus bad times) jointly to Andy and Doris. Andy is further encumbered by his promise to the dying man that he will look after
both the place and the girl. Doris, physically and emotionally exhausted (to the point that she feels no immediate interest in Andy,
and far beyond what one would have expected of a healthy country
girl under the circumstances), goes back to her aunt and uncle in
Sydney, where she endures a ladylike debility while Andy works his
heart out to save Ridgelands. Months later, the harvest in, he takes
time off to go to Sydney, and on a nearby beach the book finally
ends—not with a bang, just a meeting of eyes and hands that leads
us to believe that the couple will shortly go back to Ridgelands
together and live happily ever after.

Forever Morning is conventional "magazine fiction" such as
Frank could probably have continued to grind out endlessly. But we
can believe that only the exigency of the Depression led him to put
this one together, and there seems to have been no question of his
wishing even to "boil the pot" with more novels of this caliber. He
had proved himself, with *Man-Shy*, to be capable of higher things,
and wished to get on with them. For the moment it will be worth
our while, however, to look at how he had set his hand to making
this second novel out of a half-dozen magazine installments.

Australia's lead story in May, 1924, was "Her People of the
Bush," which would prove to be no short story but the first installment of an unannounced—possibly even unprojected at that
time—long serial. This section was to become, under the same title,
the beginning of *Forever Morning*, with little change save for a
division into four chapters. The June issue carried a considerably
longer installment, "Lees of an Elder Vintage," which, again retaining the title, became chapters 5 through 10 in the book. A brief addition was made, however (a good one, too), to help thicken the plot
to novel length: a friend of Andy raises the question with Jim of
whether the boy's professed mother was genuine, inspired by the
appropriate consideration that "I've never seen a brindle scrub cow
with a purebred calf at foot. Have you?" This stirred Jim to reflec-

tion, and the added section ends with the sentence: "After tea, he went to his writing desk."[3] This is the most dramatic sentence in the book, for we are left to guess his purpose for more than a dozen chapters, after which the result, the reassuring identity of Andy's true mother, is revealed. What a refreshing device in a book which seldom leaves us in doubt as to *what* the outcome will be but often makes us wonder *when*.

"Some Backblock Arcadians," a short installment in July, becomes chapter 11, but with a title change, this time, to "In Arcady," a hymn to rural life where man chops, saws, and splits, and woman boils the billy. "The Bangtail Muster," in August, is another short installment; dealing with Andy's adventures in Queensland, it becomes the basis of chapters 12 through 14, under that title. These chapters are considerably fattened by the addition of a long description of the cowhands' clothing and by a longer chapter on station life, including some nine pages of the bush ballads sung by the men at a spontaneous "sing-song" in their quarters, inspired and accompanied by the popular mouth organ. Stretching his material to novel length from these few magazine installments was overtaxing the author's ingenuity; the reader finds himself congratulating the writer on having been content to leave *Man-Shy* brief.

There was no installment in September; Frank was never good at meeting deadlines, and now he had the excuse of being preoccupied with major repairs as he began to point the story toward a conclusion. By October, however, he had "Andy Takes Action" ready, an installment that was to be expanded to become chapters 15 through 20, each with its own new title. Notable additions include a chapter in which Doris encounters Ella Maddison Tinsdale, the horsewoman whom she had admired so much on first sight that she had deliberately lost the high jump competition in Sydney so that Ella might win. Now (another one of those coincidences) the woman has come to live in Laffin's Creek, having married her first love, a mere trooper, after the timely murder of her upper-class but drunken husband. From now on Ella plays a dual role: friend and confidante for Doris, and exemplar of the happiness possible for a pair who, like Andy and Doris, are socially mismatched. Another chapter fills us in, through the dying Jim's reflections, on the Brunton family's past: Jim's courtship, his wife Mary's untimely death, the loss of his son in World War I. It even details Jim's subsequent attempt, in middle age, to enter military service himself, a gesture reminiscent of Frank's father but without his success.

Most interesting of these additions is chapter 21, "A Modern Cavalier," in which Andy, while in Queensland, makes a spectacular ride through fresh flood waters to deliver a belated party dress to the daughter of a new settler just as the dance is about to begin. The book could have got along fine without it, but it lay conveniently at hand as a short story entitled "A Queensland Cavalier" by "Frederick Douglas" published in *Australia* a year before the beginning of the series from which most of *Forever Morning* was drawn. Only minor changes like names were needed, and it filled space.

At the end of this October installment we read, "The concluding story of this series will appear in our next issue"—the first intimation (other than content) that these had been a continuum. Actually the end was delayed until the December issue, when the series closed with its shortest installment, "The Chequerboard," placed well back in the magazine. Most of the new writing in the novel is thus to be found late, for "The Chequerboard" is fattened by the truth about Andy's background and Jim's purchase of the Caldwell place. There is also some judicious cutting (notably of Andy's trite declaration, "I love you, Doris, and I find I can't go home without you"[4]), and some general reordering and speeding up to a more subtle close. But *Australia* had already published all of the essentials, most of the bulk, of *Forever Morning*.

The novel announced itself in its first edition as "An Australian Romance by F. D. Davison" (Frederick Douglas, Junior, still, presumably, although Frank Dalby was shortly to replace him for life) and carried the lines "To my father and mother I respectfully dedicate this book." That first edition, put out by the Davisons' own stopgap publishing company, is badly set, carelessly proofread—presumably a cheap, hasty job to get in on the Depression's depressed market. It is clearly recognizable philosophically as published by the man who had earlier edited the *Australian Post* and *Australia* by its concluding notice, which hews strictly to the original "party line":

TO THE READING PUBLIC

The Australian Authors Publishing Co. is in business to make a market for the work of Australian writers, and confidently asks the support of the Australian public. It will give its patrons cheerful reading—books that tell that life is worthwhile—the reading of which leaves a pleasant taste in one's mental mouth.

Australian life is abrim with unwritten stories based on high courage and brave achievement. If our writers will dip their pens in brighter ink than some of them have hitherto used, and will set forth those stories, there will be no lack of readers.

"Forever Morning" is a book of that kind, and its publshers believe it merits, and will receive, a friendly reception at the hands of Australian book buyers.

What ails *Forever Morning*, then, appears to be the same set of paternal strictures that kept Frank's short stories secure within the yellowing pages of the magazines in which they had first appeared—strictures from which only the red heifer, an unspoiled child of nature, had been able to escape to greater glory.

CHAPTER 6

The Wells of Beersheba

F RANK'S early work had appeared in his father's magazines under numerous pseudonyms, but by the time *Man-Shy* and *Forever Morning* were published, he had settled for his own initials and surname, and the early editions of both books appeared under the name "F. D. Davison." With some degree of literary fame upon him, however, he changed in later editions to the two names by which he would thereafter be known exclusively—"Frank" for the great-uncle with whom he had first worked on the land as a boy, "Dalby" for a cattle town in the area of his former location in Queensland.[1]

Readers who had been fascinated by the small but moving *Man-Shy* only to be disconcerted by the longer but far lesser *Forever Morning* must have waited with mingled hope and anxiety for Frank's next work of fiction. When *The Wells of Beersheba* appeared in 1933, two years after his first success, its small size gave little hint of its importance. Nor had its genesis offered any promise, since to write at his best, Frank required inspiration, and this was a minor work commissioned under mundane circumstances. Walter Cousins, then manager of Angus & Robertson, decided to put out for the Christmas market six or eight little books that would be more than a greeting card but could be sold for half a crown. Since it was his firm that had taken over the publication of both of Frank's early novels from the Davisons' Australian Authors Publishing Co., Cousins quite naturally turned to Frank, as a "house author," to provide the substance of one of these gift books.

The rest appear to have vanished without a trace, having been as ephemeral as the circumstances would lead one to expect. But Frank had for a long time been brooding over the fiction potential of an incident from World War I—Australia's Lieutenant-General Sir Harry Chauvel's cavalry attack on the Turks at Beersheba during the Palestinian campaign—and gratefully seized on this assignment as an excuse to go to work on it.

The Wells of Beersheba admittedly owes much to Frank's own military experience. As he reflected many years later, it was "written by a young man, a happy warrior who had survived the campaigns of World War I."[2] Its dedication to "A Girl Who Loved a Soldier" was presumably directed to Kay Ede, the English wife he had married while he was in the service. He wrote the book, he explained, "after waiting years for someone who was there to write it because I knew it was epic. I brought to it my knowledge of cavalry warfare, my knowledge, from Australia, of dry-country conditions, and an amount of research that would have sufficed for a treatise on the campaign; much of the research was naturally of no use to me, but it gave me confidence and a feeling of freedom in selecting what I wanted. When I sat down to write I knew everything, from the phase of the moon at the time to minor accoutremental details in which the A.L.H. [Australian Light Horse] differed from the British Cavalry" [in which he himself had served].[3] It was naturally a source of great satisfaction to him when, after his publisher had sent copies of the book to the A.L.H. at Victoria Barracks, he learned that the men who had taken part in the charge he described thought he had been one of them.

There had been some debate over how to classify *Man-Shy* because of its small size and unusual subject matter; a much greater difficulty was posed by the *Wells*. This volume is small indeed—closer to a long short story than to even a short novel. Its substance is history, but its handling is fictional. In the first edition, the subtitle is "A Light Horse Legend," and the text is prefaced by the words "This is a legend. Its aim is to clothe literal fact with those imaginative truths of which historians do not speak." In its later appearances this stated aim is dropped, and the subtitle changed to "An epic of the Australian Light Horse 1914 - 1918." Yet it is hardly epic in either content or length: little more than ten thousand words to recount a single attack of Australian cavalry on the Turks at Beersheba.

When the *Wells* was published, Frank confessed to the Palmers his fear that reviewers "will make stupid comparisons with Man-Shy."[4] Inevitably, since it celebrates Australia's horses, as the early book had celebrated her cattle—but in a very different way, true. The cattle had been on their open range, escaping men; the horses are thousands of miles from home, serving them. Too, the men play a far larger and more valorous role in the *Wells* than in *Man-Shy*, somewhat justifying Frank's remark that "It is really not a story of horses. . . . The horses gave me a unique angle of approach."[5]

Small as it is, *The Wells of Beersheba* is divided into five sections, the first and shortest ("Parade") being a brief background to the successful Palestinian campaign carried out by the combined forces of the allies under the command of Australia's Chauvel. Of this campaign, the charge made by the A.L.H. which is the substance of the book was the successful beginning. The following section ("Troop Horses") opens with "They are all Australian bred—bone of her bone," and continues with a lyrically descriptive listing of the individual mounts and their geographical origins that takes the reader nostalgically across the length and breadth of their homeland.

The grey with the neat forehand was foaled where Illawarra's hillsides tumble down to the sea. The bay mare with the white off hind ran beside her dam where Jimbour Plains sweep unbroken from sky to sky. She was five-off before she felt a girth around her.[6]

Many more are described before we are reminded that "These are the veterans,"[7] and that

There are many who are not here. There were those whose hearts broke within bodies taxed beyond their power to suffer. There were those who fell in battle—the bursting shell and the whining bullet knew no difference between horse and rider. The desert which the army has won—returned again to its immemorial silences—is littered with the shrunken frames of those who died. They lie half-buried in the sands that have drifted against them.[8]

But of the survivors who will shortly be going into battle again,

These are the old campaigners, whom Fate has spared and Time has tried. They are leaner than one would wish—worn with hard riding. A twelve-stone trooper, and half his weight again in arms and accoutrements, is a heavy burden to carry when the marches are long.

For months there has been nothing at the end of a march but a picket rope, bare to the blaze of the sun and the whip of the wind—that and a careful measure of corn. These are they who will carry the battle into the plain of Palestine against the stubborn and still unbeaten enemy.

These are the great-hearted ones.[9]

Not even the men who ride them are given so moving a series of tributes.

"Bivouac" finds man and beast settled in for a day's rest under the burning desert sun, between the long night marches. Following the order "Feed!" nose-bags were slipped on, and "There was now a brief contentment. Big dark eyes looked forth above the rims of the bags. The smell of oats wet with saliva escaped, and met the nostrils wholesomely. The rhythm of a thousand jaws, champing, engaged the ear."[10] The men crawled into their shelters for what rest they could get, save for the guards on the horselines, one of whom squatted on his haunches at the end of his squadron. Now it is man's turn to be celebrated:

His eyes were half closed against the bright light. His face and arms were burnt nearer black than brown, and were lean with the leanness of strenuous living. Though young, his face was seamed. Hardship, short food, and insufficient sleep were his portion. Yet he did not look harried. Squatting there, in repose, his hearing directed toward the horses behind him, his eyes alertly watching the scene in front, his bearing of himself was easy. It suggested a man who had found his body and spirit able to meet the demands made of them. . . . He had fought the desert and fought his way across it. He had slept on it, wearily content, with no cover between him and the stars. He knew the plains in the baking noon and the chill of night. . . .

That other life, the one that lived in memory, was a long way behind him now. It was something to which he might not return. On Gallipoli's ridges and beneath the sands of Sinai slept many a mate of his. . . . The soil of Palestine would cover many more—perhaps himself. He had grown used to that thought. He eyed it—for who was he that he should ask for special dispensation?—with a soldier's quiet and sustaining fatalism.[11]

As he became conscious that a big engagement was impending, "A tremor passed through the nerves just under his skin. Was it fear? A man didn't call it that. Rather it was the elation that comes to the brave and the near brave on the eve of battle."[12]

Next is "Night March," relating not the first such by any means but one that was made especially meaningful by the issuing of double rations, portending an engagement with the enemy before the next rest. As for the horses, "Under the saddles there was a world of courage. . . . Sustained by comradeship between horse and horse, and by a strange trusting comradeship with the men they carried, they set themselves to the unknown."[13] As for the men, they retained their typically Australian humor. Queried by a soldier who had become separated from his unit, "Who are you? Who are you?" they mingled their honest answers with "replies facetious and profane.

'We're the Bicycle Battalion, Mate!'
'We're Cook's tourists, looking for—Cook!' "[14]
They were conscious that "The tradition that the southern breed
were warrior horsemen rested with them, and under a mask of sar-
donic humor, they were proud in sustaining it. There were but few
among them who would that night have surrendered their
saddles."[15]
The little book concludes with the part that the whole has been
leading up to—"Battle." At daybreak, awaiting the order to mount
and advance, the men breakfasted hastily, sipping lightly from their
water bottles. "There was no water for the horses, although at the
sweet smell of it, an enquiring whinny came from their patient
line."[16] As men and horses moved out, the sound and sight of
fighting came from the forward distance. An advance brigade swept
on despite enemy fire. "Behind them, riderless horses galloped
aimlessly among the fallen, and horseless men ran to try to catch
them."[17] At last

Beersheba, the disputed village, lay within the plain. . . . The light-
green clouds among its buildings were pepper-trees, and the tall bronze-
green plumes were ecualypts. Its houses sprawled widely apart; except for
white mosque and tall minaret, it might have been a township in the
Australian bush.[18]

All day the battle raged. When men dismounted to storm the
ridge, their mounts were left with horse holders, four horses to a
man, the attention of these battle-wise horses divided between the
bursting shells and their thirst.

A trooper uncorked his bottle and raised it to his lips to draw a lukewarm
mouthful. There was a shuffling of hooves and four dark muzzles were
thrust toward him; one, that of his own horse, was pushed gently against his
arm.
"Sorry, old man!" A shamed sense of the fellowship of the flesh lent
sincerity to the soldier's words, as he thrust off the horse's head.[19]

At last the ridge was won, the way cleared for the attack on
Beersheba. But nightfall was at hand, and the commanding general
faced a dilemma: to rout the enemy from trench to trench in the
gathering darkness was not feasible, but to delay watering the
horses was to lose the engagement.

Water was thirty miles behind him—or three miles in front. To retire on the wells from which his horses had last drunk would be to leave victory in the hands of the enemy.

It was the moment of crisis in battle.[20]

Much more was at stake than the winning of Beersheba, for on it depended the success of the British infantry back in Gaza. The general, "not accustomed to losing battles,"[21] gave the order—for his cavalry to advance against infantry that was entrenched and supported by machine guns and artillery.

Men and horses understood, and were sustained by "a courage not of each, but of all."[22] The Turkish artillery took a heavy toll of both—until the rapidity of their advance put them under the shells. Then the machine-guns and rifles—till again the bullets whistled overhead. Then the trenches. "In the last hundred yards it seemed to the riders not that they raced to the trenches but that the trenches were drawn to them."[23] Line after line was leaped—or stumbled into, for hand-to-hand fighting—and finally, while "the failing light was sufficient to reveal the last moments of the great charge"[24] to the Australian commanders on their hilltop, the town was won.

It was a victory for men, opening up greater triumphs to come. Yet, though the author could reasonably claim that his account is not really a story of horses, it was *for* them, one might say, as well as *by* them, that the battle was won. With them the narrative opened, and with them it closes:

> The day was gone. The moon looked down on the still and silent field. In the town, men laboured. The smell of the water, cold and sweet, was released on the dusty air. Standing weary and patient, out among the ridges, the horses smelled it, and a whinny ran from line to line.
>
> Through the night the streets of the town were loud with the clatter of hooves walking. Brigade after brigade, the horses were led in, light horse and gunner, to drink with slackened girths and bitless mouths at the wells of Beersheba.[25]

No false notes are sounded in this small book. Its poetic sweep suggests that the author was caught up in the writing of it even as he had been in *Man-Shy*. But while the *Wells* may rival *Man-Shy* in power of concept and beauty of style, it has known much less success, perhaps because its theme is less universal, although Frank, pressed for its symbolism, called it a working model of communal effort. Whatever the cause, its history is brief: first published in 1933, it reappeared in a revised version in 1947 (how Frank loved to revise, as we shall see), still within its own small covers. Not until 1964 was a wider distribution achieved, when it was included as the lead piece in *The Road to Yesterday*, Frank's second and last collection of short stories. This was an appropriate enough inclusion, since it is shorter than the longest of them, and welcome, surely, since it thus became more readily accessible.

Curiously, the *Wells* is almost the only piece of Frank's writing that reflects even indirectly his own several youthful and impressionable years in military service (a much later short story, "Fathers and Sons," was written for quite another purpose and with a very different attitude toward war). This dearth is especially strange when we realize how close to the roots of his own experience both his fiction and his nonfiction lie. Perhaps he was a little ill at ease with his military experience, as an Australian in the English forces. A quarter of a century after the war he explains,

I went to England to enlist because like a lot of other mugs, I thought the war might be over before I got into it. I was homesick for the Australian Forces in the same way as I was homesick for my own country throughout the years of my wanderings. Beersheba, I think, was in the last resort an expression of that nostalgia, notwithstanding that it did not appear until years afterward.[26]

He points out, however, that even though he had been "a bit of a Kiplingesque romantic" when he joined up, the *Wells* does not concentrate on the glory of battle but rather pays tribute to the endurance of men and horses. If the reader does not altogether follow his disclaimer, let him remember that it was uttered during a later war, when Frank's thinking on the subject had greatly changed.

Despite that change, Frank never lost his fondness for *The Wells of Beersheba;* witness his including it years later in *The Road to Yesterday*. But perhaps its most lasting significance for him is to be found in an introductory note to the 1947 edition, repeated as a headpiece in 1964:

In the years since it was first written, this glimpse of an old campaign has become in a small way a memorial to a vanished arm of the service. The aeroplane, the tank, and the infantry-transport lorry have outdone the horse in range, speed, and endurance; and brought the cavalry's long and gallant history to a close.

CHAPTER 7

Blue Coast Caravan

THROUGH three books Frank Dalby Davison had become known in the early 1930s as a writer of fiction. In the mid-1930s, however, he published two travel books, both records of personal experience though far removed from one another in time and place: *Blue Coast Caravan* (1935) and *Caribbean Interlude* (1936). Though neither, understandably, went beyond a first edition, both are worth looking into as we trace his development as a writer.

We shall never know what the financial insecurity of the Depression years may have kept Frank from writing, but it was directly responsible for the existence of *Blue Coast Caravan*, for as the Depression deepened, it aggravated Frank's already serious money problems. Early in 1934, therefore, he responded eagerly to a proposal that had been suggested to him the previous year and that now promised to answer the immediate question of what to live on, even though it involved a curious kind of collaboration.

Dr. Brooke Nicholls of Melbourne was by vocation a dentist, by avocation a field naturalist; and he was also, as Frank remarked later, a "book-mad man of means."[1] He had already written part of a book on his interests, including the Great Barrier Reef. Now he proposed to Frank that they two and their wives make a leisurely camping trip of perhaps four months through northern Queensland, the major purpose of which would be the joint production of a book based on the experience. Nicholls would advance the travel expenses; Frank would do most of the actual writing of the book. In addition, the trip itself would be an enviable experience.

In a car hauling a trailer loaded with simple camping gear, the travelers got away from Sydney about the first of May, 1934, and ultimately reached their objective, Cairns. But the trip was terminated considerably short of the proposed four months, probably for personal reasons. Although he "wrote with a tight mouth" so that no hint of friction appears in the book, Frank later admitted that the experience had been an unpleasant one, personally, with two families from such differing economic strata living so closely together for so many weeks; in fact, he called the venture a ghastly failure in human relations.

Then there was the writing. The Foreword to *Blue Coast Caravan* opens with this statement:

This story is our companion of the open road. The greater part of it was written in the rest periods of our journey; on a stool in a tent; on a log by a river-bank—with the scribe's hat tilted back, or pulled forward, to shade his nape or his nose—by lamplight in the stranger's cottage; in a humpy, by the light of a couple of candles stuck in the necks of bottles; in the shade of a shed on a hill-side above a seventy-mile sweep of coast; on the veranda of a pub looking down on beds of crotons; under the palms of a coral isle. It was often overlooked by the curious minded and its course was sometimes interrupted by the conversationally inclined.[2]

If this early writing, under these circumstances, sounds difficult, it was nothing compared to the labor of shaping the material for publication. In his first letter to Vance Palmer after his return from the trip, Frank reported himself as "busy writing up from notes made along the road. I am back now with 75,000 words done and am under the need of completing it by the end of the month. I would like to finish it and then throw it in the bottom drawer for a year; but that can't be done."[3] Four months later he was still at work—had reached about ninety thousand words (Angus & Robertson wanted only eighty thousand) when Dr. Nicholls sent in twenty thousand "which he will expect to be included." Further, Nicholls's interests being particular (doodle-bugs, etc.) and his own, general, Frank feared the finished project would look like a cross between a layer cake and a club sandwich. "I hate the thought of it, but it's got to be done—and quickly."[4]

The worst handicap for Frank was that of all writers he needed to feel warmed by his material, as he had been in preparing his two successes, *Man-Shy* and *The Wells of Beersheba*, and as he had not been in writing the mediocre *Forever Morning*. Marjorie Barnard was later to analyze his talent as a "small clear spring of genius" and as "creative tides" that made it possible for him to write well only when the mood was upon him. When, early in 1935, he at last sent the finished manuscript to Angus & Robertson, it was refused—tentatively. Again, of all writers, Frank was one who needed encouragement, and he turned to the required rewriting with

bad grace. After a couple of months of this, he went so far as to turn
the manuscript over to Marjorie Barnard (he had met her the
previous year and felt a justifiable trust in her judgement) to "sub-
edit." She responded with seven pages of "necessarily brutal comment," and wrote Vance Palmer this further reflection on Frank's
personality:

Davison swallowed the seven pages with the best grace in the world. One
doesn't have to worry about his vanity. He's too proud to be vain but there
are some curious formal streaks in his pride so that friendship with him is
just a little like a game of snakes and ladders.[5]

Frank put her criticism to good and prompt use, Angus & Robertson
accepted the results, and before the year was out, *Blue Coast
Caravan* was published, with "Frank Dalby Davison" in large type,
on cover and title page, followed by "Brooke Nicholls" in small
type.

Briefly, the book is a detailed account of what the Davisons and
the Nichollses saw and heard and reflected on in the course of their
several weeks' trip. Description is its backbone, description that is
often brilliant in quality, oftener tedious in quantity. There is no
evidence of fictional distortion of fact, as in the later *Caribbean
Interlude;* the four principals, Frank and Kay, Brooke ("the Doctor") and Barbara, all appear in their own persons. But curiously,
especially in the work of a novelist-author, none of them are
developed into familiar, recognizable personalities; "The Doctor,"
particularly, is never allowed to emerge as a distinct individual. The
author himself is always "Frank," never "I"—presumably in an effort not to distract from the supposedly corporate nature of the
enterprise. Harder to explain is the fact that things are done or experienced by "one of us"—which one is rarely specified. "One of
our number went down to the sea for a swim."[6] "One of us, who
had not previously caught a fish, brought the first fish aboard."[7]
When the group debated the identity of a distant vegetative color,
"One said it was wattle blossom, but another said not at that season
of the year."[8]

The fine lean prose of *Man-Shy* disappears in a welter of passives
throughout. The travelers seldom passed cars, reached towns, and
saw things, but cars were passed, places would be come upon, and
things were to be seen. In Cairns, "An establishment in Townsville
was remembered" with a sign advertising a Chinese as a "Dinkum
Tailor." Whereupon "It was wondered if it was not a reflection on

our national character."[9] The only accident of the trip, occurring when a broken trailer axle pulled the car dangerously off a muddy road, is reported with the passive "A culvert had been crossed"; then this remarkable double passive enhanced by a highly dangling modifier: "Having had the greasy road in mind all day, it was assumed that the car had skidded; and an effort was made to straighten it up."[10] All of this rhetorical impersonality, when the author himself was driving! Enough of these—but by no means all. What a heyday Frank, the inveterate reviser, might have had with this book if only a second edition had ever been called for to give him the opportunity!

John Steinbeck's *Travels with Charley* suffers from some apparent padding provided to make a full book of a not quite full enough experience; so do Davison's travels with the Nichollses. The accounts of the variety of people met on the journey, their occupations, and the anecdotes they told are welcome, but some observations seem pointless, even in context. The boy and girl who meet and are absorbed in each other while the caravaners are mending a blowout are not peculiar to the Mary River valley but as universal as Romeo and Juliet. The travelers' speculations concerning the relationship of the middle-aged man and young girl who share their carriage on the train to Cairns could have provided an amusing interlude had the four onlookers been individualized, as they should have been long before; but as a group enterprise it has little to offer us. Still less is added by this report of an encounter as the four travelers left the Cardwell railway station, where the Italian caterers rang bells to attract trade, to go to the beach:

On our way to it we passed the fat Italian. As we did so a Chinese girl, very pretty and fashionably dressed, came out of his fish shop. Whether she was a customer or a part of the establishment we could not say. She spoke to the Italian and he stopped his bell-ringing to answer her. They spoke to each other in English.[11]

Only that and nothing more. One suspects many of these observations of having been copied verbatim from Frank's travel diary regardless of the fact that the prevailing purpose of the entire narrative was unable to accommodate them.

We would gladly exchange some thousands of words in the book, by Chinese reckoning, for the equivalent in pictures. Although both Frank and Brooke carried and used cameras extensively, not one illustration appears—perhaps a publisher's economy, but a pity for a largely descriptive book.

But *Blue Coast Caravan* had, and still has, its virtues. The greatest of these is that it looms early and high on the list of protests against what Australian man had done, and was doing, to the Australian landscape. The book need not have protested; as we have noted, its declared purpose was to record the party's experiences between Sydney and Cairns. This area being new to the author, he approached it with a kind of wide-eyed wonder, but disillusionment set in on the first day out. Although Gosford, the first town of any consequence north of Sydney, had few attractions, it wore "an air of comfortable prosperity," reminding the travelers of "a rather ordinary little female snuggled into an expensive fur coat."[12] But through Ourimbah and beyond, the scene changed.

Someone's misdirected zeal had settled a lot of people on unsuitable land. What had possibly once been a pleasant tract of forest had been cleared, only to uncover a soil that sprang a tough second growth of rushes and wiry shrubs. It was sour land, giving a grudging yield to tillage. The farms were miserably small, there being only a stone's throw between dwellings. The homesteads were old, unpainted, and in varying stages of disrepair. Their appearance suggested occupants trapped in their own poverty—too poor to get away. What the dilapidated walls concealed it was not pleasant to imagine; to look on the houses from the road seemed an intrusion upon a degree of poverty that had a right to privacy.

The memory of those homes haunted us for some time after they were passed. The effect on us was, on the whole, salutary. They suggested the thought that we, being, so to speak, in search of Australia, must not expect an unbroken idyll. We must endeavour to be realists, accepting the bad along with the good.[13]

Frank's final impressions were not more favorable. On his return he wrote to Vance Palmer that as for the country they traveled through, the trip was "something of a fizzle. We took with us about half a ton of luggage but forgot to include a supply of rose coloured spectacles. It seemed to me, as the map unrolled itself, that we Australians have plundered the delicate beauty of our continent and disfigured it with a careless, tin-shanty semi-civilization. We saw bare little farms without so much as a tree to hide their ugliness, frowsey little hamlets, and big towns that could hardly have been more dreary looking than they were. I don't know why I should so suddenly have wakened to it. But there it was. It was painful at times."[14]

In fact, these note-taking travelers intent on making a book found themselves facing certain alternatives:

Would they soothe the susceptibilities of those who might read the narrative by confining their observations to matters that were of pleasant report? Bearing in mind the adolescent eagerness with which their coun-trymen welcome anything fostering self-admiration, and their equally adolescent dread of unflattering comment, would the caravanners carefully gloze over anything that might prick their vanity? Or would they take the decent way of letters and deal adequately and honestly (so far as lay within their power) with their subject matter as it presented itself? The latter course was chosen.[15]

But not without some later trepidation. When Frank first submitted his manuscript to Angus & Robertson, he feared they might object to it as not "pretty" enough, might even be hurt in their tender patriotism. Though the editors did return it for some rewriting, "prettiness" was not, apparently, a consideration, for *Blue Coast Caravan* as published is filled with details—and grief—about what Robin Boyd, years later, was to popularize under the title *The Australian Ugliness* (1960). It would be gratifying to report that Frank was influential, in the thirties, in bringing about an im-provement—a lessening of the senseless rape of the natural bush, a beautifying of the country towns with their bleak galvanized iron dwellings, but this cannot be said. Unlike Boyd's book, Frank's was never popular enough to have much influence, and the back coun-try continued to present, all too often, the same face that Frank reported to Vance Palmer in 1934: "a great deal of mutilated beau-ty, a small amount of accidental beauty, almost no created beauty, and a very great deal of created ugliness."[16]

The book had a scattering of other virtues. It was written at a time when few Australians could travel much through their own country, not just because of the economic slump but because roads, especially in the north, were shockingly bad. Even Frank's party had to abandon their vehicle at Maryborough and proceed to their destination, Cairns, by train. To their fellow countrymen *Blue Coast Caravan* offered generous glimpses of both territory and people; its account of the mixed population of the north, with its examination into the lives and circumstances of the aborigines, was especially il-luminating at the time. The book further offers an interesting contrast between northeast Australia in the 1930s and its present state, for today's reader. Perhaps it is a pity that there aren't more of him; but it is unlikely that many will turn, or return, to this book.

Frank would not be surprised. Throughout his life he looked back on *Blue Coast Caravan* as the biggest failure of all his works. He felt that it had been written under impossible conditions: having to get out his typewriter at every stop and do his thousand words a day, writing of the place last visited while looking at the new—of Brisbane, for instance, after a day's travel and sightseeing around Maryborough. He made no allowance for the months of writing and rewriting that he put in after his return, when he should surely have begun to see the forest showing through the trees; he just remembered the entire episode as producing "something very like a nervous breakdown for the writer, altogether a tragic affair."[17] Toward the end of his life he did concede that there was *some* good writing in the book, and felt its worst feature was its bad temper—the fact that it scolded solemnly instead of satirizing or making fun of the country towns.

It may seem like idle carping to spend this much time on a book that even its author did little to defend, but it is important to recognize, this early in Frank's career, what went wrong. To Vance Palmer, friend of both, Marjorie Barnard wrote of Frank as a writer: "He's more vulnerable and easily turned aside than the rest of us. He hasn't any ready mades and every bit of his hack work is hand made, a terrible strain."[18] Frank himself wrote to Vance during the *Blue Coast Caravan* period (late 1934) that his last three years had been a nightmare—that his recurrent attacks of nerves meant that he needed both physical labor and financial security. When secure and full of an idea, he was always at "top of form," but he could not, like many of his writer friends, turn out an acceptable job at need or on demand—this, in spite of his having begun his writing as a hack journalist for his father's periodicals. Marjorie attributed his difficulty to his lack of formal education, which left him with nothing to fall back on if the spirit refused to move. This may explain why he spent his writing time "oscillating between high spirits and the dumps." It is significant that in his fifties, after his retreat from a dull office job to his beloved and relatively undemanding farm, and with steady help and support from a most undemanding and cooperative second wife, he was unable to stick for more than three months with a small weekday feature for a Melbourne newspaper, a job that he had undertaken for money, not love; yet he was to be able to spend the last quarter century of his life there on a single final novel with no certainty—scarcely a likelihood—of publication, because in it he was saying what he had long wanted to say.

CHAPTER 8

Caribbean Interlude

*B*LUE *Coast Caravan* had largely failed because it was an account of travels too recent to be properly digested; it might have been improved had its author been able to "throw it in the bottom drawer for a year," as he had wished. Further, the experience had been too unpleasant in many respects (his reaction to his companions and to much of the Australian countryside) to be a source of the inspiration he needed. Further still, it had been solely a record of personal experience, and Frank was essentially a writer of fiction. Thus his second travel book, *Caribbean Interlude* (1936), was a vast improvement: it harked back a score of years to experiences enjoyed while his heart was young and gay, and its facts were, he later admitted, freely enlarged upon. Here the author chooses to tell us what should have been (or what he feels will be most effective in the telling) against a background of what actually was.

Between his leaving his family in Chicago and his sailing to England and the war, Frank had worked as printer for a ship in which he made three trips from New York to the Caribbean. Now, writing in retrospect, he consolidates these three voyages into one and takes frankly admitted other liberties with people and events. The result is a highly readable if not great book. Marjorie Barnard, who had been frankly critical of *Blue Coast Caravan*, was enthusiastic about *Caribbean Interlude* while it was still in progress, reporting to the Palmers that Frank "has caught, by a magic that cannot be analyzed, the authentic bloom of youth." [1]It was Nettie Palmer who unwittingly supplied the title. Knowing the material that Frank was engaged with, she wrote to ask how his "Caribbean interlude" was coming along, and he felt that her phrase admirably suited the book (certainly preferable to the "Ships, Girls and the Spanish Main" by which its advent had once been announced). *Caribbean Interlude* was published in mid-1936.

Frank's purpose in writing the book was twofold: to capture the feeling of being young and going places, and to show another side to sea life than that commonly portrayed by sailor authors, who limited themselves to tedious discussions of their adulteries in port. He succeeded in both aims. While heeding his warning that his story should not be taken seriously as autobiography, the reader can nonetheless find the background—the sights and sounds of the Caribbean—and the feelings of youth agreeably authentic.

Caribbean Interlude tells of a cruise from New York through various West Indies ports to the northern coast of South America as seen through the eyes of a twenty-year-old Australian crew member (to whom I shall quite properly refer as Frank throughout). Its interest lies in its characterizations of passengers and crew, its descriptions of ports and people, its accounts of its author's adventures, and its relating of his reactions to the whole. Of the seventy-one passengers we learn that

forty-eight were school ma'ams. In the United States it was the summer vacation period, and, by a coincidence, the least popular and cheapest time of the year in which to make a voyage south. With a delight in doing things in concert which is characteristic of their nation, they had arranged this pilgrimage in mass formation to equatorial shores. These ladies were travelling with the double motive of recuperating from the strenuousness of the previous school term, and of improving their minds. Forty-eight female pedagogues! The mere thought of their combined impact against the strongholds of ignorance was impressive. I wasn't so long out of school myself but what I viewed them with a certain amount of awe.[2]

The author's main contacts among the crew were with the members of the chief steward's department, a class apart from passengers and from the ship's crew alike. The social levels on board were rigidly maintained, so much so that when egalitarian Frank innocently went to call on the ship's wireless operator, a fellow Australian, he found the man most reserved: "one of those instances in which the bond of nationality was not sufficient to bridge the chasm of class."[3] Frank and his mate belonged to the "scullions," a group that were bunked together in the "glory hole" under the fo'c's'le, to which they retired in their spare time to engage in drunkenness, gambling, and profane conversation, at sea as they did in port. All of this Frank and a young American pantryman named Marshall, his "mate" (Australian for a man's close friend and companion), are reported as having observed without participation; a chapter entitled "Two Pure Young Men in Jamaica" might have served for the whole book, even to the point of falsifying, perhaps, some of the actual behavior of the young adventurers. It might have been American fiction's Frank Merriwell reporting, when we are advised that they found the blandishments of the port prostitutes "too commercial for romantic young men such as we."[4]

Yet the two were unhappily incapable of mouthing the elaborately romantic declarations that they found to be customary and proper for a gentleman to make to an unknown lady on the street, in Spanish countries, much as they desired to do so.

Marsh and I would dearly have liked to make use of this very charming custom. Looking back after one passerby Marsh got as far as making a preliminary gesture by wiping his mouth with the back of his hand, but he wasn't equal to it and neither was I. Our up-bringing was against it. Our entire racial tradition was opposed to it. We couldn't, in a moment, bridge the gap imposed between us and opportunity by inherited ideas of how the opposite sex should be approached. In short, we were in terror of being roundly snubbed.[5]

The "authentic bloom of youth" is captured, credibly and charmingly, in the report of a passenger, a girl with sea-gray eyes traveling alone, who became the focus of this unsophisticated twenty-year-old author's thoughts.

To see her was to take away a disturbing image, which made you secretly a little dissatisfied with your place in the glory hole.

She met my glance on an occasion when I passed her and smiled. This was very cheering. It was not the sort of smile a woman passenger gives you for drawing back at the head of a companionway. It was of a personal character, something to take away with you. I took it to work with me, and thought about it while in solitude I pursued my duties. Its effect was to make me feel that I could live a better and a purer life. After that smile I lived on two planes of existence, one the lower, or commonplace, in which I ate and made merry, talked with Marsh and kept my place among men; the other in the upper atmosphere, whither I wafted on thinking of Grey-eyes. I would have made inquiries about her, but I didn't like to cause mention of her in the glory hole, nor to risk disclosing my interest in her.[6]

Marsh actually had a conversation with her, leading Frank to some unsettling comparisons. His own face he later described as having "freckles that spattered it just as if someone had squirted pea soup at me." On the other hand,

Marsh had fine hair with a soft wave in it, the nose and chin of a youthful Byron, a chin that must have given its modeller a moment of joy, and grey eyes that had an enigmatic droop. He had a smile—not a grin—and a voice so full of soft southern modulations that he could have coaxed a she-alligator to let him steal her eggs from under her.[7]

Most interesting are the author's accounts of the strange lands, strange people, encountered in the course of the trip. Among the many "niggers" on the Kingston wharf was

one whose beauty of proportion and glory of raiment claimed and held the eye. The entire scene of people, sheds, vista of roofs and sudden green hills was but a background for his splendor.

His presence was evidently intended as a gesture from authority. But beyond an occasional glance at the crowd, his duties required him only to be present and to look like something. He was about thirty years of age, coal-black, and standing something over six feet in height. He was sparely built, flat backed, and had an athletic taper from his wide shoulders to his ankles. He wore a spotless white helmet, a white tunic, with polished brass buttons and scarlet facings, fitting like a lady's glove and cut with a most decided waist. He had navy blue trousers with a broad scarlet stripe down the side, cut close to the shape of his long elegant legs. His neat black shoes had a shine that gave back a twinkle to the sun. With his little silver-mounted swagger-stick twirling, or tucked under his arm, he walked up and down the wharf like a game-cock showing himself to the hens. Standing, he stood like a living statue of the Glorious Male. If he had a wife she must have been proud of him.[8]

To the squalor still to be found in many of the Caribbean ports he visited, Frank was impervious; almost no hint here of the critical eye with which he viewed his native land and reported in *Blue Coast Caravan*. His only "cause" now was Youth, and an air of gaiety throughout pleasantly enlivens his prose, even when the circumstances he relates are not happy ones. The behavior of these Rover Boys was not altogether flawless: once, they overstayed their shore leaves and were soundly berated by the chief steward. Frank later reported that "I had been called a ——— Colonial and a ——— ———— kangaroo, but Marsh suffered much worse than that! He had been three times called a Yankee with contemptuous adjectives." In addition, the steward made trouble for the pair throughout the remainder of the voyage—but what of that? "We mustn't let it cast a shadow on our blythe chronicle."[9]

One of the noteworthy things about the book is the clear stamp, in language and outlook, of its Australian author, in this report of what was reputedly an American-owned ship operating out of an American port under British colors and with a predominantly British crew. The pilot, a big man who took them out of New York harbor, was "active as a rock wallaby." Among the crew was "a nuggety little Scot." Marsh, in a state of depression, "snapped like a dingo." At one stop a native woman, needing to scratch, "put her hand inside her dress and fossicked about." Walking inland in Jamaica, the boys found themselves in sight of "both bush and sea," and Kingston had the naiveté of "any other bush town." Cristobal-Colon, too, was outwardly "an Australian country town," and in one of its beer-shops Frank's "bush-bred eye" discerned blood marks on the wall.[10]

This story of an Australian's wanderings was obviously written for home consumption, not only in the Australian idiom but with a traveler's eye and ear for the peculiarities of behavior and speech of others, especially Americans. Of a seaman attempting to cross from the fo'c's'le to the main deck in rough weather, "In the American phrase, he had to act on a hunch."[11] The predominantly British crew is explained on the grounds that "Americans don't take kindly to work entailing the rendering of personal service."[12] The difficulties of the ship's pantrymen are compounded by "the American custom of serving each vegetable in a separate dish like a dicky-bird's bath."[13] The fifteen-inch caliber gun they saw at the Canal Zone was "said by the American newspapers—who are notoriously careless in the use of the superlative—to have been the biggest in the world."[14]

The author was alert to the weaknesses of other nationalities, too. A French widow who approached him in the hope that he might know her friend in Sydney led him to say that "People who can claim one of the centres of the older civilization as their place of birth are parochial-minded and given to thinking that remote places like Australia are as small as their knowledge of them."[15] Bert, a Canadian crew member, was, "like many of us Outlanders, born convinced that his native land was first in the minds of men."[16] The author later admitted to getting caught in his own parochialism when he tried to impress Stanton, a braggart English crew member, by claiming descent on his father's side from Bass—only to find that the boy "had no knowledge of early Australian history so the value of my claim went over his head."[17] Later Frank facetiously capped another of Stanton's tall tales with a claim inspired by his own

mother's Manx descent, asserting that his maternal grandmother
was daughter of Orry, the last king of the Isle of Man—and keeper
of the general store.

Frank had picked up some unfortunate Americanisms of his own.
It is startling today to read his persistent references to the blacks of
the islands they visited as "niggers," "darkies," even "coons," and
to have him write of a girl he met that she had "a thin dilution of
Ethiopian blood, but she wasn't nigger! She was too alert and agile
of mind!"[18] We must remember that his models for his vocabulary
and attitudes were Americans of the period prior to World War I.

Caribbean Interlude ends in Colombia, where news of the out-
break of that war is received. Only a short final chapter, "Hasta la
Vista," is needed to get the ship back to New York under hooded
lights, as was true of Frank's actual third and final voyage. Here
too, in brief, is his trip to England on quite another ship with a
cargo of war-destined Canadian horses, and his enlistment in the
British forces (ostensibly, here, for his mate Marsh as well). "Gone
was the dream of exploring the islands of the Spanish main, of seeking lost El Dorados, of longing for the brave days of Elizabethan
England. Adventure had come to us in our generation."[19] For Frank
that adventure spanned five years of military service, out of which
came, three years ahead of *Caribbean Interlude*, the smaller but
greater *The Wells of Beersheba*.

Caribbean Interlude was one of the books that Frank enjoyed
writing. The score of years between the living and the setting down
of the experience had mellowed his memories without blurring
them. If some failed him, despite his travel diary, he was able to
pad, as travel writers do, with related material. On the excuse of
having "swotted up a little"[20] on the places they were to see, for instance, he scattered pages of island history throughout his narrative.
And when, early in the voyage, the ship passed a square-rigger up
from the Horn, he escaped from the Caribbean present to the
Australian past with this reminiscence:

She was a type of the craft that carried our grandparents to Australia in the
days when tales of gold to be had for the digging brought men and women
half-way round the world. As I looked at her, wispy recollections of talk of
"on Bendigo" I had heard around my grandparents' fireside, came back to
me. Four months out from Liverpool—puddings boiled in sea-water—vegetables carefully rationed—ladies in voluminous skirts—gentlemen with
side whiskers—the Britain they were never again to see receding into
memory, and their hopes and realities drawing slowly nearer. And now the

ladies of many petticoats and the gentlemen with facial upholstery were no more, and I, who had not entered into their calculations, was on deck, and the old windjammer was sailing for Davy Jones's locker.[21]

Since the book expired with its first edition, Frank had no chance for his usual second or third thoughts in revision, and his expressions here are occasionally inept, even awkward. But for the most part this one has a lyric quality that *Blue Coast Caravan*, written a year earlier, had notably lacked. Here the archness of "The delicate reader" in his introductory note and later of "the bright eyes for whom these pages are written"[22] is all part of the game, and he plays it well.

In later years, however, Frank himself, who continued to admire *The Wells of Beersheba* and who never developed any fondness for *Blue Coast Caravan*, became somewhat ambivalent about *Caribbean Interlude*. Writing to a curious inquirer in 1942, he remarked that the book had never been meant to be more than an "irresponsible excursion,"[23] and that it had succeeded moderately well in that. Yet a couple of weeks later he was to confess that he had never been happy about the book, even at the time of writing. Calling it "nothing but a fabrication except where it is literally true" (hardly a helpful comment for the curious), he added that it hadn't quite come off—that he lost confidence and didn't push it far enough.[24] His last and perhaps his best judgment of it was made a quarter of a century later, when he spoke of it to Owen Webster as "only a trifle."[25] It seems fair to say that, weighed against the rest of his output, *Caribbean Interlude* does not add much but neither does it conspicuously detract.

CHAPTER 9

Children of the Dark People

I N June 1936, while *Caribbean Interlude* was still in press, Frank wrote to the Palmers that "I fear it will open like the curate's egg but that can't be helped now. Like *Blue Coast Caravan*, its father is in process of forgetting it. I think I'll stick to fiction after this; it provides its own supports."[1] And turn to fiction he did, promptly and joyfully. Within six weeks after receiving that letter from Frank, the Palmers got one from his good friend Marjorie Barnard saying: "Frank's *Caribbean Interlude* will be out any day now—its successor is nearly done. He hasn't been so happy in his work since *Man-Shy*. It has made a new man of him. He's happy, full of vigor and hope. These creative tides."[2] That successor, published before the close of the year, was *Children of the Dark People*.

Once again Frank had written a book that is hard to categorize. This one is fiction but hardly a novel. At something over fifty thousand words (short as novels go, yet longer than *The Wells of Beersheba* and even *Man-Shy*), it is a story *for* children as well as *about* them. The subject is especially suitable for young Australians, being their country's aborigines. Frank wrote the story, he explained later, to please "a very charming lady," an artist who was looking for a book to illustrate—presumably Pixie O'Harris (Mrs. Bruce Pratt), a friend of Frank's who handsomely illustrated this one with black and white drawings, small and large. For the story itself, Frank acknowledged that "Much of the lore of bush and blackfellow is of my own gathering, but also for much I am indebted to others. On the creative side as well as on the informative I am not without obligation. . . . My view is that I have taken from, and, I humbly hope, added to, the common stock."[3]

A children's book by Frank Dalby Davison probably came as no shock to his readers, many of whom persist to this day in looking at *Man-Shy* as such. This one is frankly subtitled "An Australian Story for Young Folk" and is dedicated "For Doris and Peter," his own two youngsters. It may have come a little late for them, as they were then well into their teens, the chief appeal of *Children of the Dark People* being rather to a younger child's love of fairy-tales. In the front matter, as a kind of text, appears this stanza from Australia's Henry Lawson, from whom Frank was always proud to trace his literary descent:

> Oh, tell them a tale of the fairies bright—
> That only the bushmen know—
> Who guide the feet of the lost aright,
> Or carry them up through the starry night,
> Where the bush-lost babies go.

In the Acknowledgments, Frank explains that "this simple tale of two aboriginal children who became lost and found their way home again, is an attempt to possess four worlds within one pair of covers, Reality and Fantasy, and the Past linked with the Present." It begins with reality in the past, a charming and useful account of ancient aboriginal daily life in its regular movement across the continent—though reality is considerably softened by being viewed through rose-colored glasses.

The two children in the story (for whose names the author gives credit to the illustrator) are Nimmitybelle, a little aboriginal girl ("Though different in appearance from white children she was very pretty; with smooth dark skin, soft dark hair, and big dark eyes in which sadness and laughter dwelt by turns"[4]), and the boy Jackadgery, her friend and playmate, who "was a little older than Nimmitybelle, a little taller, and, because he was a boy, a great deal stronger."[5] Enter the tribe's witch doctor, "the unhappy sort of person who likes to upset things"[6] and whose jealousy of this promising young pair leads him to plot to remove them from their own tribe to another, far enough away so that they could never return. "It was a wicked idea, and, like all wicked ideas, it was also foolish. The witch-doctor didn't think of this. The foolishness was to be proved to him after many days, but the wickedness had to come first."[7]

With the witch doctor's success in persuading the children to disobey their parents by going down the river in Jackadgery's little canoe, we slip from Reality into Fantasy. The two are followed by the villain himself, who is capable of making all kinds of magic over his fire, especially when he wears his magic hat. He even shifts landscapes around until the children, skilled and self-reliant aborigines though they are, become hopelessly lost. Luckily there is magic on their side, too, for all the spirits of the bush are committed to the defense of righteousness. Nimmetybelle and Jackadgery are helped, through successive and trying difficulties, by the Spirit of the Billabong (pond), the Spirit of the Caves, the Spirit of the Mist, the Spirit of the Plains, and the Spirit of the Desert. Grandfather Gumtree helps, also, and the Imp of the Willy-willy stirs up a concealing whirlwind for them.

It is the head mogul, Old Mr. Bunyip, Guardian Spirit of the Land, however, who finally arrives to work his own hocus-pocus in the matter of the landscape and thus allow the two children to return to their grieving tribe. There, elders promptly meet to render judgment on the witch doctor's sins and deprive him of his magic hat. Back to Reality, then, such as the story provides, and even a glimpse into the Future to learn that Nimmitybelle and Jackadgery, when they grow up, are to become man and wife.

The Present is least represented of the four worlds that Frank was bent on possessing here; it enters only in the Epilogue. The Prologue had already advised the reader that although the dark people have almost passed away, all of the spirits are still around, as is Grandfather Gumtree and also Old Mr. Bunyip, who "still passes through the land on his many errands." Now the Epilogue advises us that

> There came a day when, from the high ranges, he [Mr. Bunyip] saw for the first time, on the hunting-ground of a tribe, the square green patches of the white men's crops, the slow sails of their gristing mills, and their cattle, sheep and horses grazing northward, southward, and westward across the country. For a long while, without moving, he watched these things with deeply troubled eyes. Then, in his nobility, he took them also into his care.[8]

Frank had acknowledged his debt to others for part of the aboriginal lore appearing here, but credit for its admirable adaptation, in content and style, is solely his. His knowledge of back-country Australia stood him in good stead here as it had done and was to do so often, and the book is rich in native flora and fauna alike. He is as skillful in maintaining his established viewpoint here (of children and for children) as he was in being true to the animal viewpoint in *Man-Shy*.

Once in this idyll we even hear the authentic voice of the author of *Man-Shy*, in a curious footnote. Referring to Dry Weather, who keeps a half-year watch on the Land of the Summer Rains, the note reads:

Dry Weather did not become Dragon Drought until a later period when over-stocking produced times of shortage and acute suffering among the wild creatures and man's dependent animals, and wire fences prevented free movement through the land from dearth to plenty.[9]

When this pleasant little story, which had first been serialized in the Sunday *Sun*, was published in book form by Angus & Robertson, there was unreserved rejoicing. Marjorie Barnard and her writing partner Flora Eldershaw celebrated the event with a party in Frank's honor for some writer friends in Flora's "minute flat" in Bohemian King's Cross. *Children of the Dark People* proved itself well worthy of celebration. Although in writing to a student a half dozen years later, Frank modestly sloughed the book off as "just a whitefeller story about blackfellers, with some paddock lore worked in,"[10] he admitted that it seemed moderately successful in pleasing those for whom it was intended. It kept on pleasing for the rest of his life (then only a little more than half over), going through a steady series of reprints and editions to the present, and selling about a thousand copies a year—no mean figure in Australia's small population. It will probably continue to please long after Frank's death. With its native background, its engaging concepts, and its charming style, it is an established and deserving classic among its country's literature for children, and one of those several small books for which the author may well be best known and longest remembered.

CHAPTER 10

The Thirties: Critic and Polemicist

IT is well that *The Children of the Dark People* left so pleasant a taste in the mouths of its author and his friends and admirers, for though it was the sixth book that Frank had succeeded in publishing in as many years, it was to be the last for several more. Other important aspects of the author's life affected his literary productivity at this time.

I   *Difficulties*

The 1930s were for Frank at once a most difficult and a most rewarding decade. The difficulties were chiefly marital, financial, and physical. The English wife of his youth, Kay, had borne him two children, had endured the four pioneering years in a Queensland bark humpy, and had made the shift with him to Sydney, where they settled in on Diamond Bay Road, Vaucluse. Kay's attractiveness is presumably confirmed by Frank's report late in 1932, after he had lost out on a much-needed government job, that her required presence during the interview had "crueled my pitch," and that another time he would take along a "woman with cross eyes, a shapeless figure and shoes that will go on either foot."[1]

The extent to which Kay shared her husband's literary enthusiasms, however, is uncertain. Frank, whose long and revealing correspondence with the Palmers had begun in September of the same year, first met the pair a couple of months later when their ship from Green Island to Melbourne stopped overnight in Sydney. Afterward he wrote a gushing letter to them, admitting that he had been "tipsy with excitement," and that the evening had meant more to him than winning the A.L.S. medal: "I *felt* it more."[2] Kay had been with him on that memorable occasion, but he does not mention her, nor did Nettie Palmer in a later account of the meeting, suggesting that the wife may have remained very much in the background.

The Davisons did share some cultural interests. In a later letter to the Palmers, Frank told of their joint work with a local dramatics club, the Greenroom Players (actors limited to six, audience to twenty-two). Frank himself tried his hand at playwriting with a one-acter entitled "When She Came Back" ("Very modern! Bloodshed and Adultery!"),[3] which served a useful purpose by convincing him that the theater was not his forte. But Kay played the leading lady so successfully, he reported, that a pro could not have done better.

By 1935, however, the twenty-year-old marriage was in trouble, a matter that Marjorie Barnard, close friend and reluctant confidante of both, reported on frequently to the Palmers. Part of their problem, here in the middle of the Depression, was unquestionably financial; both Kay and seventeen-year-old daughter Doris were looking for work to eke out Frank's scant and irregular income. Probably more important was the fact that Frank, who was later to pride himself on having become a "man about town" in those Sydney years, was attractive to and attracted by women, and came to reject Kay's overtures. At the end of the year they left Vaucluse for a new flat on Salisbury Road, Kensington (another Sydney suburb), but they did not leave their marital problems behind.

As for finances, we have already seen how early and how hard the Depression hit Frank, robbing him of his prosperous real estate business and sending him out on the streets to peddle books. This was only the beginning of a long dry decade; Frank's early letters to the Palmers are spattered with references to his financial difficulties. In 1932 he applied for the job for which Kay "crueled his pitch," one that would have involved working with "the plurry[4] blackfellers" (the aborigines) on a federal project; but though he was one of the final seven to be seriously considered out of over a hundred applicants, he was, to his great disappointment, rejected. Early in 1933 he wrote that he was buying the Sydney *Herald* regularly—for the job ads. Later that year he travelled for a manufacturer of frocks, selling to retailers, but that work did not last. In 1934, to gain a few months' respite from the struggle to earn a living, he grasped at the ill-fated trip with Brooke Nicholls. At one point, he recalled later, rather than sponge on his father, he went on the dole, a particularly bitter pill for anyone to swallow, especially an independent and ambitious Australian. Life for Frank at this time was for the most part a continual series of odd jobs and hack work occupying the time that he wanted for writing creatively without providing any dependable income.

Physically, all this told on a man inclined at best to mental and

emotional ups and downs. Having missed out on the ripening years
of a formal education, he had been working steadily from the age of
twelve: outback, printing, war, more outback, real estate, odd
jobs—and always his writing. During the 1933 Christmas season he
had reported on his first vacation in eight years, spent with his family in a rural area near Mittagong, revelling in the chance to use his
muscles in grubbing out stumps. But in March he confessed to the
price of having done a great deal of writing: several short stories
and continued work on his Caribbean experience, with even the
dark people's children apparently beginning to trouble his mind.
"Really I have worked too hard. I cracked up about a fortnight
ago."[5] And a month later: "The old nerves went on a jazz. . . . I
was hoping to get that book of mine finished before the end of the
month, but I don't think I will be able to. I got a bit of hack work
given me so I decided to take the cash and let the credit go. Just as
well, perhaps. . . . I really was knocked groggy—couldn't sleep."[6]

The next few months the Davisons spent travelling up the "blue
coast" with the Nichollses—a welcome change, but under the circumstances hardly a rest; and on their return the difficulties of putting the book of experiences together were such as to compound
Frank's health problem. That September a letter to Vance reports:

I got so tired that I was funking the typewriter of mornings so we packed
up and went and camped at Blaxland. I took no work and no letters. Unfortunately I came back not very much rested. . . . But the last three years
[these take us back to the time of Frank's entrance into the literary world]
have been nightmarish. Of late they have discovered in me a weakness that
I did not suspect myself of having and which I do not doubt I will through
[sic] off presently—nerves. . . . A little period of security and physical
labor would be a great help.[7]

II Literary Contacts

But despite these problems, the thirties were a good decade, too,
a time of rapidly widening horizons for Frank. His close lifelong
friendship with Vance and Nettie Palmer, Australian literature's established "first family," began in 1932. Fiction-writer Vance started
it by writing to this young unknown (a habit of the Palmers in their
eagerness to promote their nation's literature) a letter of congratulation on his sudden emergence as an Australian novelist. Familiar, of
course, with Vance's work and a great admirer of it, Frank replied
in enthusiastic detail. A few days later he found occasion to write to

critic Nettie, of whose essays he had a high opinion, to thank her for an appreciative article she had written on *Man-Shy* for the Red Page (long a literary institution in the Sydney *Bulletin*). The ensuing correspondence with both meant a great deal to Frank, for as he wrote Nettie shortly in a letter whose length he felt he must explain: "I assure you it is a great relief to talk a bit of shop with someone who understands. I don't know the literary crowd."[8]

Thanks to *Man-Shy* and the A.L.S. medal, however, his acquaintance with writers broadened rapidly. He not only met the Melbourne-based Palmers in person shortly, but became widely acquainted in Sydney literary circles. Always forthright, he made no secret of his reactions to some of the personalities there enshrined. He met the Establishment's editor and anthologizer George Mackaness, of whose critical judgments he thought very little. He thought little more of the University of Sydney's H. M. Green, feeling that his *Outline of Australian Literature* (1930), an early attempt to see the subject whole, "shows that his critical faculty is not as delicate an instrument as might be."[9] But Green kindly made Frank free of the University's Fisher Library (having for many years been its librarian), and Frank found him to be "a nice fellow" even though he "tries to bring me up." Another who tried was author and editor P. R. ("Inky") Stephensen. ("Rather amusing," Frank observed, "these people who think they have a mission of bringing the young author up in the way he should go."[10] Frank thought Stephensen delightful but did not take him very seriously, as he found a streak of irresponsibility in his makeup—perhaps a perceptive insight into the character of the man whose excellent magazine, the *Australian Mercury*, was shortly to appear, only to die with its first issue.

Frank came to know numerous Australian poets: Tom Inglis Moore, friend of Flora Eldershaw, and "Furnley Maurice" (Frank Wilmot), with whom he was much impressed, reporting that "I like him immensely, a great fellow."[11] He met poet Hugh McCrae, with whom he disagreed about the poetry of Robert Fitzgerald (Frank could see nothing in it and was always honest, even about his blind spots). But he and McCrae agreed on one thing, Frank reported to Nettie Palmer: that *she* should be editing the *Bulletin's* Red Page! He came to know and like dramatist Leslie Rees. He met "G. B. Lancaster" (Edith Joan Lyttleton) at the height of her success with *Pageant*, a Tasmanian novel drawn from her own family's history, which won the A.L.S. medal two years after *Man-Shy*. He met and later worked in the Fellowship of Australian Writers with novelist Jean Devanney, of whom he was personally fond but who annoyed him with her "idea that you have only to read Karl Marx to the Wild Man from Borneo to make him fit for citizenship in modern society!"[12]

Most important to his life and work, he met the fiction-history-criticism team known as "M. Barnard Eldershaw"—first, Flora Eldershaw, whom he initially found "charming but elusive,"[13] and six months later, Marjorie Barnard, recently returned from a year in England. Finding Marjorie more approachable (they were both friends, admirers, and regular correspondents of the Palmers), he took her to lunch and reported, "I like her well. Like myself, she is inclined to be forthright in her opinions. I like that, even if I don't always agree with the opinions expressed."[14] Marjorie's reaction to Frank was equally favorable, and with Flora they became a closely knit trio, later to be enlarged for a while by the addition of poet-novelist Leonard Mann, exchanging critical opinions, job opportunities, and professional know-how, and sharing vacation trips and joys and sorrows generally.

By the middle of the 1930s, with six published books and a growing reputation as a writer of short stories, Frank himself had become one of the literary lights of Sydney. Following the custom that had introduced the Palmers to him, he too took it upon himself to write letters of congratulation and encouragement to newcomers: to Leonard Mann to welcome him to the ranks of the A.L.S. medal winners with his fine war novel, *Flesh in Armour*, the year after Frank's own award; and to J. J. Hardie, whose novels of life in the outback naturally appealed to Frank, who was first of all a "dinkum" (genuine) Australian, as eager as his mentors the Palmers to encourage any writer whose work brought their country to the fore.

When Frank first became known, Australia's leading novelist was expatriate Henry Handel Richardson (Ethel Florence Lindesay), whose *Ultima Thule* was not only the second A.L.S. medal winner but the first Australian novel to attract serious critical attention abroad. In 1932 Richardson had written from London to her friend Nettie Palmer that she had seen a paragraph of *Man-Shy* quoted and "thought it very promising."[15] But her own work drew criticism from Frank, who preferred Vance's "authentically Australian" writing, because Richardson "says in so many words 'Richard Mahoney *went* to *that* country.' And that phrase characterizes her attitude. She addresses the British public. Her story is *about* Australia but not *of* Australia."[16] This point of view was always to underlie the literary criticism of Fred Davison's eldest son, patriot to the core.

Early in his efforts to find a place for himself in Australian literary circles, Frank attended meetings of Sydney's chapter of the P.E.N. (short for the "International Association of Poets, Playwrights, Editors, Essayists, and Novelists"), but the organization offended his native sensibilities: too many members had been "home" (to England) and were given to speaking frequently of their experiences at the "Mother Club" there. He found them generally snobbish, wanting, he quipped, a sample of his blood rather than a specimen of his writing. He was much more at home in the local F.A.W. (Fellowship of Australian Writers), which he reported to the Palmers in 1933 as "a rather decent little show, really. It has its roots in its own soil, and one finds there a good deal of genuine comradeship."[17]

The Fellowship had been organized not long before (1928) under the leadership of dramatist and poet J. LeGay Brereton to honor and encourage Australian writers and writing, and had grown to a membership of several hundred, including many prominent authors in the Sydney area. At one point Frank complained that "most of the members of our association . . . are not interested in literature; only in themselves writing."[18] Nonetheless he began to work with it regularly, involving himself in its numerous business and social activities. He early became a member of the Executive Committee under the presidency of Tom Inglis Moore, and was one of the vice-presidents under Flora Eldershaw, the publicly active member of the M. Barnard Eldershaw team, when she succeeded Moore to the presidency. Marjorie reported that Frank was Flora's mainstay who did the dirty jobs. He himself became president in 1936 and was reelected for 1937.

He soon saw the job as "a case of going through vast motions in the hope of doing just a little good. I am trying to make the evening meetings satisfyingly cultural, the luncheons fellowshippy, and the parties gloriously Bohemian."[19] There was much more to his position than this suggests, however; the Fellowship was involved in all kinds of activities aimed at book and writer recognition, and it got into numerous difficulties that taxed its leader's time, patience, and ingenuity. First there was a crippling organizational debt—nobody's fault, Frank concluded, but it fell to him to get it cleared.

The biggest problem with which he had to cope was a split threatened by the appearance of a rival, the Writers League, but his energy, ability, and growing popularity proved equal to getting the two organizations to amalgamate. Probably the most noteworthy achievement of the F.A.W. in this period was the success of its long and vocal advocacy of the establishment of the federally funded C.L.F. (Commonwealth Literary Fund), which in the ensuing years has contributed ever-increasing sums for fellowships, pensions to authors, and grants to literary periodicals and book publishers.

III   Critical Writing and Speaking

During this period of his greatest public activity, Frank understandably produced no more books, but he was writing an enormous number of lesser items for publication. Most of his short stories stem from these years, and in addition he was writing book reviews, critical articles, and other "fugitive pieces" at a great rate for a variety of outlets. From the time *Man-Shy* appeared, he began getting occasional commissions for book reviews from newspapers and magazines, including Sydney's weekly *Bulletin*. Cecil Mann, its associate editor, shortly made him a "preferred contributor" at a most welcome seven pounds a week, the beginning of a long stint with the *Bulletin*'s prestigious Red Page. Reviews and critical articles of his, signed and unsigned, appeared there with increasing frequency from the mid-1930s on.

His work included some weekly lists of "Recommended Books," which would not have taken much writing time but a good deal of reading, and short reviews of current foreign books, mostly fiction and often several to an issue. Of most interest, of course, to him as to us, are his reviews and articles on Australian writers and writing. Under the title "A New Australian Writer"[20] Frank had the privilege he most cherished—that of extending a hand to a promising unknown, Dal Stivens, whose first claim to a place in authentically Australian literature was made with *The Tramp and Other Stories* (1936). This collection provided a particularly good subject for Frank, now a short-story writer himself, and after analyzing its strengths and weaknesses, he accorded it a "balance of favorable criticism." He found Stivens's best stories to be those using local settings and rooted in things the author had personally observed—the kind that Frank himself was writing. For special commendation he singled out the two-page "Grass," which he found "so slight that to indicate its nature here would be to spoil it, but it is a statement of simple truth and as wide as the continent in its application." He judged it to be not only "Best of them all," but "among the best short stories written in Australia." Coming from a recognized short-story writer, this generous opinion in an important national magazine must have given a considerable lift to aspiring young Stivens.

A few months later Frank went back into the Australian past with an article on "Tom Collins and His Books,"[21] Vance Palmer's controversial abridgment of Collins's (Joseph Furphy's) long-famous *Such Is Life* (1903) having recently appeared. Frank appeared not to approve of the project and devoted himself mainly to the original, with quotations from Bernard O'Dowd, A. C. Stephens, America's C. Hartley Grattan, and from Furphy's letters. His introduction did speak of the work as "now abridged by Vance Palmer," but the article ends with a quotation from Palmer's preface to the unabridged edition of 1917. Frank's unwillingness to express disagreement with his mentor is evident in a letter he wrote to Vance at about this time that puts the case gently: "I prefer the original myself," but "Considering the abridgement *as* an abridgement I think it is an excellent job."[22] His only expressed wish was that Vance's critics would take into consideration the delicate surgery involved.

More important, in 1937 the *Bulletin* ran a series of articles by various hands (not always specified) on "Australian Writers," stating as its purpose the fact that "So much has been written about what is wrong with Australian writers that everyone by now should be aware of pretty well all their sins. The chief object of this series is to show characteristic examples of the best of these writers' writing."[23] The first four articles were on Vance Palmer, Hugh McCrae, Katharine Susannah Prichard, and Walter Murdock. Frank wrote the fifth (the first to be signed) on M. Barnard Eldershaw.[24] Australian criticism has always suffered from the small size of the literary community; when close friends review one another's books, they are likely to fall into one of two pits: unjustifiably high praise or, bending over backward to avoid it, nit-picking. The first was true of M. Barnard Eldershaw's treatment of Frank's works in their *Essays in Australian Fiction* published the following year; the second marred Frank's discussion of the three M. Barnard Eldershaw novels available at this time. His review of their fourth, *Plaque with Laurel,* a month later, is more gracious: "a nourishing brew," sophisticated in the word's best meaning; "a serious and, in fact, a passionate book" with a surface glitter of malicious wit. Yet he curiously misnames one of the leading characters throughout (Imogene is "Jenny"), and while he recognizes the story as a "study in mateship," he says nothing of its secondary Sale theme nor of Owen's philosophy. But these omissions are perhaps less intention or lack of understanding than haste.

Frank also wrote—and signed—the sixth of the "Australian Writers" series, an article on Norman Lindsay.[25] Dal Stivens may have appealed to Frank because they both wrote short stories best from personal experience, M. Barnard Eldershaw because they were his personal favorites. Lindsay, however, was a man apart, and Frank's greatest admiration for him springs, interestingly, not from the wit and humor for which he was well known but from his candor: "He refuses to deny any aspect of life." None of Frank's own work at this time had ventured to portray any aspect that might be considered objectionable by a reader, but much of what he notes in Lindsay, such as the characters who from adolescence to old age are in conflict with their romantic propensities, might have been used by him thirty years later in defense of his own final novel *The White Thorntree*.

It is surely legitimate to draw conclusions about a critic and his own creative work from what he says about others, and each of the four preceding reviews has been in some way revealing of Frank as man or writer. His Red Page articles did not always deal with personalities and their works, however, but often with more general subjects. The question of what is fit to print, raised in the Lindsay review, was one of particular concern to Australian writers at this time, and had been taken up by Frank on an earlier Red Page called "Censor and Syndicate,"[26] prompted by a complaint from Customs Minister White to the effect that Australian writers did not want censorship for their own wares but censorship and restriction of syndicated stuff from abroad. Always a lover of causes, and a defender of writers' causes in particular, Frank sprang to a reasoned answer: responsible writers in Australia realize, he argued, that if literature is to play its proper part in our national life, we must safeguard the conditions under which it can exist. He first opposed, on economic grounds, the unrestricted and recently growing importation of syndicated stories and articles so cheaply that local writers could not compete. His second issue was even more heartfelt: censorship must be distrusted by any writer who "sees in literature one of the dynamic elements of civilized life—and it is nothing less." Novels that give false values, and are therefore bad art, may pass the censor because they avoid "certain topics," while those that attempt serious discussions of life—all life—are likely to be banned. "To judge a work of art by anything other than the canons of art is ultimately to do a disservice to humanity. No nation can become adult whose citizens have not the freedom of the library."

Frank was always at his best with subjects that lent themselves readily to analysis and organization. One of his most readable Red Page articles is "Australian Literary Currents,"[27] the theme of which is that the same energy runs through these three consecutive groups in Australia's literary history: 1) the word-of-mouth versifiers who drew pictures of early colonial life by parodying songs from the old country, and so began to domesticate a strange continent through verbal images of the life in it; 2) the later mostly native-born balladists, led by A. B. ("The Banjo") Paterson, whose songs of "the shearing shed and the droving track," printed in great numbers for urban as well as rural customers, pushed back the unknown and provided fresh images to express the new nationalism in the air; 3) the then current "landscape school," with its books on life and adventure in still unfamiliar parts of Australia, so widely popular that Frank found it to be one of the two main streams of writing energy in Australia, the other being the novel, comparable but not competitive. The landscape school seized on the obvious and readily communicable, leaving to the novel the task of "getting behind the first appearance of things, of creating the more complex images that are needed if the whole of our life is to be expressed."

Late in the 1930s Frank's increasingly independent and vociferous political views led to his separation from the *Bulletin*. But there were other outlets for his opinions. In 1939 *Australia, National Journal*, a Ure Smith venture just beginning, published his "Australian Writers Come to Maturity,"[28] a brief, competent, and readable history of Australian literature from the time it was "nascent," with Henry Lawson, to its present "renascence." Frank generously names and comments on many authors and works throughout. Again he credits Henry Handel Richardson's *The Fortunes of Richard Mahoney* with having been chiefly responsible for making Australian literature known to international audiences, but except for setting this standard of achievement by an Australian-born author, the book does not, he feels, have any special significance for an Australian. We must look instead "to writers more advanced in understanding the Australian natural and social scene." Frank does not mention the facts that Richardson had left Australia at 17, in 1887, for a life in Europe, and had returned to her homeland only once, in 1912, for what she called a flying six weeks' visit to test her memories while she was writing her great trilogy; but all of this may provide some explanation, even justification, for his judgment of her work.

When Frank was in the process of breaking into Sydney's literary circles in the early 1930s, he spoke a number of times on radio, although it was a medium he did not particularly enjoy, partly because he found final deadlines difficult to meet. Sometimes he reviewed books, as Vance Palmer was doing regularly in Melbourne, sometimes he spoke on other literary subjects. Most of these talks, of course, disappeared with the giving, but a couple reached print. One of these was broadcast during Authors' Week in 1935, later printed in P. R. Stephensen's short-lived but memorable "monthly" National Literary Magazine, the *Australian Mercury*, that July. The title, "Australian Fiction Today,"[29] unfortunately belies much of the content, the bulk of which is devoted to rather pedagogical generalities on the function of all the arts, before arriving at literature, and in particular, prose fiction. Of the ten notable Australian fiction writers that Frank finally lists, only one merits a comment, and that is expatriate Henry Handel Richardson, not as an interpreter of Australia (Frank had more than once expressed his dissatisfaction with her deficiences in that area) but as an Australian-born writer who had produced a masterpiece recognized by the English-speaking world. He goes on to fault Australian readers for not responding to an Australian book until it has been recognized by America and England. He also anticipates his later "Censor and Syndicate" article in the *Bulletin* by using Australian censorship as an example of life endeavoring to repudiate art, and by discussing the handicap to a young literature of the fact that so many imported books can be purchased so cheaply. He does see recent promise of more interest in native books and, as an example, details the remarkable popularity of a recently published novel—"A quietly told and utterly sincere story of life as it presented itself to an Australian middle-class family, living in the city of Melbourne" (obviously Vance Palmer's 1934 *The Swayne Family*, but in keeping with Frank's generalized beginning, he names no names). His conclusion introduces a very sore point as he expresses the hope that this development "may help to stop the cultural impoverishment

that has resulted from first-class writers, over many years, aban-
doning Australia, in spirit and in person."

Another of Frank's broadcast talks has been preserved in the
F.A.W. volume *Australian Writers Speak* (1942) along with those of
a dozen other well-known writers speaking singly or in pairs. Frank
was first on the series with a title even more disconcertingly broad
than before: "What Is Literature?"[30] But a comparison of this talk
with his "Australian Fiction Today" gives us a good glimpse into
how much Frank had learned, in the seven intervening years, about
putting ideas across. While he repeats some of the generalities of
the earlier talk by way of definition, he supports them with many
specific examples from other times, other countries. And before he
is halfway through, he reaches Australia, whose literary history he
retraces, naming names generously of both authors and works.
Then, returning to the question in his title, he affirms: "My personal answer is that in the field of general literature it is whatever
commands my serious and lasting attention, and in the field of imaginative literature it is whatever offers me thoughtful enter-
tainment. . . . I can only say that for me literature is that which
quickens my sensibilities; work behind which I feel a writer's
sincere attempt to communicate his vision of life to his fellow men."
He closes with a timely defense of propagandist writers—provided
the advocate does not come before the artist. Again he is generous
with examples, and afterward reminds us that it is valid to criticize a
work because it is clumsy propaganda but not because it disagrees
with our opinion. "But please," he concludes on this wartime
program, "do not accuse me of saying that writers should be
propagandists. I am only affirming the right of each to tell us of
what interests him from the angle from which he sees it."[31]

In judging Frank's scattered critical work we must remember that
in these years he was always a writer of fiction at heart though a
writer of criticism by profession, even by necessity. The retainer he
was on at the *Bulletin* was financially steadying, during a personally
difficult period, and as a principal contributor to the Red Page he
could be depended on to promote Australian authors and books
wherever possible but never at the expense of a lowering of standards. His wider comments on literature indicate the remarkable extent to which he had remedied his lack of education through books
and the company of those who knew them. But writing *about*
literature was not his first interest. It can have been no wonder,
even to him, that despite his considerable critical output he was not

included on the list of those that Clement Semmler drew up in the 1960s of the seven most important Australian critics from past to present, though both Palmers were there, as was Douglas Stewart, Frank's young successor on the *Bulletin* and a long-time editor of the Red Page later.[32]

IV   *Reflective Essays*

Writer and reader alike must have drawn sighs of relief when toward the end of the 1930s, his days on the *Bulletin* over, Frank returned to his memories of the outback and produced a pair of excellent reflective essays. Minor as they are, they challenged nothing he lacked and gave full scope to all he had, as their author was to say later of *Man-Shy*. Both are on subjects well within his competence, as they draw on the fund of experience from which his best fiction had come. Both appeared in the Sydney *Morning Herald's Home Annual*, a large, glossy magazine that drew upon some of Australia's best writers and artists at this time.

"Salute to the Beast" appeared in 1939, its exposition making explicit some of the ideas already implicit in his narratives. In its opening paragraph we find the author at the vivid, fluent, Australian best that always bespoke inspiration:

Man's journey down the centuries has been to the groaning of beasts. Perhaps nowhere does this reflection strike home as sharply as in Australia. The tread of hooves is in our literature; the volleying of whips in the dust of the slow-crawling bullock teams and the protesting bellow; the thin stream of complaint rising from sheep creeping along the hungry stock routes and the patter of a kelpie's feet; the crash of undergrowth and rattle of stones as a scrubber dashes for liberty with the stockhorse in pursuit; the smell of hot sweat—and increasing leanness—as the nodding teams plod from dawn till night, drawing a gleaming furrow or taking off the crop in the mile-wide paddock.[33]

His theme here is the mateship of animal and man, in the hard life of the Australian outback, and he uses the phrase that had first appeared in *The Wells of Beersheba* and that has continued to be associated with him since: "the same rhythms of life run through the human and creature worlds, *a fellowship of the flesh*."[34] (Italics mine. See p. 191.) After all, stock exists by virtue of human need of it. "There's a price to pay for living," Frank reminds us, "by them as well as us,"[35] but he feels that life is worth that price, for the cattle. He develops this idea in a conclusion prompted by his presence at a railway station, years after he had left cattle tailing, as a long slow stock train came creeping through:

The smell of cattle was like a breath of times gone by—a stumble of hooves in the trucks as the train jolted; click of horns as heads were raised to look above the top rails; wide, wondering eyes reflecting the dim station lamps; soft lowing sounding through the measured panting of the engine. They were on their way to the city saleyards at Homebush, and then to the abattoirs. Tough luck? Yes, but not cruelty—which brings me back to where I began. Like all flesh, they were going their predestined way, at a time not chosen by themselves.[36]

The difference in point of view and effect between this exposition about cattle in general and *Man-Shy's* narrative concentration on one red heifer makes a revealing study.

"Still Waters of the West," appearing in 1940, is even more heavily descriptive. It begins with Frank's boyhood love of the water hole, with its insects, birds, animals, and even indications of aborigine days. Now a middle-aged man, he finds his thoughts going back to such water holes:

They are the life-centres of man, beast and wilding, those western waters. Camp, hut and homestead lie by them. Life comes in to them and life rays out from them. In time of drought they are where the last grim stand is made—as a scattering of white bones around so many of them will prove. If you could see them from above you would see each the centre of a patch of bare ground, where the grass has been walked off by daily comings and goings. Beyond that—as a spider's legs are attached to his body—you would see the little tracks going out, where the beasts make their way to the quiet reaches of the paddocks. And there might be others, wheel-tracks, leading off and away, if you followed them far enough, to some other waterhole, some other camp or homestead.[37]

The essay gives the author a chance to describe nostalgically not only the animal but the human callers at the water hole, giving us a glimpse of an earlier age.

The company at a waterhole may be a teamster with his waggon, a kangaroo shooter, a station manager looking over his paddocks, a police patrol with dog-eyed tracker in attendance, or a family party, women and children on their way to a week of high life at the nearest township. It may be an Oriental hawker with a waggon loaded with goods from Bradford and

Birmingham, or an itinerant clergyman, a Bush Brother, in his pocket the
Word from the Orient. There may be nothing at the waterhole but cattle
camped placidly under the trees, but at least human travellers will have left
signatures of varying degrees of freshness, little circles of ash with half-
burnt twigs around them, where the fragrant billy has been boiled.[38]

Frank goes from the natural water hole to the man-made,
describing the equipment and work of the tank-sinkers as we find
them later in one of his short stories. These tanks, he feels, help to
make up to wild life for the harm that settlement as a whole has
brought, since they add to the water available in arid areas. At his
own tank he had seen of a morning the tracks of kangaroo, wallaby,
dingo, even koala: "It was rather pleasant to find oneself dispensing
this sort of hospitality."[39]

. . . but it is to the natural waters of the west that thoughts go most often
and most fondly: the waterholes with their gnarled and ancient trees, their
mingled shadow and shine, their cool still depths and air of peace. Beside
natural water you feel you are at the heart of the land, that you are where
something that is the very spirit of Australian earth has its dwelling
place—the sacred grove.[40]

Like Frank's early accounts of the process of settling in his
father's *Australian Post* (but for less practical, more esthetic
reasons), these rare essays leave one wishing that there had been
more of them, so rich they are in the sights and sounds of Australia's
early days, and that they might have remained in print, as so much
of his fiction has.

V *Political Interlude*—While Freedom Lives

In these late 1930s, as the world moved from threats of war to war
itself, Frank had other concerns, less literary. He would not have
been his father's son if his interests, especially in this distressing
period, had not gone beyond literature, either critical or creative.
There are few hints of the polemic in his fiction, but with the approach of a second world war, he turned his attention for a while to
the body politic. In August and September of 1938, he wrote and
paid for the publication of a twenty-four-page pamphlet entitled
While Freedom Lives, recalling his publicist father.
    Frank remarked, years later, that all the Australian writers of the
thirties had anti-establishment views, he himself having been the

palest of the pink. He never joined any of the frankly leftist literary groups of that period, but he put forth in *While Freedom Lives* a set of highly unconventional views. For some years the Depression (particularly traumatic for Australia, not least for Frank) had given clear indications that the status quo was far from flawless economically. Now, with the advent of Fascism in Europe followed by the increasing threat of war, many people began to question the validity of the established order socially and politically as well.

While Freedom Lives was inspired, Frank wrote the Palmers, by social discussions with Marjorie Barnard and Flora Eldershaw. Neither was responsible for his way of thinking, but the talks induced a long period of systematic thought on his part by way of arriving at the social foundations for a play that he aspired to write. The major thesis that he arrived at and presented in his pamphlet is that economic nationalism is breaking down and must be abandoned for an international economy, under either socialism or fascist capitalism: "There is no third way."[41] The result must be a United States of the World, ultimately a United Socialist States of the World, a conclusion that led the author to take refuge, however, in the remark that he hoped "it will not be said that I 'advocate' socialism, I merely point out its inevitability."[42]

As for the current situation, Frank was convinced that while professional armies might start a war, civilian populations everywhere, "a sadder and wiser generation than were their fathers and mothers,"[43] would mutiny rather than allow conscription again, so that "within a very few months war would shift from the international to the home front."[44] The alternative to such revolution, he felt, is social evolution—reform by constitutional means. He concluded that "the possibility of Germany risking revolution in an attack on the Western Powers is remote in the extreme."[45] But Frank misjudged his generation: World War II was to erupt within a year, with capitalism intact and no mutinies.

These published theories made no perceptible change in Frank's life or work. He even relied, on the title page of his tract, on some very unrevolutionary credentials: the publication of six entirely unpolemical books, his two-year presidency of a literary society, and still more conspicuously "Establishment," the "M.B.E." after his name, a British decoration he had recently received for his services to literature.[46] By May, 1939, he had sold about half (some nine hundred copies) of his stock of *While Freedom Lives*, but its contents had aroused no conspicuous following. In nothing else he wrote is his lack of formal education more evident, for he had to fight his way through vital social issues with no systematic grounding in anthropology, sociology, psychology, economics, government, or even history to guide him. The results are naive oversimplification of issues, wearisome verbosity of style. Only four years later he was to call the tract "the Forever Morning of my political writing and thinking. I have advanced from that a long way and would now repudiate it in greater part."[47] Late in life he was to conclude, "I'm not really a political person."[48] This is surely true, despite his family background (his father was to continue speaking and writing on public issues almost to his death), for here in the age of the problem novel, scarcely any politics seeped into his creative work (the play "The Home Front," for which *While Freedom Lives* was to be an expository statement, did not materialize).

Frank's interest in politics continued rather longer, however, than his later memories implied, although his point of view did some shifting. His article "Australian Writers Come to Maturity," appearing in mid-1939, closed with the revealing assertion that we do not need a "mass of rabid radical writing," for "Radicalism and conservatism are inseparable companions, really, counterpoises in any workable plan of social or personal life."[49] For some months he was very much involved as co-editor with an F.A.W. publication by various hands, *Australian Writers in Defense of Freedom*, which appeared late in 1939 after much organizational difficulty, having finally proved restrained enough for even Angus & Robertson to publish. Here, to his editorial duties, Frank added an article of his own, "Alternative to Fascism."

In *While Freedom Lives* Frank had disavowed Communism, choosing rather the title of liberal, one whom the Fascists oppose because he wants reform, and the Communists hate because he wants it by constitutional methods. But a year later he confessed to Vance Palmer that "I find myself getting closer and closer to the Communists" through admiration for their social philosophy, but that he is hindered from joining them by the "jesuitical side to their activities."[50] Vance replied (the day before England and France declared war on Germany) that it was Marx and Engels who had the social philosophy, that he feared the Communist Party to be only a political party like any other, and that he despaired of the expediency on which its policies had been built for seven or eight years.

Frank always had a profound respect for Vance's opinions, and we hear nothing more of his interest in Communism.

Early in 1940, with the war several months old but still in its "inactive" period, he continued to maintain to Vance the conviction he had expressed in his pamphlet—that "if it reaches the point where the people have to be called on to really fight, it won't be long before France and Britain have revolutions on their hands. . . . I think next spring and summer will very likely tell the tale."[51] But France was to fall and Britain to fight on without fulfilling his expectations.

Later in the year, revolutions failing to materialize, Frank (the "happy warrior" of World War I and the celebrant of one of its notable military campaigns) was rooting for surrender! To Vance he praised the French for having "taken the right road; a dark and difficult one, but shorter and less dark and difficult than if she had set herself for a long war."[52] To Nettie Palmer (who couldn't have agreed with him less) he went farther, wishing that the French had not fought at all but had saved themselves from much distress, disorganization, and loss of life. He questioned whether a British victory at arms would make the country any better off, and even went so far as to advise that if the Germans came, it would be best not to fight or run away. Such a course, he admitted, might be uncomfortable and dangerous for a while (some might even be killed), but out of it might come better ways for the world to deal with difficulties. Besides, he was sure that the Germans would find something ironic among the fruits of victory. Whether he was able to endure the later long dread of an invasion of Australia by the Japanese with equal philosophical calm I have been unable to discover.

The year 1941 found Frank appearing, with numerous other prominent Australian writers, at an Aid-Russia Cultural Conference in Sydney attended by a couple of hundred delegates representing more than fifty cultural organizations. The emphasis of the conference was all on stepping up Australia's friendship with and aid to the U.S.S.R., an ally in the struggle against world fascism, and the atmosphere was thick with compliments. Of the speakers assigned to Literature and Drama, novelist Miles Franklin prayed that God would help the Russians and save from total destruction "their vast social experiment on which the hopes of the world are set," and (incidentally) keep Australia from the "final horrors of invasion."[53]

Novelist Katharine Susannah Prichard, herself a Communist Party member, said, "Let us do all in our power to demonstrate that the will of the Australian people is with the Soviet Government to defeat Hitler, and to maintain the standard of the highest and finest civilization the world has ever seen."[54]

Following these two, on the assigned subject of literature, Frank, who had not had time to write a paper, spoke less enthusiastically. He fulfilled the requirements of the occasion by stating that he wanted personally to give all possible aid to Russia, "the great and courageous ally of my country," but then he turned to the more universal view of his *While Freedom Lives* by grieving not only over what Russian soldiers were enduring to keep Sydney safe (no mention here of the advantages to Sydney of an early capitulation), but also over what the enemies' people and soldiers were suffering. All of this was happening because of the lost opportunities between the two great wars, he affirmed, for "movement toward worldwide sharing of what life has to offer." His main theme was not literature, as assigned, but politics, which he viewed as the very peak of culture—man's highest activity, being concerned with the great problem of how to live together. At its best, he felt, politics embodies both art and science, so that he had been driven as a writer to interest himself in it. His expression of regret over the difficulty of getting hold of books on Russia's political and economic foundations gave him an opening for another attack on Australian censorship, and a chance to speak up for the restoration of the Communist Party in Australia to a legal position.[55] His remarks were published with the proceedings of the Conference by the N.S.W. (New South Wales) Aid Russia Committee in 1942, and again, as a separate pamphlet ("slightly furbished," trust Frank) by the N.S.W. Legal Rights Committee.

One who knew of Frank's opinions and activities during these several years might have expected that after the close of World War II he would devote himself to the cause of those earlier "lost opportunities" in an effort to promote the world view of which he had been writing and speaking. But if his political interests did not expire as suddenly as he later recalled, neither were they long sustained, being overridden shortly by personal matters that were to change the course of his life and even of his writing. First, however, let us look at one of his major achievements of this period, his short stories.

CHAPTER 11

The Short Stories

I The Woman at the Mill

I was one of the accepted short-story men of the thirites,"[1] Frank was to state without exaggeration in the preface to a collection published many years later. He had been writing stories for a long time, beginning with those for his father's periodicals in the early twenties. Even after he achieved literary fame with a novel, the short story remained one of his chief preoccupations, the source of much success and of some income. In early 1934 he wrote Nettie Palmer that in two months' time, during which he had written fifty thousand words of what was to become *Caribbean Interlude*, he had also written—and sold—four short stories. Throughout the 1930s and on into the early 1940s, his stories appeared frequently in a variety of Australian periodicals, notably the Sydney *Bulletin*.

When M. Barnard Eldershaw honored Frank with a long treatment in their *Essays in Australian Fiction* in 1938, going into detail about each of his then six published books (fiction or no), they added that beyond these "there is a scatter of short stories that have appeared in various journals, rare both in incidence and quality, which, it is very much to be hoped, will some day be collected into a volume."[2] Only two years later, like an answer to that hope, Angus & Robertson brought out a first collection of the best work of this "accepted short story man," *The Woman at the Mill* (1940).

The book is gratefully dedicated "Out of my recollection of groping years . . . to Vance Palmer and Nettie Palmer, whose lamps have burned with a clear and steady flame." To Vance, presumably, as one of the finest and most prolific writers of the Australian short story in this period, to Nettie as one of the earliest and most discerning of Australian critics, and to both in recognition of their warm and encouraging friendship of almost a decade. Of the fifteen stories included, all but two had seen previous publication: one each in the *Sydney Mail*, the *Sydney Sun*, and the *Newcastle School of Arts Journal*, the remaining ten in Sydney's *Bulletin*, which since its founding in the late 1800s had been the chief source of encouragement for Australia's short-story writers.

One of the earliest judgments of Frank's short stories came from that astute critic Marjorie Barnard, who wrote to Nettie Palmer in 1935 that Frank had showed her more of his stories and that she found them all good and all thoroughly alike. The reader of *The Woman at the Mill* is likely to agree with this opinion and to reflect in all justice that its contents would be more effective uncollected—read one by one, here and there, now and then, as they originally appeared, rather than one after another in a single volume.

The reason is that however different their characters and their themes may be, the settings and the tone of these stories are, on the whole, quickly identifiable, even predictable. Frank was not a highly imaginative writer but one who stuck close to his own experience. This had so far fallen into six major periods: in Victoria as a boy, in America as a youth, in Europe as a soldier, in Queensland as a selector, in Sydney as a business man, then as a writer. Among the fifteen stories in this collection America never appears, Sydney and Europe share one, Sydney and Victoria another, and a third has an unidentified urban setting (presumably Sydney) with a rural inset (the Illawara coastal area). The remaining dozen are set on the land—the outback Queensland of their author's years as a selector. In his Author's Note to the volume, Frank speaks of these as having "the same setting as *Man-Shy*. Readers of that tale may recall that it ended when the waterholes on which the wild cattle depended were cut off by the incoming settlers. These are stories of the settlement." The result is something of a monochrome of brigalow trees and belah scrub, high hopes and brutally hard work. All good, yes, but of a sameness.

Another source of similarity is their author's fondness for the first person as narrator. This he also explains in his Author's Note:

My frequent use of the first person might suggest, to the uninitiated, that I am writing from life. *Nothing could be farther from the truth.* [Italics mine.] Life doesn't transpose like that. These are all works of imagination, stories of things that never happened and of people who have never lived—except that I have been studious to avoid doing violence to the probabilities. There is no allusion to any person living or dead, and *even the narrator is not to be identified with the author*. [Italics mine.] The use of the first person in fiction is just a technical device, and one, it so happens, that I often find apt to my subject and comfortable to my idiosyncrasies.

Grant him all of this—with some reservations, but even his use of the first person tends to follow a fixed pattern. The narrator is inevitably a man, a Queensland selector, and one who, regardless of his shifting identity, always has the same manner of speaking, expresses the same points of view. He is never the central character nor yet a mere observer, but something in between: an intimate who plays a more or less minor role, seldom one that affects the course of the action. Of the relatively few stories told in the third person, only a couple avail themselves of that popular stance among authors, omniscience. The rest, limited to the viewpoint of a single character, have much the effect of the first person. None of these remarks are intended to pass judgment on any of these choices, only to point out that concentration on a single technique, as on a single setting, does not make for the richness of variety.

II *Queensland*

The dozen Queensland stories in the collection form a kind of treatise on the newly opened settlement: the way its people lived and the work they were required to do. The several installments that Frank had supplied to his father's early *Australian Post*, written under the pseudonym "T. Bone" while he was still in Queensland,[3] had given an account of the choosing and early occupation of the typical 1200-acre selection—purportedly a factual account although apparently laced, like *Caribbean Interlude*, with fiction. Now come the later stages of selection life, in fiction certainly based on fact, the two never very far apart in Frank's early work. We get some glimpses into the building of homes, from bark humpies up, but the women who occupy them are relatively scarce in these Queensland stories, mostly playing very minor roles when they do appear. It is a man's world and work that is detailed, and what work! Clearing the land meant cutting the trees (both down and up, in our curious idiom), burning them and digging out the stumps, and cutting the brush and getting rid of all roots to below plow level—all of this without modern power machinery. Then the splitting of posts and the building of fences. Then the erection of dams and the sinking of tanks for a water supply—if it rained. Then the encouragement of grass for pasture, the buying (by going into debt) of stock, the planting of crops. And *then*—the long, long waits between rains—the hopes, the uncertainties, the failures, the departures.

Frank once admitted to an early fondness for America's O. Henry, with his emphasis on plot and his sudden endings, but no one could list that writer among his later influences. Most of Frank's stories run to some length, not so much because of what happens in them as because of their author's love for building up a background and fondling its details. The result is that the reader of the collected stories is likely to emerge as much with a feeling of "I certainly know the fabric of life on a Queensland settlement in the twenties" as with vivid recollections of particular characters and the events they were involved in.

Not that Frank neglects his characters; he draws some notable ones. Commenting on the superiority of *Man-Shy* over *Forever Morning*, he once explained that in his early days as a writer, he understood animals better than he did people. But by the time he took up short-story writing seriously, in the early thirties, his understanding of people had been enlarged considerably by a decade of urban living. Nevertheless, the men and women that he wrote about during the next decade are rarely city dwellers; those, he would concentrate on later in *The White Thorntree*. The Queensland people, however they may vary, are all deeply rooted in the circumstances of the new settlement, and presumably (regardless of any sea changes resulting from their journey through the mind of their settler-author) in his experience as well, whether he chooses to portray the narrator as a neighboring bachelor or as a family man whose wife is of little if any importance to the story. Who his characters are, what kind of people they are, is usually a matter of more moment than what they do.

III "*Sojourners*"

His range of characters, within the limits of his chosen background, is considerable, and his treatment of them grew in sensitivity and understanding. They are never stereotyped, even when their circumstances might lead one to expect such treatment. Take Captain Vachell of "Sojourners," who could so easily have been portrayed as the typical "pommy,"[4] or "new chum," favorite butts of Australian humor—but he isn't. Vachell worked with the best of the settlers, despite having been at "home" (England) "the dull boy of the family, apparently, the unfortunate inheritor of nothing but good breeding."[5] On his selection one could find "nothing cockatoo about his workmanship. His fences and shed were quite up to the best bush standards."[6]

But our interest centers rather on his wife, a rare emphasis in the Davison short story. She had dutifully joined the Captain in his adventure but could not for a moment forget the England she had left in order to learn to tolerate the Australia she found. The selector-narrator, a neighbor, repeats her views: "What was wrong with the country? More things than I had imagined. It was upside-down on the earth's surface to begin with. The wind blew from the wrong direction. The sun came up at a skew-whiff corner. The people! The accent! The manners of the shop girls! The women's clothes! . . . The tasteless food in the restaurants! The inane newspapers! The ignorance of the populace!"[7] Yet the narrator concludes, "She wasn't a bad sort; just taking badly to being transplanted."[8]

IV "*Soldier of Fortune*"

"Sojourners" is neither a typical treatment by an Australian author of the "pommy" immigrant nor is it what some of Frank's literary contemporaries occasionally settled for, profitably, the slick magazine story. It is real, it is human, it is understanding, it is tolerant. The same qualities pervade "Soldier of Fortune," in which the courtly Campbell, of poor but educated parents, had worked his way up from teamster to stock dealer to station manager and at last to holder of a grazing lease on Loch Lomond. This was twenty thousand acres which he stocked with the finest cattle, compared to his neighbors' modest twelve-hundred-acre farming selections (like Frank's own). Yet his dignity and kindness were such that no one envied him, and everyone grieved when a serious slump sent him back to his teamster beginnings, a fall that he endured in middle age with no complaint, no loss of spirit.

V "*A Letter from Colleen*"

Frank's more endearing characters are not the outsiders nor the social superiors but "dinkum Aussie hard grafters"[9] like himself,

struggling single-handedly to turn wild scrub land into productivity. Old McShane in "A Letter from Colleen" is such a man, alone
on the four or five acres that were all he had succeeded in clearing
of his wooded twelve hundred. He had been a family man, but his
wife had died while their only child, a daughter named Colleen,
was a mere infant. The girl had been reared by friends and was now
married in faraway Melbourne, but she still wrote loyally every
week to her old father. The story hinges on the failure of Frimwade,
the stationmaster, to produce the weekly letter, sending the old man
empty-handed down the lonely seven miles of foot track to his
homestead. When the letter is shortly discovered by the narrator
where Frimwade had carelessly dropped it, Harry Marchant, a
young man from a family that were "reckoned a bad lot," [10]
volunteered to ride after the old man and deliver it, to keep him
from living a week in uncertainty.

This slight incident is the shortest story in the collection—less
than three thousand words. Yet there is time and space for the
author's typical leisurely development: a long description of Old
Mac's small but productive handful of cleared acres on his large and
heavily wooded selection; of his walking four miles, in dry weather,
to carry two small cans of water from the narrator's tank to his
camp; of his Irish background and his own history of hard work in
Australia; of his long weekly hike solely to get his letter from
Colleen; of the disdain of the stationmaster for any but the scrub
aristocracy, to whom he kowtowed; of the dubious family background of the Marchants, whose Harry thoughtfully and generously saved the day. Altogether the story is an account of place and
people that goes far beyond the little incident related and that adds
to the intimate picture to be found in this volume of the developing
Queensland settlement out of which most of its stories emerge. It
would be damning the author with faint praise to say that a by-
product of these stories is a revelation of settlement life as valuable
as Arthur Upfield's whodunits are, especially to an outsider, of
Australian outback life generally, but it would not be without some
truth.

VI "Here Comes the Bride"

Frank did not always find the short story an easy form. "It is
more than a high-brow aesthetic theory that form and content must

flow together; that content demands its own form; it is a plain fact of sound narration,"[11] he once wrote, when most of his short stories were behind him. He held up "Here Comes the Bride" as one of his best-handled stories, but admitted that it had cost him many attempts over a five-year period. His problem had been where to begin, and when he found the point, "the story came out like a telescope."[12]

Where he began it was, as in more than one of his other stories, close to the end of the action, with a vivid description of a farmer caught out in the first drenching rain to follow a frighteningly long drought:

> Clouds like a big bruise had risen above the ranges, towering up like the wrath of God, thunderously growling, spreading like coils of sulphurous smoke, shutting off the sun, casting an unearthly light upon the distant scene, wafting a scent of rain on the cool gusts of wind that were driven from their lower darkness. Now they were rolling low above the treetops.
>
> With his axe, straining fork and a couple of loops of wire over his shoulder, Pa Pettingell, who had been mending a fence at the back of his selection, was stumping home through the drenching storm. He plodded through a rain-striped gloom in which wet tree-trunks glistened darkly. From his sodden old hat the water trickling down his face carried the taste of sweat to his lips. Water squelched and bubbled from the laceholes of his boots at every step. His shirt and trousers clung to him like a half-sloughed skin.
>
> But Pa's heart was light.[13]

Not that his trouble had been just an ordinary drought; it had all centered around the approaching wedding of his youngest daughter. Their two years in Queensland had not yet justified his having uprooted the family from "the green hills of Gippsland," and it had become a matter of personal pride with him to encourage as good a wedding for Rose as her two sisters had had in the South. Hence he did everything he could to protect her and her mother from the knowledge (all too clear to himself and his neighbors) that he had overstocked in this uncertain season; and the women, accustomed to a more hospitable country and thoroughly absorbed in preparations for the wedding, did not notice. Pa even encouraged them to spend generously—while he was dragging bogged and drought-struck beasts from a shrunken waterhole, and skinning a £10 cow to salvage a ten-shilling hide. Only in his imagination did he shout at his wife, "My God, woman, have a little mercy on me!"[14]

The story is well built, in other ways than its introduction, alternating Pa's cruel troubles outside with the women's sole concern for the wedding, inside. Then came the saving downpour with which the story opened. "Forgetting that they who had been shielded from sharing in his anxieties could hardly be expected to realize the measure of his relief," Pa stepped to the threshold to announce "Hey, Ma. It's rainin'!" Ma's dutiful reply was "Very nice, isn't it?" and Rose's, "Hadn't you better get your wet things off, Pa?"[15] A suitable conclusion to the story whose beginning had cost its author so many thoughtful years. "Here Comes the Bride" is the nearest to a study of family life the volume provides, but even here the emphasis is on the man and his trials.

VII "Nobody's Kelpie"

"Nobody's Kelpie" gets away from the grueling work of the owner's selection to the labor of putting through a road on a government contract—which leaves time and strength for other troubles. This story is marked by Frank's increasing skill as a teller of tales. When as "Frederick Douglas" he wrote in the early twenties for his father's magazine Australia a story called "The Regeneration of Jimmy" (p. 38), he portrayed an unusual outback character, the man-who-wouldn't-fight. At that time, however, youth and the requirements of his editor-father suggested nothing better than the pat ending of Jimmy's finally being goaded (not by repeated personal insults but by a kick to his dog) into squaring off to his opponent—and of course to win. But by the 1930s, not only freed from Australia's policy of the happy ending but also more experienced as man and writer, Frank was able to produce a far more perceptive, study of the noncombatant bushman in "Nobody's Kelpie." Here, not even the abuse of his dog by Bill Connolly, to say nothing of the alienation of its affections, could make of Lou Cody the kind of man he wanted to be. He couldn't bring himself to fight and "He was not helped by the reflection that had he the easy confidence other men possessed, such provocation as existed at present would not have been offered."[16] So—he loses his dog, and his job, and his self-respect; he does not even have the satisfaction of being around to see Bill, his impudent young baiter, get from other, bolder hands the beating he so richly deserves.

VIII   *"Return of the Hunter"*

Frank explained in 1942 that "Return of the Hunter" was a development and elaboration of a column story published in the *Bulletin* six or seven years before. As it appears in *The Woman at the Mill* it is well developed indeed—a full-fledged character sketch of Tug Treloar, emerging from both past and present events. The story is told in the third person but entirely from Tug's viewpoint: we learn of his bravery as a sniper during the war, of his returning to woo and marry Bonny, of his giving up further opportunities for adventure with his wartime buddies in order to stay with her and protect his interests. Now he "was irked by the plodding sameness of a settler's life."[17]

The story begins, as Frank's often do, near the end of the action, with the hunter skinning a cattle-killing half-breed dingo sought by many for the challenge, the bounty, and the pelt. For Tug there had been the added inducement of wanting money to buy the pony and sulky his young wife had been yearning for. After days of tracking, he used his kelpie bitch Topsy as a lure. Now, having skinned his victim, Tug started for home. "Neither then nor at any moment during the long wait in the shadow of the brigalow, had any sense of fellowship with the warigal stirred in his mind. It was hunter and hunted, and when his shot rang out the hunter had triumphed."[18] And yet, stopping on the way, he is almost a convert to "the fellowship of the flesh": "Perhaps more thoughtfully than he had ever looked upon anything, Tug studied the scalp dangling limply at the end of his up-thrust arm; the coat, the bloom of life still in it, gleaming dimly in the moonlight." He seemed almost on the verge of a reflective thought, this man whose mind had always been busy only with images, but the moment passed and he was himself again, noting "A skin without a dog in it. Rather funny—but withal a noble trophy!"[19] His next image was of his imminent arrival at his camp where his wife was waiting: Topsy, then Tug holding out the scalp for Bonny's unbounded pleasure and approval.

Tug's complexities make him a welcome change from the simpler hard-graft selectors of the other stories, and the "Return of the Hunter" has been widely anthologized.

IX   *"The Woman at the Mill"*

The title story, "The Woman at the Mill," however, is the most

important in the collection for the study of an author who was later
to produce a huge novel on sex. Women, as we have noticed, have
been rare in the collection; sex, even rarer. But in this story, though
still set in Queensland, the central figure is a wife and mother, and
the story an analysis of her emotional reactions to what proved to be
a brief illicit sexual episode.

The beginning is typical Davison—at the end of the action (we
hear the finality of his cantering horse's hoofbeats as her lover rides
away). But the ensuing story concentrates on Irene Lawrence, wife
of Mat the miller, once a cattle dealer and years her senior. Now the
mother of three, she looked distastefully on her marriage. "She had
a feeling that in spirit, if not in fact, she had been part of a deal
arranged between Mat and her father; a feeling that Mat had led
her from her father's farm as he might have led a well-grown and
promising heifer."[20] Dissatisfied with her life with him, she began
to "look around," with indifferent success until she met Bert
Caswell, a wandering drover. He was younger than she and "better
looking than any man had a right to be."[21] Besides, he seemed as
drawn to her as she to him, being inexperienced, we learn, save with
"girls of fourth-rate country pubs; housemaids whose employers expected them not to be above entertaining guests on terms to be
arranged between them. This matter of his encounter with a very
desirable married woman was in a different class."[22] From a dance,
they withdrew into the woods and made love. Then he left on a job,
and "For a while, afterwards, Irene was lost in her feelings between
being something aghast at what she had done, and taking pride to
herself in that she had gone, daring worthily, where most women
ventured only in guarded excursions of the imagination."[23] As the
days passed, "there were times when doubt tortured her"; when she
felt "She had given too much too readily."[24] But learning of Bert's
return, she was overwhelmed with longing, and when he appeared
(knowing that her husband would be away for the day), "Her eyes
were idolatrous."[25]

Since this is one of the relatively few stories Frank told in the
third person, we are able to explore Bert's reactions as well: his elation when "a very desirable married woman" had responded to him
so readily on their first meeting, his doubts as to his reception when
he returned, his need for the "reassurance of repetition." But after
their prompt second love-making, at the mill, Bert was thoughtfully
uneasy. "He had become aware of a difference between himself and
her; a difference of intention. She didn't want just to nick an oc-

casional orange from the tree. She wanted all of him." [26] While she was making tea, "He was thinking how, by half-truths, evasions and direct lies, by both feigning to answer, and stifling questions with caresses, he had misled her in the bedroom. But what else could he have done? He didn't mean to be unkind—you couldn't think unkindly of a woman who had taken you to bed with her—but she was a bit of a mug!" [27]

Irene saw that he was afraid of a scene, and spared him that. As she said goodbye to him, she even forced herself to smile. "She must appear to take what had happened between them in the spirit in which he intended—at any rate until he was gone." As for Bert, as his eyes were held unwillingly by hers, "He saw in them pain, and resignation to pain that was yet to be endured; he caught a glimpse of reaches of human feeling he hadn't known to exist." [28]

X "*The Night Watch*"

In the years after he wrote *Forever Morning*, Frank had obviously learned a good deal about people. Yet he had not dealt much with women characters; even in "Lady with a Scar" his major character is a man. In the miller's wife, however, he not only produced a mature, infatuated woman but also sharply outlined a credible emotional distinction between the sexes. "The Woman at the Mill" goes so deeply and skillfully into the reactions of both man and woman, in fact, that it is hard to believe it was written not long after another of Frank's infrequent love stories, "The Night Watch." It may seem unfair to examine this one, since he did not include it in his collection, but it has other credentials: it appeared in the *Australian Writers' Annual*, a volume published in 1936 under the auspices of the Fellowship of Australian Writers and the editorship of Flora Eldershaw. This included contributions by a wide variety of authors, greater and lesser (even including a rare short story by Frank's younger brother Douglas).

"The Night Watch" is like "The Woman at the Mill" in that its setting is Queensland and it tells of an illicit attraction between a mature pair. Charlie Wardroper is a wandering laborer who, like Bert Caswell, has thus far known only prostitutes, and Grace Grover, like Irene Lawrence, is a wife and mother. Charlie, once a mate of husband Tom, is now working for him briefly on the Grover selection, and between him and Grace "something was trying to work its will." [29] On this day Tom (like the miller) being away on business, they grew increasingly aware of one another, went for a walk in the woods together on the pretext of Charlie's going hunting, and he, after leaning his gun against a tree, took her in his arms. "She protested when he sought consummation of their embrace, but that was only the voice of nature, whetting the edge of conquest and surrender."[30]

Here the likeness between the two stories ends. Had this been "The Woman at the Mill," Charlie would shortly have left the selection (he was due to go soon anyway), leaving Grace emotionally bereft. "The Night Watch" is more eventful, however, even melodramatic: husband Tom, returning early on quiet hooves in the soft earth, discovered the pair, jumped off his horse, and grabbed the gun—Charlie nobly threw himself between Grace and the rifle with an "I wouldn't make matters worse, Tom,"[31] whereupon Tom solved their immediate problem by putting the muzzle under his own chin and pushing the trigger with his thumb. During the inquiry Charlie and Grace avoided each other's eyes, and Charlie ended his reflective "night watch" by taking the morning train out of Wilgatown.

This story of violent action must have been far easier to write than "The Woman at the Mill," with its subtle revelations of fluctuating emotions. Frank chose wisely in omitting this one from his collection while making the other his title story. But shades of the melodrama here, so rare in Frank's early writing, will haunt us through his much later novel, *The White Thorntree*.

XI "The Wasteland"

"The Wasteland" deserves special attention as the least typical of the Queensland stories, having virtually no action and only one character of note, other than the usual selector-narrator. The "wasteland" itself is Lot 32, an impractical piece of land that had inevitably been selected, but not yet developed, by de Burgh, an impractical man. The story concludes with "It struck me that men like de Burgh have something of the character of Lot 32—a high resistance to practicality. They carry their wasteland inside them."[32] But even de Burgh is not characterized at much length—he appears only once, full of a variety of unsuitable plans, then disappears.

The center of interest is the "wasteland" itself, several hundred acres of a variety of conditions that would not justify development. But it served a purpose, for "Down on the good lands the bush was wasting before our attack," so that the woodland and the wild creatures it had supported were both disappearing before the cultivation of the selector-settlers. The narrator, who had first regarded Lot 32 as "one of the Creator's obvious blunders,"[33] came to value this piece of unspoiled country as "an escape, and a condition of mind."[34] Page after page is devoted to lyrical descriptions of its variety of elevation and growth, its native inhabitants, and the joy and peace that the narrator finds on his rides through it. It is his good fortune, after de Burgh forfeits the land untouched, to win the right to it, on a draw, and to know that his possession of this "worthless" land will secure it from maltreatment. In his other writing Frank had been notably kind to Australia's animals and people; this is his major tribute to her undisturbed earth. It is hard to believe that its poetry is from the same hand as the workaday economics that we shall find in "Fields of Cotton."

XII *"Further West"*

In his *Social Patterns in Australian Literature* (1971), critic T. Inglis Moore includes Frank's name among those short-story and novel writers "with radical sympathies" who "indict the social and economic system at many points."[35] Frank certainly had radical sympathies, especially in the late thirties and early forties, as *While Freedom Lives* and some of his public addresses demonstrate. What is surprising is that these leanings are so rarely reflected in his fiction. The plight of the aborigines, for instance, was beginning to be treated sympathetically by creative writers (Xavier Herbert, Katharine Susannah Prichard, and others) in this period—a nest of problems with which Frank was presumably somewhat familiar (he had once applied for work among them). Yet "Further West," the only story in the collection in which these native Australians appear, has little bearing on a people's condition; rather, it looks into the depths of a white man's pain.

Emma, an aborigine from a mission station, was happily situated as the wife of Dave Chandler, an itinerant hunter and trapper in the Queensland outback, and mother of their half-caste brood. All their lives they had camped out, but as Dave, approaching middle age, discovered that part of his hunting territory was being opened for selection, he became enthusiastic over the idea of joining the new settlement, with its social and educational advantages. He had just decided on a selection when, at the railhead store, he was waited on by Mrs. Thorpe, newly arrived widowed sister-in-law of the store-keeper. At first sight of her, "It was just as if she had been living somewhere in his mind all his days, and had suddenly appeared before him; as if all his life had led up to this moment. It had been the same with her—he saw and felt that. The reserve with which women ordinarily veil their eyes in meeting the glance of a man had not been there—only startled recognition."[36] As he was leaving after finishing his business, he realized that she had been interested-ly asking about him, for he overheard her say, with a quiver of horror, "Not that old black gin!"[37]

Dave, who had known only flickering dissatisfactions with Emma in the past, now recognized them as "evidence of buried discon-tent; of the need of a mate of his own kind and colour. The discon-tent had become imperative only when the woman he would have chosen had appeared before him in the flesh."[38] As the days passed he convinced himself that Mrs. Thorpe's exclamation had been one of sympathy, not repulsion; but on his second trip to the store she waited on him without a sign of recognition. Back at camp, he packed up his family and their gear. As he stood by the wagon ready to leave, he found himself running through the advantages for them all of going "further west"—even as he had earlier per-suaded himself of the virtues of settling down. For the rest, he realizes philosophically, "He must flog himself forward to forget-fulness—it would come. Contentment would return. Sometime, no doubt, in camp or going around his snare line, memory would swoop on him. It would bail him up, like a cattle dog bails up a goanna. He'd face that. The fact of it would be proof of something steadfast in himself."[39] To a passerby's inquiry about his change of plans, he answered, "Too many people around for people like us."[40]

XIII   *"Fields of Cotton"*

There is nothing "radical" about the perceptive treatment of the human heart in "Further West." For that matter, Frank mostly por-trays the problems of the Queensland settlers as the fault of nothing, as he explained his own, but ignorance and the weather. Only one story mildly indicts the System: "Fields of Cotton" recounts at length the local farmers' desperately hard work as the result of a government project to encourage the raising of cotton. It failed, in most areas, including the one of which the story is told, and the narrator reports on the disillusionment that followed:

> We saw through the game a few weeks after the end of the cotton season.
> It turned out that one special part of Queensland—the Dawson
> Valley—was best suited to cotton. The farmers there did very well out of
> the crop; and thitherward went the ginning mills, the brokers' agents, every
> one who had anything to gain from cotton in bulk—the bright commercial
> lads! Get the idea? The whole of the State had been used as an experimen-
> tal plot. There had been some lobbying. . . . The public had been per-
> suaded to provide the information, the seed, and the guaranteed price. We
> had supplied the soil, the sweat and the blasted hopes. It is possible, of
> course, that the full terms of the great cotton experiment were fully set
> forth to us at the beginning, and that we forgot about them in our rising
> enthusiasm, but I don't think so; even thinking hard I can't recall anything
> of the kind. Of course, the nation was presented with a splendid and
> valuable addition to its range of industrial crops but I can't help feeling
> that those smart business chaps put one over on us simple country folk.[41]

This is social criticism of the kind that we might expect from Fred
Davison's son, a kind of essay on agricultural economics with
responsibility for failure duly assigned. As such, however, it stands
almost alone in the volume, and as a short story, near the bottom.

XIV   "Fathers and Sons"

Only one story in *The Woman at the Mill* is the kind of indict-
ment that Moore's remark about radical tendencies and our
knowledge of some of Frank's thinking at about this time might
lead us to expect. One of the longest in the book, it is the only one
drawn from Frank's personal experience of war. In "Fathers and
Sons" he is no longer the "happy warrior" of *The Wells of
Beersheba* days; the narrator here is a disillusioned veteran of
World War I, reminiscing in dismay from the vantage of World
War II. The framing experience is his visit to Sydney's impressive
Shrine of Remembrance, and the substance of the story is the experience of an idealistic American boy, Mitch, who has come over
to "join up" early in the first world war, encouraged by his English-
born father. The boy reads with shining eyes the older man's letter
(inspired, the narrator adds, by "vicarious heroism"), directing that
"when you reach the field of war, my boy, do not expose yourself
unnecessarily; but if it comes to the charge, let no man show you

the way."[42] The narrator further observes of the father: "He was willing to serve his country at least by proxy. He was innocent enough in that, I daresay. We all, fathers and sons, were very innocent in those years. We had very high-flown romantic notions about war."[43]

Inexplicably, however, from being the best of soldiers, Mitch became the worst, and ultimately deserted. Later caught and reinstated, he was sent up to the front where he rejoined his friend shortly before being killed. As his closest comrade, the narrator had the duty of going through Mitch's things, and there found clippings from "the New York gutter press" that explained everything: the boy's father, with his son at war, had left the mother for some young thing. For Mitch, "The pillars of his faith had been thrown down."[44] For the narrator, "I know now that the only difference between Mitch's old man and the fathers of the lads lying over the top was that the elder Mitchell's betrayal had a sharper edge. In every case life was in the arms of the older man, not only the anonymous fathers, but also the fathers of state: for the boys, the kiss of death."[45]

Here at last is fiction that reflects Frank's political thinking at the time. We can hear unmistakable echoes of *While Freedom Lives* as the narrator looks at the Anzac Memorial, having "reached the end of my recollections and reflections of war as the bloody excreta of competitive nationalism. With the new war in mind I was disposed to reflect on statesmen as scurrying lackeys of greed, on ancient political lechers scraping the pot, on their accomplice the hail-fellow Judas of the editorial chair, on the jiggery-pokery that stuffed words like vested interests out of sight behind words like freedom, honour, justice. I wanted a devil to scotch, a villain to break. But it went deeper than that; the blame was on us all; our common selfishness and stupidity. Hadn't I, who might have known, and had the power to speak, gone unmoved for half a lifetime?"[46] Once more inside the shrine, he goes on to criticize the three grieving female figures who hold the dead soldier aloft on his shield, for the fact that their grief, so profound, is also wholly personal. "Of a sense of responsibility, of rebellion, of attempted understanding, their faces showed not a vestige, not a glimmer."[47] He concludes (with the words of British nurse Edith Cavell as she faced a German firing squad in 1915): "Patriotism is not enough."

The surprise here is not the violence of Frank's expressed stand but the fact that it appears nowhere else in his fiction. We must remember, however, that he himself admitted later that he was not really a political person (as his father was), and that the *While Freedom Lives* period, violent as it sounded, was just a phase. This admission helps us to understand a nagging problem for the literary historian: why, when he did so much leftist thinking for a time, he seems to have done it as an individual, and never appears to have been connected with any of the steadily leftist fiction writers such as Katharine Susannah Prichard and her coterie.

XV *"Lady with a Scar"*

Frank arranged the stories in *The Woman at the Mill* in three parts, the first and the third each containing a half-dozen Queensland stories, the second, presumably to break the monotony (he labels them "An Interlude"), a group of three with vastly different settings. One was the "Fathers and Sons" we have just looked at, with its Sydney frame around a long story of World War I in Europe; another, "Lady with a Scar," in which he proves again his ability to write without the usual Queensland background. Here, from an urban setting we are taken briefly to the scene of a country childhood. Beyond that, the locale does not matter. In this story, as in none of his others, the author is preoccupied with the psychological, even the philosophical, and a universal theme.

When Frank reviewed the novel *Plaque with Laurel* (1937) by his friends M. Barnard Eldershaw (p. 95 - 96), he curiously omitted any mention of the basic theme of the book, which is clearly stated in the lives of both central characters, Richard Crale and Owen Sale: briefly, that the real evil in the world lies not in what we intend but in what we do unwittingly. This view was apparently important to Marjorie Barnard and Flora Eldershaw, for it had appeared briefly in one of the inset stories of their previous novel, *The Glasshouse* (1936). One may wonder, then, if it was not the result of one of the many interchanges of ideas in their tight little circle that led to Frank's "Lady with a Scar," product of about the same period.

In this story middle-aged Jim Durrell, attending a Sunday night musicale to please his wife, sees a lady whom he notices not only because of a disfiguring scar on one side of her face but because she haunts him with a sense of earlier familiarity. Finally he remembers her—Jennie Marshall, a girl whom he had loved while he was a country schoolboy.

He had forgotten her in adolescence—that rather churlish abandonment of childish things—and had remembered her often in maturity. She was one of a score of wispy recollections; things that flitted across his mind in moments of mild bodily activity and complete mental relaxation—at such times as when he was shaving, or when he was watering the garden.[48]

When he finally gets to speak to her, he learns that it was he who, in childhood, had caused the scar by shoving her against a piece of galvanized iron in a moment of boyish bravado. But "he couldn't recall the incident." Later he is led to wonder "if hell contained a daintier torment than stumbling on the forgotten acts of one's life—not the big things but the little mongrel acts that had inflicted unguessed injuries upon others."[49] But he has comfort—comfort of the same sort that Frank had allowed Dave Chandler in "Further West" after he had resigned his dream of Mrs. Thorpe (p. 120):

The matter was going to ride his mind for a while. He knew that. He knew also that there would be eventual escape. Work. Life wasn't so relentless but what a man could elude the pursuit of memory. But sometimes, he knew, the memory of Jennie Marshall—the child and the woman—would return to him unexpectedly, catch up with him. At such times as when he was shaving, or when he was watering the garden.[50]

"Lady with a Scar," like "The Woman at the Mill," shows Frank's growing ability to get below the surfaces of life and explore, at least briefly, the deeper levels that he was to reach more frequently in *The White Thorntree.*

XVI *"The Yarns Men Tell"*

The third "interlude" (relaxation from a steady diet of Queensland) is "The Yarns Men Tell," an echo, the introduction explains, of Henry Lawson. The narrator here is now "in Gippsland, swagging it through the ranges"[51] with his mate Tom. At their campsite one evening they were joined by another knight of the road, obviously a city man, "and presently he was entertaining himself telling us lies,"[52] such as laying claim, curiously, to a Sydney column written by the narrator. Soon, "as was almost inevitable, he got around to the subject of women"[53] (one not to sensitive Tom's liking), and told them in detail of one of his personal exploits—"a particularly callous betrayal of a particularly trusting girl."[54] Whereupon Tom turns the tables with a long story (his mate recognizes it as at least part fiction) about a girl he had known in

Sydney who had been seduced and left pregnant. Tom's description of the seducer is made to tally at every possible point with their visitor at the campfire, until the braggart gets uneasy and departs. The narrator is left to conclude that "there's mostly a core of truth in the yarns men tell."[55] Frank never denied his debt to Lawson, although he did say once that "Lawson is immeasurably the greater writer but—and I say it in all modesty—I have a few qualities that he lacked, enough to warrant me adding my scrawl to the general page."[56]

XVII "*Meet Darkie Hoskins*"

Of the fifteen stories in *The Woman at the Mill*, all but one were to reappear in a second collection a quarter of a century later. That one, "Meet Darkie Hoskins," is especially worth looking at here as evidence (greater than his continual revisions) of Frank's shifting taste. Written before *Man-Shy* and *Forever Morning*, it too had its origin in one of his father's magazines. This time he had gone back to the short story "Shifting Sands," which had appeared in the first issue (March, 1923) of the then *Australian* (p. 35 - 36). He chose to revive it, he said, because of his father's fondness for it, and proceeded to rewrite it, vastly improving it, he felt, only to have the old man like the new version less! Strange, since Frank retained the happy ending (one of editor Fred's requirements for fiction); he even began the story with it, in the revision, as if to help tide the reader through the pain of Darkie's brutally hard work during a long series of reverses. In substance, both versions were an account of a settler's increasingly desperate efforts to assure himself of a water supply—but just as repeated failures had led Darkie to face giving up his selection, a fortuitous rain storm at last built up his dam instead of wrecking it, and his future on the land was assured.

Within a couple of years after his inclusion of "Meet Darkie Hoskins" in *The Woman at the Mill*, Frank was calling it "a petit bourgeoise success story," probably written "under the influence of that bloody awful rag the Saturday Evening Post."[57] He wished that he retitled it "The Skin of His Teeth," as he had once intended (perhaps) because Darkie was a misleading nickname for an English Australian in the land of the aborigine). He even wished that he had left it out entirely, and when the publication of a second collection gave him another chance to omit it, he did. Thus *The Road to Yesterday* is happily free from any direct det to his paternally influenced literary beginnings.

Back in 1932 Frank had admitted to Nettie Palmer that when he first started, "I hadn't the faintest idea about technique in writing. I just began at the beginning and quit when I had finished."[58] In becoming "one of the accepted short-story men of the thirties," he had learned a variety of techniques well. In this collection only in "Fields of Cotton" (one of the weakest) does the action follow a straight time line from start to finish. In "A Letter from Colleen" and "Sojourners" the action is related chronologically when it starts, but is preceded in both stories by long and leisurely introductions devoted to the backgrounds and personalities of the central characters; in "A Letter" this occupies almost half the space. In "Fathers and Sons" the present appears only as the introduction and conclusion of a past story—a kind of frame around it to handle it by, to give it significance; in "The Yarns Men Tell" the present has more narrative meaning of its own. It is the important thing in "Lady with a Scar," but it encircles and depends upon a long reminiscence of a distant past.

One of the lessons Frank had taken to heart was the dramatic value of beginning a story at or near—even just after—the end of the action. This was his answer to the problem that he admitted having arrived at slowly: where to begin "Here Comes the Bride." As he solved it, the reader knows the happy outcome of the long wait for rain before learning of the particular concern the drought had caused. The major change its author made in reworking "Shifting Sands" into "Meet Darkie Hoskins" was to start with the solution of the critical water problem that, the story then proceeds to detail, had almost robbed the selector of his land. Campbell, the "soldier of fortune," has lost his place before we know who he is, how it came about, and what his reaction is; and Dave Chandler is preparing to go "further west" before we hear about his hopes for settling down and their defeat. "The Woman at the Mill" begins with the departure that spells the end of all the hopes the story itself raises, and "Return of the Hunter," too, starts near the end with the skinning of the dingo, the story itself being thoroughly developed later through a variety of revelations of earlier events. There is no question of the virtue of these reversals of time order; most of them furnish a kind of bait to entice the reader and keep him reading to find out not *what* happened, which he knows, but how and why and to whom.

XVIII   The Road to Yesterday

Since this study deals with Frank's life and works chronologically, some explanation is required for moving now from 1940's *The Woman at the Mill* to 1964's *The Road to Yesterday*. Both are collections of short stories, but more than that, the second contains, with the one exception already noted, all of the contents of the first, adding only a reprint of that small book from 1933, *The Wells of Beersheba*, and four new stories written in the early 1940s. Thus the "new" collection is not very new, and all of it belongs to the 1930s and early 1940s rather than to the 1960s in which it appeared. Yet it was published twenty-four years after *The Woman at the Mill*, sixteen after Frank's last book-length publication of his first period, *Dusty*, and only four years prior to the appearance of *The White Thorntree*, on which he had been working ever since.

What prompted the publication of this second collection is hard to say, since it added so little to the first; perhaps it was to recall the Davison name to a long-neglected public in preparation for the appearance of Frank's monumental novel. But whether it was inspired by author or by publisher, *The Road to Yesterday* apparently sold well (*The Woman at the Mill* never went beyond a first edition), for four years after its appearance it went into a paperback edition (1968) which was reprinted, with a new cover, in 1970. Its chief attraction for many buyers may have been less the additional stories than the inclusion of what was far more than a short story, save in length—the remarkable *Wells of Beersheba*, which had never been available save in the tiny volumes of the 1933 and 1947 editions.

All of the new stories had already been anthologized. This was owing to the fact that the 1940s saw the beginning of a great source of encouragement for the short-story writer in Australia: the institution of a published collection of each year's best under the title *Coast to Coast*. Put together by a succession of well-known authors and editors and published by Angus & Robertson, it appeared annually from 1941 through 1948, biennially from 1949-50 through 1969-70. A few of the better-known short-story writers—Vance Palmer, Katharine Susannah Prichard, Dal Stivens, for instance, and Frank—had already published collections of their own stories, but most of such writing was doomed to an ephemeral existence in newspapers and magazines. Now a couple of dozen writers a year were recognized and their work perpetuated in this lasting series. It was probably the greatest boost to short-story writing in Australia since Sydney's *Bulletin* began to promote the genre in the 1880s and 90s. It came a little late for Frank, but each of its first five volumes carried one of his stories, "Return of the Hunter" in the 1941 issue having already appeared in *The Woman at the Mill*, the other four now being included in *The Road to Yesterday*. They are among his best, and being also last, lead the reader to regret that he wrote no more.

XVIII   "*The Good Herdsman*"

In three of the four we return to the familiar Queensland background. One is "The Good Herdsman," which Frank himself as editor of *Coast to Coast 1943* chose to include.[59] Reminiscent of "A Letter from Colleen" in that its chief character is a lonely old landsman, it is far superior in theme and sensitivity. Isaac, the good herdsman, is no widower leaning emotionally on a distant daughter, but an elderly bachelor who in a couple of years of husbandry becomes so attached to a small herd of heifers he had bought for profit that he cannot face parting with them. Colleen's letter was ultimately delivered to her father; no such happy ending for Isaac, who finds himself forced by the jeering of his neighbors to agree to the sale of his beloved herd. In the *Coast to Coast* version, the story ends with the sentence: "Isaac Burgess had no word for the act of renunciation, but he knew its pangs."[60] A dozen new concluding lines were added in the 1964 revision, but the final sentence, like many of Frank's revisions, is hardly as effective as the original. They read: "He knew himself, now, for an old man who was being hunted onwards against his will."[61]

XIX   "*Tank-sinkers*"

"The Good Herdsman" is remarkable for its understanding, its tenderness, and the keenness of its author's perception of character. "Tank-sinkers," the last to appear (*Coast to Coast 1945*), is a more typical Australian short story, a hymn to the laboring man, with toughness and character variety rather than depth. Frank was duly proud of his place in the Lawson tradition of Australian short-story writers, but as a writer of outback life more than a generation later than Lawson, he necessarily reflected in his themes the changes that had taken place in that world. Men like Lawson and Furphy ("Tom Collins") saw the outback developing in pastoral days, when men, pressing on ahead of their families in the pushing out of the great grazing properties, found their chief human tie to be with each other in that peculiarly Australian relationship of mateship. Frank's review in the late thirties of M. Barnard Eldershaw's *Plaque with Laurel*, a novel of urban literary Australia, shows his sharp awareness of this tie, for he chooses to stress as the principal feature of that book what would have passed with most readers for mere friendship. In his own Queensland stories there is little mateship because life in a settled area did not encourage it. Men were good neighbors, exchanging work as need be, but they were also husbands and fathers, working mostly alone, and more concerned with their own families than with other men. In "The Yarns Men Tell," two mates (the inevitable narrator and his companion) were "swagging it" together through Gippsland, but their relationship had little part in this framework, none in the principal "yarn" told within it by the companion. "Tank-sinkers" stands as close as we get in the Queensland stories to that old tradition of loyalty among men.

Frank's early "Shifting Sands" and its expansion into "Meet Darkie Hoskins" had centered on the difficulties encountered by Queensland selectors in getting and holding water through dam-building and tank-sinking. The "tank" was no manufactured container but one laboriously scooped out of the soil. "Tank-sinkers" describes in detail the work of "sinking" one—labor of men and of horses used in twelve-horse teams for only a half day of each two because of the rigors of the work for grass-fed animals. It involves the usual unnamed settler-narrator and the crew of three who are working against time to get his tank completed before the imminent rains arrive. The men are Peter the horse-tailer, whose job it is to bring in for each half-day's work a fresh twelve-horse team; Hughie Penton, who handles the scoop itself; and Don Crake, who drives the horses. Don is the stuff of which mates are made; his loyalty to his co-workers and their employer is complete. But as a new settler he is also a family man who resents the work that keeps him away so much from his wife, son, and daughter. When word reaches him of an accident to his children, he sets out unquestioningly on horseback for home, after scrupulously leaving a message for his employer.

Much of the story takes place during the long evening hours of the second night when the men wait, hopeful for Don's return. His fellow workmen, having carried on as best they could without him for a day and a half, are more than usually exhausted. But no one thinks of going to bed (which they normally did at eight), for their mate might be coming in, and it wouldn't do to have him find a dark camp without hot tea, food, and companionship. So they sit around an open fire reckoning up his chances and good-naturedly "chiaking" each other in the rough, affectionate manner of Australian men. And at midnight Don arrives, having fulfilled his two obligations: to make sure that all would be well at home, and to return to the job with all possible speed. It had meant a 128-mile ride in thirty-six hours—a source of great pride to the others, for this "was a mate of ours."[62]

XX *"Transition"*

In this final group of stories in *The Road to Yesterday*, Frank twice demonstrates his concern with political and economic problems. "Transition," which had appeared first in *Coast to Coast 1942*, is framed by a meeting in a Sydney pub, in the mid-thirties, of two old friends from the "new settlement" days in Queensland. One is the narrator, the other Con Whatley, a character who had appeared in "Soldier of Fortune." There, in a minor role, he had been identified as "our local radical":

While trying to get ahead—"A man's got to live!"—he despised himself for the effort. In his view Campbell was a land-grabbing bastard if he succeeded and a victim of the economic frame-up if he failed. The financial people who had backed him in the first place and now taken him over were bastards first, last and all the time.[63]

In "Transition," Con becomes a central character. The narrator (who bears a remarkable similarity to the author in detail after detail) admits that while he himself agreed with the Opposition in Queensland, he always voted Government, like his neighbors, out of pure self-interest. But Con was marked in that community of self-interested settlers by his loud concern for the underdog all over the world. His views once led him close to becoming a victim of Joe Sinclair, the settlement's leading Tory—so close that Con moved his family away from the area. The narrator shortly left, too—"failed and left" (one of the numerous details in which he resembles his author). Now, a decade later, the two meet as city men. Here the present frame brings us up to date on the past story: whereas the narrator had been a Government supporter while Con put his faith in the Opposition and constitutional reform, there has been a "transition"—a couple of them, in fact. The former Government man, now in real estate, has switched to the Opposition, only to find that Con, now a journalist, has gone beyond into Communism.

XXI   *"The Road to Yesterday"*

The title story of this second collection deserves special consideration. "The Road to Yesterday," which like "Tank-sinkers" first appeared in the *Bulletin*, then in *Coast to Coast 1944*, is not only the longest story in the book but also provides us with a refreshing new setting, the mountainous rural Victoria of Frank's early adolescence. While the Author's Note in *The Woman at the Mill* disclaimed the autobiographical element with a forthright "Nothing could be further from the truth,"[64] here in the second collection the disclaimer is modified, wisely, to "This is true only to a very limited degree."[65] We noted the similarities between author and character in "Transition"; in "The Road to Yesterday" the middle-aged narrator "after many years and much wandering,"[66] visits a selection in the Plenty Ranges "where I first put down roots in the earth,"[67] and where "I was the boy about the place, wide-eyed, and with a mind as receptive as soil to water"[68]—obvious similarities to Frank's own experience of living and working in this area from the ages of twelve to fifteen.

The story is simple, leisurely, and deeply significant. The narrator is a "baldish man in city togs" who, through the kindness of Melbourne friends willing to use their car to explore indifferent old mountain roads, revisits the scenes of his youth. Some of the author's most beautiful prose is to be found here. The contrasts between the past and the present give him an opportunity for emotive description of a high order. There is the new road, "a modern mountain highway, a black stream of bitumen that loops and sidles along the flank of the range. . . . Each cutting and embankment is like a brown cicatrice on the aboriginal body of the mountain, but the road passing between these earthy scars is smoothly purposeful in its upward course."[69] By contrast the old road, "unsurfaced earth, a pioneer track," had been "a long stiff pull, and raised the sweat on a horse. . . . You must needs walk beside him to help lighten the load, and you had to give him a spell at the top, where he would stand with quivering chest and dripping belly."[70]

The trip by car is only a framework for the bulk of this narrative, which is devoted to the past, chiefly to life and work on the hundred-acre selection of Mr. Sims, no "good herdsman" this time but an excellent husbandman whose cultivated acres were immaculate. "Just as the company of well-bred people gives you the feeling, 'Here is gentleness,' or a library, 'Here is learning,' so when you came to Mr. Sims's place you had the feeling, 'Here is husbandry.'"[71] Sims was from Kent, whose beauties he had left with some regret for the sake of the freedom of "the Colonies." On his relatively small selection in Victoria "hard graft" was as much the order of the day as later in Frank's Queensland. After four years Sims and his sons had cleared only ten acres of their heavily forested land, where "in addition to the living trees there were the stumps of the dead, like great half-decayed teeth, to be dug and wrenched piecemeal from the earth and piled for burning."[72] The cleared land was devoted to fruits and vegetables, with some rye for winter fodder. This, Sims cut by hand, of course, and the boy watched fascinated "while the rye subsided in dark swaths above the shining arc of his blade."

The use of the scythe is an art and beautiful to see. It takes skill that has become part of nature to wield that python handle so that the blade neither stabs the earth with its point nor raises the dust with its heel, but shears close and even. The movements of the scytheman's body are rhythmical like those of a ritual dance. His arms and shoulders swing wide above rigid hips, and the movements of his feet are timed to the sweep of the blade. In watching our scytheman we forgot his stooped shoulders and stiff gait; youth and grace had returned to him. In the return swing his blade came clean from under the swath, leaving the windrows smooth for the binders who would come after him.

Twice in his first strip off the side of the crop Mr Sims turned to look back over his work in careful self-criticism; and when he had turned the corner of the field and was lost to us across the green from the chest down, he upended his scythe to whet it. His left forearm lay along the back of the blade to steady it. In his right hand the whetstone flashed back and forth as if it had a life of its own, and the blade sent a keen song into the morning air. After he had slipped the stone into the holder on the back of his belt he paused to mop his brow, and stared briefly over the crop. Perhaps the shades of old scythemen had come to swing their blades with his; at any rate before he reversed the scythe he lifted his voice in a bar or two of his favourite lay.[73]

Nostalgia is much in evidence in "The Road to Yesterday." For a boy (presumably, like Frank, city-reared) life was all new and exciting, if strenuous. When, in a moment of discouragement, Sims wondered whether he himself had done wrong in coming to this part of the country, he asked the boy "why I didn't work in the city and grow up to sit at a desk and wear a coat and be a gentleman; and I had difficulty in making my preference for cleaning out stables and splitting fence-posts sound very sensible."[74]

The boy even gloried, with the Sims children, in a sudden violent hailstorm, oblivious at the moment to the ruin it was bringing to the Sims's hopes. From such a catastrophe Sims might well have recovered, but "People round about were not doing very well. The cold clayey soil just didn't seem sufficiently responsive to cultivation; crops seemed, as a rule, rather uncertain, and orchard trees seemed to run more to wood than to fruit."[75] With constant labor and Kentish husbandry Sims, who had not taken up his selection until his late fifties, managed a living until his seventies, when declining strength required a remove to the city. None of the sons being interested in the place, it was abandoned, and by the time of the narrator's return, the buildings were gone, the fences collapsed. "The road to yesterday had brought us to the end of tomorrow—all tomorrows. It seemed odd that I hadn't counted on that. . . . Little by little' the bush was reclaiming its own—though there would be an open green place in the wilderness for many a year."[76] Now, for the visitor and his companions, there was a return to the city on "the new road, gliding swiftly and smoothly around its sleek curves."[77]

In his Author's Note in each short story collection, Frank stressed his belief that some of the atmosphere of *Man-Shy* was to be found in his Queensland short stories. Certainly the larger purpose in "The Road to Yesterday" is reminiscent of that early book. *Man-Shy* recounted the history of western Queensland from the open ranges to the enclosures, a story of man's success (though of defeat for the "scrubbers"); "The Road to Yesterday" told of mountainous southern Victoria from the first attempts at cultivation until its abandonment—a record of man's effort and failure.

CHAPTER 12

The Forties: Marie, Melbourne, and Dusty

THE 1940s were to see great changes in Frank's life, as wage-earner, as writer, as man; at their close he was to be firmly established in the new circumstances of life and work that were to be his for the twenty years still remaining to him.

An early encouragement was the fact that in 1939 he had been awarded for the following year one of the first of the C.L.F. (Commonwealth Literary Fund) fellowships. As early as 1908 the young Federal Parliament had established a fund from which to make small grants (which became known as "literary pensions") to destitute authors or their widows and orphans. As the F.A.W. gathered strength in the thirties, it urged a broader program of assistance, and one of Frank's Red Page articles in mid-1938 was concerned with a "Deputation to Canberra" (Flora Eldershaw was one of its three members) to ask for a variety of literary subsidies. A one-time Prime Minister, J. P. Scullin, was sympathetic to their cause, and largely through his initiative the scope of the fund was much enlarged, to include several grants of up to £600 to established authors to enable them to complete specified projects. It was such a grant that Frank himself received, a welcome if temporary relief from the financial strain of the Depression years, as it meant a monthly payment throughout 1940 while he was getting together *The Woman at the Mill*. With his first check he bought a much needed suit; after the second he wrote to Vance, "The Fellowship is a godsend to me. I don't know what I'll do at the end of it—and I'm not caring! I'm just plugging ahead, doing my stuff." [1]

Not that his integrity was to be compromised. Years before, he had expressed scorn for prolific Ion Idriess's indication that his incentive for writing was royalties. Now, Vance Palmer having written to ask Frank how he would feel about a possible opening as a writer with the military, Frank answered as one who, like his red heifer, preferred freedom to a sure living.

I wouldn't do for it, Vance. It seems to me essentially a job for a bright young journalist, a keen imperialist, who would please authority by writing about the awfully jolly times the boys are having on active service. Perhaps a better type of man could make the job yield a small dividend in social betterment, but he would need—unlike myself—to have the language of diplomacy well ingrained in him.[2]

So, after the security of the fellowship, back to odd jobs—briefly. Early 1941 found him at Mittagong for six weeks, relieving the storeman at the Farm Home for Boys and able to send his family a couple of pounds a week. The evenings, he confessed, were very dull, but he improved physically from the early and regular hours, the "enforced regularity and sobriety," and he found that he enjoyed "just doing things—not living out of my head." He was convinced that he did not want to go back to journalism and that "It would suit me very well if I could get a clerical-cum-light manual job in the city."[3] Back in Sydney he shortly got another six weeks of work at the Health Department—washing bottles, but with a 37½-hour week and full Saturdays and Sundays off, a schedule so hard to match in private enterprise that he began to look for further work in public service.

He found it shortly, along with more permanence. The war being now well under way and the demands for manpower increasing, Frank was employed in mid-1941 as a clerk at the Commonwealth Aircraft Corporation's Mascot factory. With the steady income from this work he emerged at last from ten years of continual financial straits; but his joy in the new security was marred by the pressures of war, which in less than a year put him onto a 60-hour week—a long way from the "light" program that he had envisaged, certainly leaving little leisure for writing.

I *Fred Davison's Later Works and Death*

Fred Davison's magazine editorializing had ended in 1925 with the death of *Australia*, but that had not permanently stilled his pen. In 1932 his Australian Authors' Publishing Co. published his *Storm Bradley, Australian: A Story of Yesterday, To-day and To-morrow*. This three-generation romantic novel, "a story with a purpose," shows "a man of the people" doing his "full share through changing times," and is generously interspersed with discussions of Australia's financial condition.

In 1937 Fred Davison's publishing house had also issued its *One-Story Quarterly Magazine*, "A 6s. novel for 1/6." The novel was *Public Enemy No. 1*, another fictional attack on the financial and political situation in Australia. One comment in this work sounds like an apologia for the interrupted education of the author's eldest son: "Yes—if education is the fitting of a man to adapt himself to life's changing circumstances, then Jim Redpath was educated. But if education is the acquisition of the knowledge contained within the covers of a few textbooks, then he was unlearned."[4] Fred Davison paid for this publication and gave copies to six hundred members of Parliament and a thousand newspapers, selling the rest at a loss—with no regrets. This was in 1937; it was only a year later that Frank yielded to a similar impulse to publicize his own views on the world situation, and paid, during what was still hard times, for the appearance of *While Freedom Lives*.

An interesting addendum to Fred's publication, recalling some of his earlier magazine appeals, stated that the Australian Authors' Publishing Co. would consider book-length manuscripts of novels dealing with Australian problems. (No short stories were wanted, the editor having perhaps discovered, as Frank was doing at the same time, that it was too limited a form.)

Fred's last novel, *Duck Williams and His Cobbers* (1939), es-chewing social problems for the adventures of a bunch of Australian boys in the Bendigo area, was published by Angus & Robertson. In the last year of its founder's life, however, the Australian Authors' Publishing Co. reappeared to issue his *Australia's Fifth Column??*, a story about banking. Like his son, Fred was not averse to using the same material twice: the first part of this book was an abridgement of his earlier *Public Enemy No. 1*. This was his last published work, as he died in 1942.

In the year of his father's death, Frank was searching his own past for D. C. Meacham, a student at the University of Melbourne who had chosen Frank Davison as the subject of a B.A. thesis on a modern Australian writer. Meacham had written Frank asking questions about his life and works.

Frank's three generous replies, written over a period of two months (mid-August to mid-October, 1942), are not only invaluable to the Davison biographer, being presumably more accurate than some of his later memories, but they also had the effect of making him, in his fiftieth year, sit back and evaluate his life and works—for himself as well as for Meacham. Suffice to notice at this time Frank's explanation in October that after having spent the preceding fifteen months at "hard labour"—as a receiving clerk with the Aircraft Production Commission, and nearly two years without writing, he had just had a three weeks' holiday resulting in a lyric, a short story, and other works in progress.

Later Frank obtained more appropriate and congenial work as an editor in the publications section of the Department of Labor and National Service under his friend and fellow-author Leonard Mann. Before the end of the war this work was to take him to Melbourne, the city of his birth and boyhood, and he stayed with it there until, some time after the end of the war and with consequent dismissal imminent, he resigned. It was the last regular employment that he undertook. From that point on he was to be his own man, and while he never became wealthy, he had said goodbye to the grinding poverty he had known so long and so well.

II *Marie*

Frank himself marked the 1940s as a happy turning point in his life, as both man and writer. Of first importance was his meeting at a party in 1942 a Sydney girl named Edna Marie McNab, the "Marie" of his life from then on. At that first meeting he had found her "shapely, fair, and fragrant, an accomplished dancer . . . a stylish dresser, with an elegant coiffure and a most interesting taste in hats."[5] He later found that she could also "lose herself in a good book, take a well-painted picture to her heart, laugh at a funny story, cook an interesting meal, wash and iron, sew buttons on a shirt, or darn a pair of socks."[6] These domestic skills she had developed as the housekeeping daughter of a fairly large family.

She was 29, he 49, when they embarked upon an eighteen-months' courtship. But they were "ready for each other," and the path of true love ran very smoothly indeed—except that a number of serious outside difficulties had to be overcome. The most critical one involved Kay, Frank's wife of twenty-seven years. Their marriage had, as we have seen, been increasingly unstable since the mid-1930s, and they had for some time been going their separate ways socially (though "not financially," as a friend observed); in mid-1942 Frank left the family home to live in an upstairs room with kitchenette in an apartment house on Macleay Street in Potts

Point. Here his now-grown children, of whom he was very fond, visited him regularly. So did Marie, who helped him to entertain old and understanding literary friends like Vance Palmer and Leonard Mann. In 1944 Frank's marriage to Kay was formally dissolved.

Another problem was location. For nearly twenty years Frank had lived, worked, and written in Sydney, and had become much involved in its literary and social life. Now, as a public servant with a regular editorial job at a good salary, he was threatened by his superiors with a transfer to Melbourne. This was the place of his birth and boyhood, but he confessed to Nettie Palmer that it was now a foreign country to him, and that "Melbourne affects me badly. I leave at 15 and return at 50, and feel as if 35 years had fallen down a hole, and that I have jumped from adolescence to the undertaker's anteroom."[7] From its first mention he fought the idea of the move, even threatening to resign from the department rather than lose touch with his children and break up the "safe and satisfactory"[8] pattern of life that he and Marie had achieved in Sydney.

III   *Melbourne*

But move he did, despite his many protestations to the contrary. He worked all day and from his lodgings wrote letters to Marie at night (a correspondence that they later modestly burned to keep literary people from ever "messing with"). Before the year was out, all problems had been solved, and the pair were married on December 8, 1944, a marriage that was never to be regretted by either and that greatly enriched the lives of both.

Unable to find a flat or apartment in wartime Melbourne, they set up housekeeping in a large front ground-floor room with kitchen privileges down the hall; they remained in these limited accommodations for five years. At first they felt like visitors, in Melbourne, and went back to Sydney on weekends at every opportunity. Later both conceded that the move had actually been a good one, as it got them both off to a fresh start, away from old associations. New friends in Melbourne they did not long lack, since Frank was already well known in literary circles, and they were soon being entertained by (and even entertaining, in their cramped quarters) numerous literary and artistic figures—including historian Brian Fitzpatrick; *Meanjin's* founder and editor, Clem Christesen;

and of course the Palmers, when they were in residence.

Frank later confessed that when his intimate friends saw how complete was his absorption in his new wife, they feared he would never get back to his typewriter. Actually he came to feel that "our coming together marked the beginning of the most mature and fruitful period of my life as a writer."[9] He was referring particularly, of course, to his last huge novel. But even during their rather hectic courtship he wrote two of his best (and almost last) short stories, "The Good Herdsman" and "The Road to Yesterday."

IV Dusty

During the first year of their marriage, despite their small quarters and a steady job, Frank settled in happily to nights and weekends of sustained writing. The result was another short novel, *Dusty*, ranking with *Man-Shy* in subject and in appeal. Published in 1946, fifteen years after *Man-Shy*, *Dusty* nonetheless belongs to Frank's early period, even while terminating it. Those who had been waiting for years to find out what kind of writing Frank Dalby Davison would eventually settle down to had found each of his previous books a new enterprise: an animal story, a love story, a war story; a factual report of recent travels, a fictionized report of travels long ago, a mythical treatment of the aborigines for children, a collection of short stories. At last, in *Dusty*, he can be said to have repeated himself, for while its subject and theme differ widely from those of *Man-Shy*, it is a second account, from its author's Queensland days, of the life of an animal—this time "A Dog of the Sheep Country," as its subtitle announced. In *Dusty* man plays a larger and more sympathetic role than in *Man-Shy*, but in both the animal is the central character.

Dusty tells the story, from conception to death, of a half-breed dog, offspring of a wild dingo mother and a domesticated kelpie father. He owed his mixed heritage to the fact that his mother, having lost her wild mate to a rancher's poisoned bait, wooed a farm kelpie to satisfy her need, only to turn on him and kill him shortly thereafter. Saved by a young man who discovered the lair, scalped the mother for the bounty, and destroyed the rest of the litter, the pup was sold to old Tom Lincoln, an itinerant station hand (in the Maranoa district from which so many of the author's short stories had sprung) and a good hand with a dog. Tom took the pup home with him to the Morrisons, who were running sheep in the Brigalilla country, gave him a name "which seemed to come to his lips of its own accord,"[10] and set to work patiently to educate him as a sheep dog. Here he was helped by the veteran dogs of the station, who taught the pup by example the things that no man, however skilled and patient, could teach him alone. Together they gradually brought Dusty to the peak of his career: the winning, from a field of eighteen, of the trials held at Brigalilla homestead to determine the most intelligent sheep-handler in the area.

As Dusty had grown in strength and skill, however, his problems as a half-breed were compounded. In him, even as a puppy confined to the homestead,

there was taking place the ancient battle between conflicting heredities, and between early influence and present environment; the mother against the father, nature against art, something derived from the mother and reinforced by her during early weeks against the need to partake of life through adjustment to the inevitable. Something in the father's strain was not wholly against the mother, for the working dog—like fruit, grain and garden flower—is a product of art; and nature, if man fails in toil or vigilance, hastens to reclaim her own.[11]

As a little dingo, Dusty was glad of seclusion, in his enforced confinement; but as a little kelpie he was lonely, and "the little dingo and the kelpie [were] alternately looking through his eyes."[12] Escaping by accident for a free run in the bush, "A change came over him, small but significant, a slight crouch and a slight drooping of the tail that changed him from a kelpie pup to a rather strangely marked little dingo."[13] But "When he became hungry the little kelpie would come to life in him again."[14]

The author, who had once experimented with playwriting, showed that he knew his drama when he let us suspect with Tom, just before the Dig's triumph in the trials, that Dusty might have become the one thing no sheep dog can be forgiven—a killer of sheep. "Though Dusty had accepted the life of a kelpie and had distinguished himself in it, his mother was still alive in him."[15] When suspicion became fact, no one, least of all Tom, who by now loved Dusty with all his "thwarted paternalism," questioned the necessity of the dog's death. But when Tom's boss, undertaking the execution to spare the old man, only wounded the dog with a first bullet, Tom wrestled with him for the gun, quit his job, and left the homestead. Dusty, in the meantime, recovered from his wound and returned to his outlawry, becoming the object of many pursuits and leading to the conclusion that "Just as a dog's worth five men in the paddocks, one dog turned killer's worth five dingoes when it comes to cunning and daring."[16]

Dusty, the half-breed, was still drawn to men as to the bush, and when one day he happened upon Tom, their joy was mutual. Without hesitation Tom packed up and left sheep country for cattle land where his companion would be safe from temptation. On an old friend's place he camped out, doing odd jobs for the leaseholder and trapping possums. "It was a pleasant enough life. The thick bush was an old friend and you had the company of horse and dog; Piebald who had drawn or carried you many a mile, and Dusty who was content these days to lie at your hearth or trot at your heels."[17] But one day, caught by a cold, heavy rain while shifting camp, old Tom was taken sick and became sicker. Dusty was intelligent enough to go to the homestead, where his very presence, being unusual, alerted the homesteader, who went to Tom's camp to investigate; but the old man lived only a few more hours.

Then began Dusty's last period: Dr. Jekyll once more became Mr. Hyde. The dog's dual nature kept him close to man's activities, but every man's hand was against him. His notoriety grew until he was blamed for killings he didn't commit (unlike a true dingo, he himself killed only at night, only for food), and a considerable price was put on his head. But Dusty lived on. We learn at some length of his courtship of a young female dingo with whom he finally mates.

A mate was almost as fresh an experience in Dusty's life as in that of a young dingo. There had been general friendships with the dogs of the Morrison homestead; acquaintances, agreeable and otherwise, among dogs that he had met on his travels with Tom, a special liking for Sapper [another dog at Morrisons], and of course a deep attachment to Tom, but not the experience of sharing life completely with another of his kind.[18]

Yet in their shared life, "The dingo went some way to becoming a dog of the paddocks, and the dog some way to becoming a dingo of the scrub frontages."[19]

The pair were easier to track than Dusty had been alone, and hunter Railey Jordan got close enought for a shot: it killed not Dusty, however, but his mate. Later Jordan used his own kelpie bitch in an effort to bring Dusty within range, but the dog had already been distracted by another female dingo, whom he won in fair battle from her dingo mate. While their pups were still young, Dusty was struck by a falling branch and killed. "No man accounted for Dusty.

He had been born of a chance rise of the sap; his way had been as
fortuitous as the winding of a creek; and his life ended with the falling of dead wood."[20]

Dusty attained prompt publicity as the fortunate winner of the
Melbourne *Argus's* novel competition. Unlike the A.L.S. medal
awarded to *Man-Shy*, this was a cash award as well as an honor—a
welcome five hundred pounds. The Davisons celebrated with a
large party of literary friends in their one-room dwelling. Angus &
Robertson promptly published the book, which has gone into some
nineteen editions and reprints since, at home and abroad. Among
all of Frank's works, *Dusty* has been second only to *Man-Shy* in
popularity.

In more areas than success, comparisons between *Man-Shy* and
Dusty are inevitable. In both, the author shows an extraordinary
ability to get within the mind and motivations of an animal without
sentimentality or even unjustifiable anthropomorphizing. *Dusty* is
more than twice the length of the earlier story but not altogether
the better for this; some sections suffer from rather too much detail,
such as the pages relating the dog trials, which recount the progress
of not just one but two other dogs through all four stages of the
competition, in order, presumably, to make us the more appreciative of Dusty's winning performance; and such as Dusty's
long and repetitive wanderings, chasing and being chased, between
Tom's death and his own. Otherwise, the writing shows no falling
off in the author's ability to portray animals, despite his years of city
life since the earlier book. Who but Frank could devote two pages
early in a story to the feeding of a farm dog by his mistress and keep
it engrossing?

Both books enjoy a universality of theme that outreaches their
particulars: through the red heifer we are reminded that the price of
freedom may be very high indeed and through Dusty of the inner
conflicts which in one way or another disrupt the lives of all of us.
But the close of *Dusty* is, not just by comparison with *Man-Shy*, un-
satisfactory. Perhaps no man had earned the right to "account for
Dusty"; his end from a falling branch may have been a concession
to his maternal "nature" side, as opposed to the paternal "art" that
a bullet or a flailing stirrup iron would have represented.
Dissatisfaction arises not from the nature of the conclusion but from
its inept handling. Four pages from the end, after Railey Jordan,
Dusty's most skilled enemy, has failed to prevail against him, we
suddenly learn (as if the author, as well as the reader, was getting a

little weary of the pursuit) that Dusty will die from a falling branch. Then back to Dusty and his duties as husband and father, until in the course of his hunting, he "had come to rest under the old dead gum that was to put out his light as quick as wink."[21] We don't see Dusty's end occur; the book closes with his mate, come to mourn his loss, startling a trooper on patrol. Maybe it is unfair to the author to wish for a more suitable epitaph for Dusty—something closer in appropriateness and poetry to *Man-Shy's* "Gaunt and solitary, she stood, waiting to join the shadowy company of her kind—the wild herd that had passed from the ranges forever."

According to Owen Webster, long-time student of Frank's life and work, part of the reason that Frank was able to write *Dusty* so rapidly was that he had the material descriptive of the country at hand. It seems that in 1944 Frank had carried on a correspondence with Jack Cumming, the crown lands ranger of his Queensland days (p. 00), and out of Jack's three long letters he had developed a six-thousand-word story centering around a man in such an office. Projected titles for this piece were successively "The Level Road," "Moonlight," and finally, "Crown Lands Ranger." But Frank found that it had led him to the larger theme of love that had long obsessed him, and he recognized that neither short-story length nor country setting was adequate for its development. So he withdrew his typescript, unpublished, saving the theme for what was to become *The White Thorntree* much later, and incorporating the descriptive material into *Dusty*.

The narrative had much older roots, however. Like *Man-Shy*, it stemmed not only from Frank's much earlier experience but from some of his earliest writing. It too was one of the "two or three novels" that he recalled, in his last autobiographical manuscript, as having grown out of his life as a soldier-settler in the Maranoa district of Queensland. But again he had more than personal memories to work from; the subject matter and the theme of *Dusty* had been not only in his mind but on paper from his youth. This material did not exist in great ready-to-use chunks, as *Man-Shy* did, but in scattered pieces: first, those narrative verses written, printed, and distributed to a society of Australians in Chicago while Frank was still a printer's apprentice there; next, the short story "Ted Allen's Spud" in the *Australian Post*, where an injured man is saved by his dog's having the intelligence to go to people for help, even as Dusty went to the Pattersons when old Tom was taken seriously ill. In several of Frank's "Frederick Douglas" stories in *Australia*, dogs played important roles: as something man is willing to fight for ("The Regeneration of Jimmy"), as old Tom fought his employer to save Dusty; even, like Dusty, as the central character ("One of the Dinkums"). In one of Frank's best-known later stories, "Return of the Hunter," Tug Treloar succeeded in getting his dingo (another one with a price on his head) by the ruse of the tied kelpie bitch, a device that failed in Railey Jordan's effort to shoot Dusty.

The direct literary ancestor of *Dusty*, however, is "The Killer" in *Australia* (June, 1923), which announces the major theme of the later novel briefly but clearly: Peter is a black and white sheep dog who, like Dusty, is a competition winner and is discovered to be a half-breed dingo, hence a "battleground of forces struggling eternally."[22] Like Dusty, he turns killer; like him, he is shot but gets away; like him, he is chased unsuccessfully by a rider swinging a stirrup iron. But Peter's end is that of Dusty's father, rather: "The wilderness had won him, yet the wilderness would not accept him. Fearful of the dilution of pure dingo blood by the tame dog Nature demanded his death as the penalty of his mingled strain."[23] Consequently the female dingo with whom he mated, "after the manner of her kind when they have mated with a tame dog,"[24] fatally tore his throat. (A more fitting end, one might observe, than Dusty's from a gratuitously falling branch.)

An examination of these origins is not intended to detract in any way from the credit Frank deserves for his skill and perseverance in producing that fine novel *Dusty*. but it does reflect interestingly on his methods as a writer, on his habit, as we have seen in numerous other instances, of drawing heavily on earlier works to produce bigger and better ones later.

It is no insult to *Dusty* to compare it a little unfavorably with its companion-piece. *Man-Shy* is not only its author's most popular book, still, but also, in the opinion of many, his best; *Dusty*, however, runs it a close second. If, as its opening "Acknowledgment" states, its writing owed something to Frank's C.L.F. Fellowship of 1940, "that year in which I had free time to work and grow," the "fellow citizens and the community of letters" to whom he here expressed his gratitude should have felt well rewarded. Frank's friends M. Barnard Eldershaw even thought highly enough of *Dusty* to include a section of it, under the title "The Good Season," as a short story when they edited the anthology *Coast to Coast 1946*.

Dusty's dedication reads "For Mareeba." This is a name familiar to Frank's readers as that of the little aboriginal girl of the coastal tribe in *Children of the Dark People* who was a special friend of Nimmitybelle. However, the word as Frank uses it at this time is a logical, affectionate extension of "Marie," the name of his new wife, and none of his dedications were better deserved. When Frank first went to Melbourne alone, he left his typewriter with Marie, who learned to use it by typing letters to him. As he wrote *Dusty* after their marriage, Marie, proud and happy that his friends' prediction that he might give up his writing because of her had proved groundless, went into training as the versatile helpmeet of his later years by typing clean copies of his labored originals. *Dusty* was thus a kind of initiation for her into the far greater labors that would be hers as Frank worked on his next and last book, *The White Thorntree*, which was to occupy and preoccupy them both for nearly twenty years.

V Meanjin

Frank wrote little during the remainder of the 1940s, save for a few interesting contributions to periodicals, chiefly to *Meanjin*. This was (and is) Australia's most notable literary quarterly. Begun in Brisbane in 1940 by Clement Christesen, who remained its able editor for thirty-four unbroken years, it was moved in 1945 to Melbourne, where it has profited by support from both the University Press there and the Commonwealth Literary Fund. Frank's first appearances in it, in 1946, were minor: a couple of letters of typical F.D.D. protest. One denounced a biscuit company's unscrupulous inducements to get Australian authors' endorsements (complete with picture, list of publications, and sample of writing) of its products—"commerce doing its shabby best as a modern patron of arts and letters."[25] The second had a title, "Intellectual Snobbery," and took severely to task a lecturer in English at Sydney who, in an address at the University of Melbourne on Joseph Furphy's famous novel *Such Is Life*, commented on his use of allusions to Shakespeare with an "I wonder how many other Australian authors have ever even heard of Falstaff!"[26] Frank was justifiably outraged to the extent of mentioning, rather unkindly, that the lecturer's fee for the evening was being paid by the Commonwealth Literary Fund at the instigation of the Fellowship of Australian Writers.

The only major review from Frank's hand published by *Meanjin* appeared the next year (Summer, 1947) and dealt with M. Barnard

Eldershaw's fifth and final novel, the remarkable and remarkably complex social, political, and economic study entitled *Tomorrow and Tomorrow* (1947). Frank's discerning treatment of this difficult piece of work is gratifyingly more capable than his Red Page review of their relatively simple earlier novel, *Plaque with Laurel*, before. There is no sign of his own preachments from the earlier *While Freedom Lives*, as might have been expected. Furthermore, Frank presumably knew that the name Knarf, novelist and principal character here, was derived from "Frank" spelled backward; but friendship alone does not appear to have prompted his judgment that "no other Australian novel—and few recent novels written anywhere—holds within one pair of covers so large and so significant a picture of our times."[27] Certainly no Australian novel had approached it.

In its next issue (Autumn, 1947), among several "Comments on *Rigby's Romance*," *Meanjin* published Frank's delightful "Letter to Joseph Furphy" (dead since 1912), in which he reminds that author, "Dear Joe," that he had always been abridged, even by his own hand in his own day, as the publisher had required that his original huge manuscript of *Such Is Life* be cut sharply. Furthermore, *Rigby's Romance* (a second novel made from some of the leavings of the first) had been abridged from its serial form in the Broken Hill newspaper *Barrier Truth* in order to make it into a book. "Abridgements have played a large part in getting you into print and keeping you there, haven't they?"[28] The letter takes note of the new *Rigby* (1946), to which much of the omitted material has been restored, but under his banter Frank has another purpose: a rather belated support of Vance Palmer's 1937 abridgment of *Such Is Life*, still a subject of dispute. Frank claims that he had wanted to welcome it to the Red Page but that his main points had been quietly blue-pencilled. This being true, we can understand why his 1937 article on Tom Collins is so noncommittal; but we still have his letter to Vance to indicate his own preference for the original (p. 95).

One of Frank's few critical works in this period, and his most ambitious, began as a lecture and later appeared in print. From 1940 on, the Commonwealth Literary Fund's widening projects included a series of lectures delivered by various literary figures at Australian universities; Frank gave one at the University of Melbourne in July, 1947, on Vance Palmer and his work. It was biographical as well as critical, containing excellent choices of material from his friend's life and writing. He gave Vance credit for the wide range of his considerable output, and even more for his great influence on his generation of writers in the production of a truly Australian literature. In analysis and organization this was Frank at his critical best; the lecture became a long article in *Meanjin* the following year[29]—his only major contribution to that worthy quarterly and a particularly happy choice of subject, since circumstances were to prevent him from contributing to its Palmer number years later (p. 155 - 56).

Frank ended the decade with another article on Vance of a very different sort—the first of a series called "Our Authors' Page," by and about authors, projected by *Walkabout*, a successful illustrated monthly journal launched in Melbourne in 1934.[30] Not a literary magazine, it was no place for a critical examination of Vance's works; Frank wrote instead a warm, informal description of the man and his Melbourne home, with a summary of his output and his influence—a good popular treatment for a good popular magazine. An interesting result of Frank's mention of "brown tones" and a walking stick was that Vance purchased a gray suit and took to strolling unsupported!

This article, appearing in 1950, found its author and his wife half in, half out of Melbourne; in the second half of the century they moved into the folding hills.

CHAPTER 13

The Folding Hills

WHEN Frank and Marie first met and loved, neither had any idea of living in the country; he had been in Sydney for twenty years, and "her acquaintance with the earth had been limited to picking a bowl of peas or tomatoes in her father's suburban back garden."[1] But from Melbourne, after their marriage, they began to watch the ads for country property. With the end of the war approaching, Frank took a serious look at the future, for he recognized that temporary civil servants like himself would shortly be dismissed. Then what? From an unpublished manuscript we learn what he was thinking:

I had neither trade nor profession. Much as I admired and valued good daily journalism I was no hand at it. I couldn't write about a set subject, at a fixed length, and to a deadline. I was by nature a freelance. That meant doing literary journalism; that is, writing for the week-end supplements and the magazines. Like writing books, it was precarious; but I reckoned I could make a do of it for us both if I had some other source of regular income, such as a small farm might provide. The cost of housing is the killer in city life, and a little farm, if it had a habitable dwelling, would be rent free. The alternative was to find myself a place in commerce, helping to sell Whosit's products in competition with Whatsaname's. I had no stomach for it.[2]

I *The Farm*

Marie, fortunately, always left the major decisions up to Frank, unquestioning. ("She is not an initiator. Her talent is for the follow-up and the follow-through.").[3] And so began the search that was to end in the sixty-one acres they would name "The Folding Hills," Frank's home for the rest of his life, and still Marie's. And how they earned it!

The cost in money was the least of it, although it was something that Frank could not have managed earlier. Now he had a good weekly wage, the *Argus* prize money for *Dusty* was a lift (though more than half of it—a shocking £275—went for taxes), and a rising interest in Australian literature after the war had increased his royalties. The hand-to-mouth days were over, and he had built up a substantial savings account. First he bought a second-hand "utility" (an open truck) and working together, he and Marie fitted it so that they could camp out on weekends. It was their first experience of shared manual labor, a harbinger of what lay ahead of them in the country. Frank built a wooden framework, covering it with plywood and canvas (and pleasing his wife with the discovery that a writer could use his hands skillfully); Marie fitted out the interior. Thus equipped, they began a search of the surrounding area, some of which Frank had known as a working boy, for a homesite—one that would combine the quiet of the country with accessibility to the city. They found places that were too much in ruins, too expensive (Frank in his fifties would not go into debt), too remote ("I wasn't planning for us to become a couple of hatters.").[4] What they finally settled on fell just within Frank's savings—sixty-one acres in a pocket of hills out in the Plenty Ranges near the village of Arthur's Creek, which was to become their postal address. It was only an hour from Melbourne by road, or five miles to Hurstbridge and fifty minutes by train, and it had satisfying views over the surrounding sparsely settled countryside.

There was much to be done to make the house habitable, the land productive, but the Davisons were not deterred. Of the acreage twenty were cleared and cultivated (but the soil was lean and "cropped to poverty"), another twenty was half-cleared, and the remainder, bush—all a proper challenge to a man who still, in the second half of his fifties, liked to use his muscles. The buildings challenged him, too: the house was substantial but in need of renovation, the outbuildings fit only to be razed and replaced.

One of Frank's haunting fears had been that his government work might give out before they got the farm onto a paying basis; actually, he felt able to resign six months before the job ended. But first the couple had two years of living with one foot in the room on Albert Street, the other on the homestead that, picking up a visitor's chance remark on the view, they were henceforward to call "the Folding Hills." They would drive out of Melbourne after Frank's office closed on Thursday afternoon, and he would make the trip back alone on Friday and Monday, giving him a four-night-and-two-day weekend, Marie a full four days as well as nights. The house necessarily came first. They remodelled it more to their liking, throwing two small rooms together to make a large living room. The bath, which former owners had made into a dairy, was restored, with a tub and a kerosene heater. "We also shifted the earth closet, which stood like a sentry-box in the open paddock, to a more secluded position."[5] Then Frank glazed all the windows and painted the whole.

Next came the land. Neighbors who called them "Collins Street farmers" and gave them six months did not know their man—nor their woman. Marie, the city-bred girl, now in her mid-thirties, worked side by side with her husband, clearing and fencing—or alone, in his absence. "Dressed in what she described as her cossack outfit—a green belted jacket and loose yellow slacks tucked into gum boots—she must have looked a colorful figure to passers-by, in a countryside where women sometimes help in the dairy but are rarely seen at work in the paddocks."[6] It was all "hard graft," surely, for both, but they revelled in it for its tangible results. For Marie it was "progressive, not repetitive"[7] like housework, and for Frank, it satisfied his creative instinct on a simple but agreeable level. Certainly he did not do much writing at this period. Ten years later he was to admit that he could easily spend the rest of his life doing things on the farm, and never writing a line.

For two years (1949 - 1951) they commuted after this fashion, working steadily to get the farm into operation. But if Frank wasn't writing, in those days—or nights, his mind was never far from it, as a letter to Vance early in the project makes clear. Having a bulldozer in to do the worst of the clearing reminded him that he could write a story about its two operators which he would call "Bulldozer," comparable to his earlier "Tank-sinkers." More important, he admitted that he had two projects side by side now—Folding Hills and his proposed next book—and that soon the book would be calling for more time, and "will wither if it doesn't get it."[8]

II *"Bush Diary"*

His only published writing at this time was the kind of journalistic stint for which he had pronounced himself unsuited. In 1950, as a buffer against his resigning from a well-paid office job for the financial hazards of farming, he undertook to supply a short daily piece about country life to the Melbourne *Argus*, which paid him a welcome £5 a week. It cost him the Saturday mornings of his Folding Hills weekends.

The *Argus*, for whom he had been a prize winner only a few years before, must have felt it had made quite a catch when, on July 22, it printed a box introducing the author of its new feature, "Bush Diary," as "the author of two of the most famous contemporary Australian novels," *Man-Shy* and *Dusty*, and a man who "knows Australia, particularly its bushland, and loves it—as his writing shows."[9]

The installments are brief indeed—only four or five column-inches—but the episodes they relate are authentic Davison. The first was "One of the Family," an account of Frank's saving a kangaroo from a hunter by implying that it was a pet. "Outside the Law" told of the red fox for whom everyone else was hunting, this being lambing season, but who drew from Frank the conclusion that "I have a weakness for outlaws [red heifers? half-breed dogs?], and a little of my heart goes with him."[10] But that does not keep him from being moved—to beautiful description, at least—by "Wobbly Legs of Spring," when the paddocks are white with newborn lambs:

Each lamb, like something out of a toy-shop, wobbles along beside its anxious mother on legs not yet quite under control—almost as if the toy-maker had fitted the leg-springs a little carelessly, but the swinging tail, when they drop on their knees to suckle, is a piece of mechanism perfectly adjusted to express contentment and delight.[11]

A pleasant piece of proof that the old master had not lost his touch.

Later contributions dealt with cats, with details of farming operations, with Frank's heifers, with country neighbors, passing boys, birds, trees, scenery ("We can see across three or four miles of folding hills."[12]) All were grist for his small mill—authentically perceptive Davison observations related in authentically sensitive Davison prose. At under a pound each, the *Argus* was no doubt well satisfied with its part of the bargain. But less than three months later, on October 18, it was obliged to announce that "because of Mr. Frank Dalby Davison's ill-health, his feature, 'Bush Diary,' has temporarily to be discontinued."[13] The discontinuance was permanent; as to Mr. Davison's health, here is his own later report on the project:

The feature proved a popular success, and the paper's editor received a number of appreciative letters about it; but I had to give it up at the end of three months. It was the sort of small daily stint that a trained journalist does with his left hand, even while thinking about something else, but to me it meant living at cross purposes with life. It put me in the position of having to examine each incident of the day, every day, with a view to suitability for publication in next week's paper. Perhaps some people can live like that, but for me it was impossible. I felt that I was swimming upstream all the time, and not accepting the natural flow of life, taking things as they come and writing of them only on reflection, as they come into perspective and in natural relation to other things. There came a Saturday lunchtime when my typewriter held nothing but a black sheet of paper. Something in me that I was too dispirited to analyse had psychologically jacked up. I terminated the agreement, gave up thinking about it, and in my opinion returned to normal life. . . .[14]

Even Marie's faithful listing of possible subjects for these tiny essays did not help. Material was not the problem; the author needed inspiration and time for reflection.

Before we leave "Bush Diary," let us notice again that Frank was not one to let his work rest after it had served one purpose if it could be used for another. In 1967 the periodical *Westerly* published his "Vignettes from 'The Folding Hills' " with this note: "The six sketches printed below are part of a work now in progress, which will consist of 'rural and literary recollections' over the period 1949 to 1957. The title is the name of Frank Davison's farm at Arthur's Creek in Victoria."[15] Of the six, five, with no more than slight changes in a couple of the titles, are early selections published seventeen years before in "Bush Diary." Only one is newly minted, "Man and Dog," an affectionate tribute to the third member of the Davison household, their beloved helpmeet Sheila, who shared with Frank at nightfall the task of turning the milked cows out into the main paddock. "From behind me come the cattle in obedience to a small drover as yet invisible to me. They pass out quietly, in single file, their breath sweet on the air and their big heads swinging like dark tongueless bells." The task complete, "we come in shared fun and affection to the lighted kitchen, the close of day, and the meal Marie has ready for each of us."[16]

In 1951 the Davisons finally left Melbourne—both figuratively and literally for good. "A farm doesn't *give* you a living," Frank reflected years later, "the living has to be won from it."[17] He himself built a considerable array of outbuildings and did the heavy work in the fields, but Marie (who continued to look more like an actress than a farmer) increasingly took over the care of the livestock In fact, her enthusiasm for stock management reduced him, Frank observed, to the "lowly status of a farmer's husband."[18] She was tender and personal with the animals, compared to Frank, who had been accustomed to the whip-and-club persuasion in Queensland; in fact, the only creature she ever struck was her husband! Both were able to laugh later about the occasion when, seeing him kick a difficult heifer, she hit him with a leg rope and yelled, "Get out of my dairy!" Together, however, "we gradually turned that hungry patch of earth into a well-pastured and prosperous little farm,"[19] producing large and increasingly profitable quantities of cream, eggs, pigs, and hay. But all of this took several years.

The farm and the farming never ceased to engross the Davisons, but they shortly felt the need for the "world of opinion" they had left. More and more they found refreshing the company of writers and artists who came out for a meal, for overnight, for a weekend, and the hospitality at Folding Hills made it a mecca to many of their city-bound friends and acquaintances. One of the best pictures of the place and its inhabitants at this time appears in the memories of fiction-writer John Morrison twenty years later:

I used to look forward immensely to those periodical invitations to spend a weekend at "Folding Hills." The name was well chosen, with its suggestion of rest and peace. Set amid softly rolling hills, and with only one (distant) homestead in sight, the property gives a pleasant illusion of being 300 miles out of Melbourne rather than its actual thirty. If I were asked to sum up in one word its attraction for me in the 1950s I would say it was quiet. Quiet. I was working very hard then, with long hours of travel to and from, and a peck of anxieties to boot. "Folding Hills" was a badly needed breather, an escape. It was mellow, warm, low key, like everything else about the Davisons. A very typical, old, work-worn, Australian small homestead, updated a bit in Marie's excellent taste, but retaining a quite spartan simplicity. Books in every room, and none of that often kitschy conglomeration of odds and ends known as bric-a-brac. A quiet man who would as soon listen as talk, who made you feel he really wanted to know what you thought of this or that. And a quiet woman, a woman of great charm, who went unobtrusively about the preparation of a first-class dinner without for a moment losing place in whatever was under discussion. Marie knows her books—and human nature—as well as any of us, and conversation was always three-sided.[20]

III   *The Novel*

And besides, there was the book—always the book; it hadn't "withered," as Frank had feared earlier, it was just biding its time.

In the first letter in the Palmer collection to be headed from Folding Hills he writes to Nettie of his joy in a rain that has ended a worrisome drought for them. But he goes on to make clear that no drought has struck his creative powers: "You will be glad to know, I am sure, that I am pushing on with the novel. It is a great luxury to be able to sit down each morning and give the freshness of my day and strength to it. Only once before do I seem to have enjoyed such good times. I am making satisfactory progress—and I mean *satisfactory!*[21] And four months later, "I've been getting in some good licks on the novel—provisional title *Other Lives*."[22]

Yet another four months brings the inevitable: a report from Frank of what appears to have been a particularly severe nervous collapse of the kind he had suffered occasionally much earlier. "I was all right for the first month or two after we came here, busy about the place and working hard on my book; and then it seems as if the three-year effort of getting here caught up with me, and I have been very debilitated—no strength for anything." Thanks to Marie, who carried on with their outside work (including the milking of seven cows), he was able to rest, as he could not have done had he been still at a desk in town. The one thing she could not do was the writing, and his disappointment over his illness lay not only in having to give up all the jobs that he had planned to do about the place, but in not "getting on with the book."[23]

For years the reports from Folding Hills ranged from the confidence of good seasons to the discouragement of bad, from Frank's good health and spirits to his spells of nervous exhaustion. But there were two constants: the never-failing Marie, who took increasing charge of house and farm, and "the book."

In his first fifteen years as a celebrated and serious writer, Frank Dalby Davison had published eight books, the last of which was *Dusty* in 1946. At that point, which we may call his "first period," he disappeared from view, for most readers. True, a few literary-minded people would have seen his occasional appearances in *Meanjin* during the late 1940s, more would have noticed him in *Walkabout*, and Melbournites reading the *Argus* would have had a few weeks of brief glimpses of him in his new surroundings through "Bush Diary." But no more short stories, no more novels, and little other evidence of him save for the continued presence of several of his earlier works on the bookstore shelves.

Rumors inevitably spread, however, that Frank was working on more than the land, out there in the folding hills, and having noticed that "a lot of people seem to know a lot about this book" that he had been writing at, off and on, ever since he left Melbourne, he wrote a long letter about it to the Palmers in mid-1958 to inform them about the project firsthand, in some detail. That he had not done so sooner, close friends that they had long been, would seem to suggest an earlier lack of certainty about its outcome. In any event, the account of his progress and his problems at this time must be of interest to any later reader of *The White Thorntree*, still ten years from publication.

I am well into it; about 150,000 words done, much of it marginal notes and heavily interlineated—but all as clear as daylight to me, and needing only to be turned into a clean copy. Much the hardest part is behind me. The premises have all been established, the architectural problems settled; there remains the work of picking up each thread of interest in due turn and giving it its chapter, and just keeping going until the end is reached. I am not anticipating any writer's hold-ups. It will run to something more than double its present length. I feel rather apologetic about that—but it just so happens that the story I have to tell is a long one, so there is nothing else to do but get on with it. I am making it as lean as I can, both in narrative method and style of writing. With costs as they are I may have trouble when it comes to publishing, but that fence will have to be taken when I get to it. Its not one you can even think about while you are writing. At present I can only report that form and substance are in a happy state of flux. It will be called *Land of Blue Horses*. . . . Never having tackled anything as complex as this before, I had to learn that novels are *built*, and that the writing of them is the least part. The building problems are behind me (I think!) and I don't think I have ever written better than I am now. I do notice that interest is unavoidably dispersed where you have a number of characters—there is much to be said for the Manshy and Dusty type of book with its steady focus on one character![24]

In 1955 another of Frank's appreciative essays on Vance Palmer had appeared, this time in the quarterly *Overland*, a literary magazine published in Melbourne. In 1959 he began work on a more serious biographical study of Vance to be included in a forthcoming special issue of *Meanjin* honoring both Palmers for their long and invaluable service to Australian letters. In April Frank wrote Vance an appeal for more autobiographical data for his article, but a month later he wrote again indicating that he had given the project up: Vance still had not sent enough material for the purpose, the Davisons had been very busy, first with guests, then with a camping trip (their first holiday together after ten years

at Folding Hills), and as a result "I felt that if I touched biography
in the coming Meanjin the occasion would call for something much
more solid than I could supply."[25] This was to be Frank's last letter
to Vance, who died suddenly on July 15, shortly before the special
issue appeared. When it did, it was a notable number, amply illustrated (starting with portraits of the authors on the cover, for the
only time in *Meanjin* history) and containing critical articles on
various phases of the works of both Vance and Nettie by a dozen
literary notables, appreciative personal essays by a dozen more.
That no word from Frank appeared was an unfortunate conclusion
to a close thirty-year literary friendship. Nettie lived for five more
years, and Frank's letters to her continue into 1964, when our best
source for checking on his writing progress comes to an end.

That progress must have come to seem more and more painfully
slow. In April, 1960 he reported to Nettie on the end of numerous
interruptions that he had suffered since the first of the year—bush
fires, flu, and a "scourge of visitors" ("Turning on sociability from
breakfast to bedtime is v-e-e-r-r-y exhausting"), all of which left
him "looking forward to getting back to myself and a bit of creative
writing."[26] A year later he spoke of himself as "one of those ap-
pointed to turn a daily grindstone before I can think of getting
around to the imaginative work I wish to do."[27] But by November,
1961, he wrote that he had reached the end of the first volume of
his long novel—*Land of Blue Horses*, had revised its "250,000
words of untidy manuscript,"[28] and had submitted it to the
publisher of all his previous books, Angus & Robertson, from whom
he was waiting daily to hear. By the end of the month he had had
their rejection.[29] Nothing daunted, he reported that he was planning to send the manuscript off to New York (we hear nothing more
of this), and was hard at work on its sequel, *The White Thorntree*.

Others of the Davisons' friends, of course, knew that Frank was
still writing, and even something about his hopes and plans, but
there was not much publicity. In 1962, however, readers of John
Hetherington's charming and useful "Profiles of Living Australian
Writers" entitled *Forty-Two Faces* got an intimate glimpse into
Frank's current work and circumstances. This was through "A Seat
in the Kitchen," so-called owing to Frank's having chosen, in a
house that could easily have provided him with the privacy of a
study, to do all his composing on a typewriter at the kitchen table,
with Marie often across the room at stove or sink and the faithful
Sheila at his feet. At the time Hetherington came to Folding Hills

for an interview, Frank had given up the idea of trying to publish the finished *Land of Blue Horses* separately. Instead, he would wait until he had finished *The White Thorntree*, too—"perhaps by the end of 1962."[30] This was not the first time, nor the last, that he seriously misjudged his timing.

IV   *End of Heavy Farming*

Again, a circumstance interfered over which he did not have complete control—his health, and not just nervous exhaustion this time. In November, 1961 he wrote Nettie that, having found himself in "very low health," he had gone to his doctor for tests and was diagnosed as having a "tired heart," from which (at sixty-eight) he could hope to recover only if he avoided overexertion. "This added up to no more loading rambuctious pigs, handling sacks of feedstuffs, or chucking bales of hay about—in effect, no more serious farming,"[31] for even the dauntless Marie could not run their whole operation alone. There were compensations: the change meant more time for guilt-free writing, for Frank, and the decline in income was partly overcome when the Commonwealth Literary Fund granted him a literary pension. The payments began in September, 1961, and continued throughout his remaining nine years. Like his earlier fellowship, they were a small but welcome share of the fund that he and others in the Fellowship of Australian Writers had worked so earnestly to establish back in the 1930s. Furthermore, the freeing of Marie too at this time from the constant demands of their hitherto involved agricultural operations was a blessing scarcely disguised. Now she too could devote herself to Frank's writing; she became his amanuensis across the kitchen table, copying (time after time, often) on her typewriter what he wrote and revised—always revised—on his.

In a later account of their cooperative effort, Frank generously acknowledged the extent to which Maries's share went beyond mere copying. "We sometimes worked together, on opposite sides of the table, I on some advanced part of the novel, she making yet another clean copy of some earlier portion. She has an ear for prose and a high estimate of my best qualities as a writer; and would sometimes pause—quite often to my then annoyance—even if to my subsequent approval—to read out some infelicitous paragraph which was the probable result of my writing when tired, and ask, 'You could do better than that, couldn't you?' I would ask, 'What do you suggest?' She would reply 'I don't know. That's your business!' 'I would say resignedly, 'Hand the bloody thing over!' I would then shove my typewriter aside, take up my ballpoint, and devote the next few minutes to doing a bit of literary spit-and-polish—bringing myself up to my wife's idea of me as a novelist!'[32]

No more dairying, pigs, or chickens, only cattle-raising, was a change that not only greatly lightened their farm work but left them much more free to come and go. Early in 1962 they attended the Adelaide Festival, where Frank gave several lectures—a great success, he felt, but a great strain, combined with camping out in the caravan that they hauled behind their remodelled truck on the thousand-mile trip. He returned in a state of such complete collapse that for almost a year he wondered if he would ever recover. But by July, 1963, he was able to write that "Happily, I felt my strength returning a couple of months ago, and have been busy on what I believe my friends have come to regard as 'Frank Davison's never-ending novel.' I am within sight of the end now (I can smell the stable) and am in hopes of finishing it before the end of the year." Actually it still required four more, and even Frank must have begun to feel a little discouraged, for he confessed: "I am looking forward to coming to the end of it, Nettie, and will never again [he was now seventy] undertake such a long and complicated piece of work. I am a sprinter, not a marathon runner, and have found the long distance rather exhausting. However, with 360,000 words behind me, I feel I can manage the rest."[33]

Despite this pressure, Frank took time off to write a foreword for a new edition of Mary E. Fullerton's *Bark House Days*, a personal account of pioneering life in Victoria originally published in 1921. This task would have been both simple and congenial. But his work on the novel must have suffered one considerable interruption at this time: the preparation of *The Road to Yesterday* for publication. Not that anything new went into it, but that he had to make decisions, decisions, about what to omit, what to include. Then, more arduous still, the revisions: "My stories have all been revised for this edition," read the last line of his page-long Author's Note, and they had—revisions large, revisions small, and all time-taking.

V   The White Thorntree—*at Last*

He was continuing to work on the big book, too, and finally, in a letter to Nettie dated February 11, 1964, there appears what should have been the Great Moment: "I finished that long novel on which I have been at work for years past—off and on." The moment is marred, however, by the inevitable "But it needs some revision and for the time being I am too tired to undertake it. No doubt I will get going on it as soon as the summer passes." Four months later, in his last letter to her (she died before the year was out), the news is still that "It is in need of some revision, and I am hoping to get around to that shortly."[34] And sure enough, in only three more years, *The White Thorntree* (now the covering title for the whole great "Other Lives" and "Land of Blue Horses" project) was adjudged to be finished, revisions and all.

Frank had recognized that the growing size of his book would make finding a publisher increasingly difficult. What had originally been planned as two books was now combined into one, the whole totalling well over five hundred thousand words. Both the problem and the eventual solution were detailed by the author in a prepared speech delivered to an audience of a hundred and twenty on the occasion of his last great honor—a dinner given for him at Union House, University of Melbourne, on November 12, 1968, celebrating the first publication of *The White Thorntree*.

Until 1962—about six years ago, when it was half-finished—I had an idea of publishing it in a series of volumes. But then I saw that I had committed myself to writing a long novel as a single story and that it wouldn't lend itself to serial publication. I saw, too, out of my close knowledge of publishing conditions, that my book was going to be so long that it was very doubtful indeed if I would be able to find a publisher. He would need to print and sell such a large edition to clear costs that he would be afraid to touch it. There was still time to chicken out by recasting my book. I could deal with my various themes *seriatim* in a succession of volumes. This had been done by many writers, especially overseas notabilities, but I felt that I would lose the effects of juxtaposition of themes, and for the good of my soul I decided to push on, publisher or no publisher. This was my book and this was the way I wanted to write it. . .[35]

This was not the first time that Frank stood up for his literary principles regardless of cost. Now it looked as if the price might be having his masterpiece go unpublished. He has left a moving account of the ensuing difficulties: how, certain that no publisher would consider anything of this length, Marie made three clean final copies (an original and two carbons, running to five volumes of typescript each), the copyist finishing on the heels of the author in mid-1967; how these were intended for the Mitchell Library in Sydney, the National Library in Canberra, and the Davisons; how they debated publishing the book privately by subscription, a project they were willing to put their savings into though not the farm; how Frank went to see a Melbourne printer, an old friend, Robert Cugley, of the National Press there, for estimates on binding the three typescript copies and on a possible printed edition; and how, on his later return, Cugley smiled and said, "We'll publish it for you, Frank."[36] A year later this private edition of the book, five hundred ten-dollar copies of a single fat, double-columned volume, appeared. Two more years, and Ure Smith of Sydney made it available to the general public in a two-volume commercial reissue—but not, typically, until after "the author went through it and made various text alterations. . . ."[37] It is this revised 1970 edition of *The White Thorntree* that we shall examine in detail in the following chapter.

CHAPTER 14

The White Thorntree

I F Frank Dalby Davison's writing career had consisted only of the first eight books he published, starting with what has been generally regarded as his best, *Man-Shy*, and ending with its companion *Dusty*, which runs it a close second, how much easier the task of the literary historian! But his active writing career extended considerably longer after *Dusty* than before, and *The White Thorntree*, the one book that he worked on throughout his last quarter-century, is not only a little longer than the other eight combined but raises far more problems. As "a fictional investigation of our sex culture," it represents such a change of subject matter, such an apparent change of purpose, from his early output that one is tempted to write a book on "The Two Literary Careers of Frank Dalby Davison."

But Frank would not have approved of such a division. In the speech he gave at the University of Melbourne to celebrate the private publication of *The White Thorntree*, he spoke of *Dusty* as "a sort of trial gallop for the large one that was eventually to follow. *The same philosophy informs both.*"[1] (Italics mine.) This statement inevitably gives pause to the reader of the two books, one about a dog in the outback, the other about sex in Sydney. But one is reminded of Frank's phrase in the earlier *The Wells of Beersheba* (repeated in substance elsewhere): "The fellowship of the flesh." It is apparent that all life faces conflict of one kind or another, some outer, some inner. In *Man-Shy*, it rose between beast and man—for the one, the yearning for freedom, for the other, the need for beef; in *Dusty*, between the two diverse sides of the dog's inherited nature—the kelpie love for man and his work, the dingo need for life in the wild. In *The White Thorntree*, as the author makes abundantly clear, by precept in his Foreword, by example in his narrative, it rises between the natural desire for sex and the restrictions placed upon that desire by society.

161

In earlier statements in the same lecture, Frank traces the very beginnings of the *Thorntree* to the time when he was a young man living in Sydney, with "two main preoccupations, the world of men and women, and what we call the natural world." He had dealt successfully with the latter in *Man-Shy*, less successfully with the former in *Forever Morning*, published the same year. For, he continues, "it was not until the late thirties that I felt sufficiently experienced to come to grips with life in its more complex manifestations. I wrote a number of short stories about men and women, and felt I was working with a satisfactory degree of perception, and what is more, with a steady hand."[2]

It was in his collected stories, he continued, that the *Thorntree* had its roots. But, as his ideas developed, he found that the short story form was too limited (these remarks seem to take us back to the "Crown Lands Ranger" incident in 1944—p. 143), and he began to experiment with the novel. After writing some thirty thousand words of one set in a country town, he found the locale too limited and abandoned the project. It was in this period that he met, wooed, and wed his second wife, Marie, however, and "our coming together marked the beginning of the most mature and fruitful period of my life as a writer—even though *The White Thorntree*, the greater part of the literary harvest, has been somewhat delayed in reaching the marketplace."[3] That "mature and fruitful period" included *Dusty*, and as soon as it was finished, Frank "made the first tentative beginnings"[4] on the far larger novel.

In the same 1968 address Frank called *The White Thorntree* "the chief product of my meditations and literary labors over the last twenty-two years,"[5] of which he estimated that about eight were actually spent at his typewriter. He had expected the book to run to around 200,000 words and take him three or four years to write, "but a large book is just something that happens to you. You become engaged with a theme. In the course of progressive writings and re-writings, and in the course of brooding over it between whiles, you come to see its prospective dimensions, and you either accept the challenge or you chicken out and tackle something easier. I accepted the challenge because I recognized it as the book I had been wanting to write since I was a young fellow—this book and no other."[6]

When *The White Thorntree* finally became available to the general public on the shelves of Australian bookshops, it was a novel remarkable in many respects. First, it was huge, especially by local standards, the two volumes totalling more than eleven hundred large pages of small print—not a book to pick up lightly. Second, it was an urban novel, exclusively of city people, by an author whose literary reputation had long since been established as a portrayer of animals and men of the outback—not the book Davison devotees had come to look for. Third, despite its size it dwelt with a single subject, sex—not one to be expected in a nation that has long been known, at home and abroad, for treating sex more casually than most.

I *Sex in Earlier Works*

This phenomenon inevitably set off a critical flurry, with second looks at Frank's earlier works resulting in such brilliant discoveries as that the red heifer bore a calf and Dusty sired a litter of pups. It may be more profitable to look for early signs of the treatment of sex in his books about men and women, but even here the pickings are rather slim. The novel *Forever Morning* is, says the subtitle, "An Australian Romance." But, despite the hero's astonishment, in the final pages, at seeing how much was to be seen when the heroine appeared in a bathing costume that "was a study in the art of omission,"[7] the book closes with a mere holding of hands. The hero himself, we must remember, is found to be a bastard, but neither that word nor the mechanics of his making appear in print.

There was no time for breeding, by men *or* horses, in *The Wells of Beersheba*, the cast of *Blue Coast Caravan* is limited to two staid middle-aged couples, and *Caribbean Interlude* deliberately spared its "delicate reader" the kind of tale that all too many sailors relate, accurately or not, of their shore leaves. True, when a girl passenger he called "Grey-eyes" gave the youthful narrator a smile, "It's effect was to make me feel that I could live a better and a purer life."[8] But that is only a touch of the most sublime puppy love, not explicit sex; besides, when the girl reached her home port she was met by a husband. Nimmitybelle and Jackadgery, the children of the dark people, were so young as to be unmindful of sex; in the end they were promised to each other, but adult fulfillment was still a long way off.

We may begin to look seriously through the short stories, however, for hints that their author might some day devote himself to the problems of sexuality. No more than a third of the nineteen stories in the two collected volumes reveal any occupation with sex, however, and only one, "The Woman at the Mill," a preoccupation. We needn't pause over the narrator's memory in "The Road to Yesterday" of "the first startling kiss of adolescence"[9] exchanged in the twilight of the barn between his boyhood self and Jessie, the fourteen-year-old Sims daughter, since it was a brief and "virtuous attachment." But in "Blood Will Tell" a more mature pair, Hilda Morgan and Jack Munster, are caught by his employer's wife in the tall grass beside the creek "very tenderly preoccupied" indeed. Then follows the conflict between nature and society that is the basis of *The White Thorntree*, with the narrator clearly on the side of nature:

The lady was shocked speechless—so she said afterwards—though why she should have been so affected by the spectacle of an act that is fairly frequent in the affairs of the living, and one with which she was herself presumably not unfamiliar, is difficult to imagine.[10]

The "poor children," on their part, "were hoodwinked by the pathological jimjams of an elder rather more comfortably situated in respect of such matters than themselves," and "slunk off in opposite directions; a latter-day Adam and his Eve, prompted by nature and shamed by man."[11] Learning of the event, Mrs. Morgan was for taking a pick-handle to her daughter, and when the girl proved to be pregnant, her mother threatened to get a warrant out for the boy, who had left town. But Jack returned of his own accord for a "pathetically hasty wedding."[12] At last report (two years later), the couple was living happily together with yet another child.

This sexual incident in "Blood Will Tell" is only part of a larger story, the same being true of "The Yarns Men Tell." Here the narrator was a roomer in the very modest home of a mother and daughter in Sydney, and became like one of the family for a time until he was forced to leave for lack of work. As he left, daughter Jean went to the door with him, and "At the moment of parting she lifted her face and I kissed her. It was one of those all round sad and sorry moments, and I didn't reflect that that kiss might mean more to her than to me."[13] When he returned a couple of years later, he found that one of a succession of later roomers had seduced her with promises of marriage, and left her pregnant. "She didn't put any blame on to me, but I knew how it was. If I hadn't come into her life, stirring up dreams, it wouldn't have happened. That kiss I'd taken from her at parting weighed on me . . ."[14] Here the emphasis is not on the seduction but on the emotional consequences for a girl of a kiss that had meant little to the man. This is reminiscent of the distinction made between the principals in "The Woman at the Mill." But by the time Frank wrote *The White Thorntree*, he was bending his efforts, rather, to equate the sexual experience of men and of women, and seduction is by no means one-sided.

Sex is only secondary in "Fathers and Sons," too, a story of World War I. The narrator here recognized that his soldier-mate, Mitch, "couldn't perform the lofty rite of physical intimacy with a woman on a commercial basis—and the other sort of girl you treated as if she were a vestal virgin. I'd had difficulty myself with the effects of being well brought up, as the saying is."[15] What upset Mitch when they came across an elderly general "spooning" heatedly in a car with a girl of perhaps twenty was not, we learn later, the circumstance itself, but its reminder of news that his own father, in America, had just left his mother—"cleared out with some young thing."[16] Nonetheless, the narrator is led to a discerning reflection on wartime sex:

Lots of the lads, knowing they might be killed, were desperate to have a woman before they went to the front. It wasn't what is called depravity and it was much more than physical craving. It was the knowledge of their uncertain tenure of life; all that life might have been and might not be crowding in about them. It was just young life, away from the khaki, under the hardness and the sunburn, crying out against being cut off, feeling that it could look death more steadily in the eyes if it had known the solace of a woman's flesh. I think the girls must have understood, too, with the boys going away. It would explain much of the so-called immorality of those years; the happenings of his last night on leave.[17]

"So-called immorality"—this is Frank early passing on society the judgment that plays so large a part in his last novel. It did not bother him that for Tug Treloar and his wife Bonny, in "Return of the Hunter," "The baby arrived prompt to the date of the engagement rather than that of the wedding."[18] From the beginning Tug had been "unable to take his eyes off her. Always an admirer of a full figure, Tug was goggle-eyed before the exclamatory nature of Bonny's feminine characteristics. She had such a lot of everything."[19] Even after their marriage Tug had to resign his dreams of further foreign adventure because she would not promise to wait for him. "He almost wished Bonny's charms weren't so sumptuous. He would feel safer about leaving her."[20] Later he

yielded to her wish to accompany him when he went to hunt the
Black Dingo, and as he returned to their camp successful, his mind
was on her reaction. The original version ends with his happy
thought that "Bonny's pleasure and approval would be unbounded,"[21] which is expanded in the revision, years later, to the
slightly sexier "Bonny would raise bare white arms to him. Her
pleasure and approval would be unbounded."[22]

Sex is mostly muted in these early stories, however, even when it
appears. It underlies, of course, the pain that Dave Chandler, long a
husband to an aborigine woman and father to a family of half-caste
children, knew when he realized that he had found, too late, a
suitable mate in a white woman, the widow Thorpe; but the pain
was greater than mere sex. Not a word of feeling, much less a touch,
was ever exchanged between them, but on their first meeting,
"From the moment when she stood in the door and his eyes and
hers had locked, . . . something had happened. Dave couldn't
give it a name."[23] Restless as he was in consequence, however,
"Rightly or wrongly, one thing comforted him. He had no furtive
designs. Whatever part his body might eventually require in his
feeling for her—and was it ever without part in the relationship of a
man and a woman?—it did not insist on immediate recognition. His
thought of her was sublimated. He wanted only the fullness of spirit
her companionship would give him."[24]

Unless psychiatrists choose to find suppressed sex in the good
herdsman's excessive devotion to his heifers (which would not be
difficult), this is the end of our examination of the subject in Frank's
early work, save for "The Woman at the Mill," the only one of his
collected stories in which it is all-important. Irene's yearning and
Bert's brief response would have to be called sex rather than love
(although it is often difficult to distinguish between the two), and
twice the two indulged in illicit intercourse—but this is still a long,
long way from *The White Thorntree* in explicitness. Emotional
states are thoroughly analyzed here, but the sex act is only hinted
at. Their first coupling occurred almost immediately after they met
on the track outside the dance hall. At the sound of approaching
voices "They withdrew among the trees to one side, and there she
had both encouraged and yielded to Caswell's ardour. She wasn't
sure whether she was doing the best thing. She felt she hadn't
meant to come so quickly to this part of it. But she couldn't bring
herself to say no to him, and she wanted to, herself, anyway."[25]

Euphemisms, euphemisms, but nonetheless more explicit than

the report of their second meeting, some weeks or months later. Irene's husband away, Bert came to her home, and they chatted, "looking at each other all the time with questioning eyes." Then

> Caswell rose and came over to her. He was thinking how nice she looked, and was wondering how soon he could come to the point. His uncertainty vanished when he went to take her in his arms and found with what eagerness she accepted.
> The yellow-faced alarum-clock had the room to itself for an hour before the door leading to the rest of the house opened and Bert and Irene re-entered the kitchen.[26]

Between these two paragraphs is a blank that most readers have little difficulty in filling; we would not have expected the author to go into the anatomical detail that was to be commonplace in his big novel—not in 1940.

II   *A Novel of the 1930s*

In the speech Frank made on the occasion of the first appearance of the book, he concluded that "It is possible that *The White Thorntree* will eventually be read, not as a novel of the late sixties but as a belated one of the late thirties. I'd settle for that. It wouldn't be the first novel to be published successfully out of its period."[27] The fact is that the book could not possibly have been published *in* its period, the two decades between World Wars I and II. The novel is presumably true to Sydney life then (these were years in which the author himself was living it fully), but neither its subject nor its language would have been acceptable then. Frank took full advantage of the freedom accorded its appearance in the late 1960s, but no one knew better than he, surely, how recently that freedom had been gained.

Frank himself had spoken out numerous times in those earlier years for freedom of expression, but not much existed, especially in Australia. Even in England the now relatively innocuous *Lady Chatterley's Lover* of 1928 appeared in an expurgated edition in 1932. In a Red Page article in 1937 Frank had spoken very highly of Norman Lindsay's candor; he did not add what was then common knowledge, that Lindsay's novel *Redheap* had been banned because of it in 1930. The book went on to publication in England and America that year, but in Australia not until 1959. Or take the more recent case of novelist Kylie Tennant. Her novel *The Joyful*

Condemned appeared in 1953, but not as she had written it. Established writer though she was, with six earlier novels to her credit, she had been required to cut her manuscript by more than a third, not just that "paper was hard to come by" (this was years after the war shortages) but because "censors [were] unduly sensitive." Yet only fourteen years later the entire manuscript was published as *Tell Morning This* (1967), apparently without hesitation—in fact, being a paperback, with the words "An explosive novel of Sydney's underworld of vice, violence and prostitution" on the cover as a come-on.

What had happened in the interim? Perhaps the sociologists could give a full answer; a rough guess would be the impact of the Kinsey reports from the late 1940s on, the publication of which in turn had been encouraged by the rapid changes in mores, the liberation of both language and behavior, in the years following World War II. One has only to go back to Frank's own stories of the 1930s to note the delicacy common to those times, in contrast to his unabashed frankness in dealing with the same period thirty years later.

The reader begins *The White Thorntree* with no misapprehensions, for the author clearly explains his purpose in a detailed foreword: to explore, without giving advice or pointing a moral, the effect on our lives of our culture's attitude toward sex. "Our culture" here is that of Sydney in the 1920s and 1930s, later social changes between the action of the book and its publication being dismissed as only raising new problems. The mores here portrayed by the author in his later years are the ones he would have been subjected to in his prime, as he was of an age with most of his main characters. He could, then, speak of their problems with authority.

Frank wrote here not only of his own time but of his own kind of people, the middle class—chosen, he explained, because their values, social and domestic, have worldwide dominance. For them the family is the primary social unit, romantic attraction is the approved basis of marriage, and marriage is assumed to be the answer to all interest in the opposite sex. In his own opening words,

To put it briefly my story deals with the predicament of a number of persons in a social culture—our own—in which, notwithstanding the urgency of nature, there is no generally approved and openly arranged outlet for sexuality between the cradle and the marriage altar, and no endorsed and socially viable outlet for romantic proclivities between the marriage altar and the cemetery . . .[28]

That "urgency of nature" can lead before marriage, he continued, to socially unacceptable couplings and even to perversions; during marriage, the accepted escape that all too soon begets the boredom of stale routine, to a second era of antisocial behavior. Both situations Frank treated of repeatedly through both precept and example.

A novel can have its genesis in a setting, a character, an event, a theme, a purpose. *The White Thorntree* avowedly began with a purpose: the exploration of sex experience in a given time and place, the characters and situations being created as needed to illustrate certain facets of that experience. The entire story is divided into seventy-five chapters grouped into four parts, the first, "Babes in the Woods." The first chapter presents briefly the engagement, wedding, honeymoon, and settling into married life of the typical young man and young woman who will remain foremost among the innumerable characters who subsequently appear: Jeff Mitchell, age twenty-four, and Norma Sherwood, twenty-two. The reader who feels that this is a good deal of ground to cover in a few pages has much to learn of the author's method, which is to return endlessly, by flashback and flashahead, to an amplification of every aspect of these two lives, in childhood, youth, and adulthood—every sexual aspect, that is. And Jeff and Norma prove to be but two of many.

With the second chapter we begin to see what we are in for. Leaving the newly married pair, the author takes us back into the Mitchell and Sherwood family trees to give fingernail sketches of a couple of dozen relatives. None of these have any later importance in the story; few are even mentioned again. But they serve to illustrate the sexual conditions that can prevail, unknown or known and quietly overlooked, in sober middle-class families. From these "typical" individuals, the author indicates, sprang our "normal" wedded pair—no wonder there is trouble ahead. There is the young man who wants to be a young woman, the aging woman who hires a gigolo, the aged one who is rabid for information about sex, the respected old judge who accosts young girls. Through these and others are sounded many of the aspects of sex to be expanded on later: unfaithfulness, desertion, adultery, bigamy, infatuation, philandering, masturbation, fantasy—not to mention a rare case or two of chastity, celibacy, and even happy marriage. The remaining four chapters of part 1—a hundred and thirty large pages of rather fine print—are required to relate the sexual background (education *and* experience) of that normal pair, Jeff and Norma, up to the time of their marriage—not that they represent the unusual but that the usual had never before been so deeply plumbed.

The unusual are introduced in the second section of *The White Thorntree*, entitled "The Fringe-Dwellers," relatively brief presumably because accidents of personality and social pressure have produced fewer of them. Here we are introduced to Shirley Beighton, bisexual; Leo Taunton, heterosexual-turned-homosexual; Allan Kimpton, homosexual-turned-heterosexual; Phyllis Gurney, lesbian; and David Munster, confused. Shirley, we are told in the first paragraph, was having "affairs of sorts" with three of the others—Leo, Phyllis, and David—one way, surely, of making this tight little society tighter. Another was to have them all connected with those normal Mitchells: Shirley as a child had loved Jeff, her uncle; David as a boy had worshipped Norma, a neighbor, whom Leo in his prime had gently deflowered and whom Phyllis had failed, despite some effort, to interest in a lesbian relationship.

Shirley appears to have been worthy of the title nymphomaniac, although it is not accorded to her. From the time of a triple rape by young toughs whom she had encouraged and rather enjoyed, at age thirteen, she had been involved in countless couplings, always for sex, not love. Phyllis Gurney, a confirmed lesbian despite a brief experiment with marriage, proved to be a stimulating partner for Shirley for a time, taking her to dances in men's evening clothes and to bed without. Leo's intimacy with women was as extensive as Shirley's with men, beginning in early youth when he impregnated the family maid and extending into middle life, interrupted only briefly by the intolerable, for him, confines of matrimony. This precocity and endurance would hardly have earned him a place among the fringe-dwellers save that as he approached middle age and sought at last for love, he found it, *with* sex, in a violent homosexual relationship with young Allan Kimpton.

The most complex of the fringe-dwellers is idealist David Munster, who as a "sprouting" boy worshipped, in turn, two older women: first Norma, a little later, Shirley. The latter considered initiating him into sex, an act which, we are given to understand, might have set him on the road to normality. As it was, he went from masturbation to a homosexual relationship with Allan Kimpton (which brought him a short jail term, to his parents' dismay) to a series of perversions including fetishism, voyeurism, and exhibitionism. In a couple of attempts at normal sex with hire-girls he failed miserably. Even a later reciprocated love for the middle-aged wife of an elderly husband was insufficient to elicit a normal reaction from him when they finally bedded down.

We leave the fringe-dwellers (but only temporarily) to enter "The Promised Land," the third section of the book that is a formidable piece of fiction in itself, totalling fifty-eight chapters covering nearly nine hundred pages. In this section the novel enters its second stage, where it particularizes at great length the general announcement in the Foreword, that "even in an acceptably successful marriage boredom is a possibility."[29] Like part 1, part 3 opens with the Mitchells, now some years into their marriage:

> In its later years the Mitchells' marriage—like so many others—had been held together by joint parenthood, shared interests and responsibilities, good principles, the general example of other couples of similar age and condition with whom they socially consorted, the law of the land and, equally with these, the simple habit of association which had grown upon them.[30]

But now the situation is changing, and

> What the Mitchells needed at this stage of their lives was for persons more experienced than they to put to them firmly, and with warning emphasis, that the promiscuous impulse, in its many disguises, was universal—powerfully inhibited in some, less so in others—that it was most likely to manifest itself seriously in persons approaching middle age, and could have devastating consequences.[31]

The chapter "Just Friends" introduces us to two other couples, relatively recent acquaintances encountered by the Mitchells in their "quite small social round." The earlier lives of these are now probed, intensively and extensively, as Jeff's and Norma's had been, in order to provide diversity in the *Thorntree's* study of marital love—and sex.

One of these pairs is the Gillespies, Tom and Pamela, whose apparently happy marriage endured a curious psychological blight. They had met in youth at a ball, and for Pamela it had been love at first sight confirmed by numerous delightful excursions together thereafter. Her only concern was that Tom never made a date in advance and that his appearances were unpredictable. She could not know that he was still irregularly (though virginally) involved with Sylvia Cullen, with whom he had fallen desperately in love before he found that she had a husband and a child. Still, Sylvia had continued to string him along for months, until he was separated from her, physically by her leaving for Hong Kong with her husband and emotionally by his discovery that she had betrayed his devotion (in his eyes) by becoming pregnant again shortly before. Now he was free to go back to Pamela; but her early ecstatic ardor had declined seriously, not only from the uncertainties of their off-and-on courtship but from a strenuous premarital weekend to which he subjected her in order to wear off his long-pent-up desire. Still, she was fond of him; they were good friends, and they married, built a home together, and had a couple of children. But the gap between his passion and her semifrigidity widened, especially after she inadvertently learned of the Sylvia Cullen affair, now long, long past, and realized that what had puzzled her during their courtship had been the fact that she had, unknowingly, been the Second Woman, only a standby. She could neither forget nor forgive; but Tom was faithful, making do with masturbation during the long dry periods between their infrequent couplings.

The marriage of the Tesdales, Roger and Margaret, serene as it appeared on the surface, was far more seriously blighted: it had never been consummated. Romantic young Roger had scrupulously maintained his virginity and had looked ahead, during his engagement to Margaret, to the tender care with which he would initiate her—and himself—into the mysteries of married love. But Margaret, he discovered shortly before their marriage, did not share his virgin state: passionate Margaret, who had for a long time "accepted the innate ardour that had always plagued her as matter-of-factly as she accepted the colour of her hair or the size of her gloves";[32] frank and honest Margaret, whose answer to Roger's shocked direct question was "Yes. Haven't you with girls? I thought most people had."[33] Roger was finally able to bring himself to terms with reality to the point where he could go ahead with the legalities of the union, only to find himself impotent—a condition that Margaret's eager efforts to overcome served only to perpetuate. Their mutual affection and respect, however, were great enough to give them a good many years of faithfulness to their hollow marriage bed.

Yet another couple, Guy and Diana Moorshead (he was Jeff Mitchell's business partner), appear shortly. These two had met in youth at a resort where both were vacationing, always amorous Guy "for the joy of the hunt," scholarly Diana to recover from an abortive (and aborted) affair with a somewhat older—and married—scholarly man. The courtship was brief: their eyes met, and five hours later they were "busy in bed."[34] Guy was inferior to Diana, socially and economically, but so potent and charming that she found herself in love with him. He, less susceptible to romance but impressed by her superiority, gladly joined her in matrimony. Within a couple of years, however, as she settled in to correcting and improving him, her sexuality began to ebb, and his interest in other women, always strong, to quicken. He would have been quite willing for her to be equally promiscuous, had it been her nature. But both adapted to circumstances, and their marriage, like the others, remained placid on the surface.

III   *Sex and Love—Only*

So much for our principal characters (there are dozens of lesser ones), four couples thrown together socially at an age when the confines of marriage were growing increasingly inadequate, even oppressive. A single liquorous party at the Brownleys, attended by the Mitchells, the Tesdales, and the Gillespies, lighted the fires between Norma Mitchell, who had begun "looking around" at this period, and Tom Gillespie, whose rationed love life with Pamela had become increasingly unfulfilling. The same evening, Jeff Mitchell was seduced by Margaret Tesdale, understandably starved from her years of loyalty to impotent Roger. Jeff was later to turn from Margaret over a rival and attach himself to Diana Moorshead, whose husband Guy, Jeff's partner, got involved, in turn, with Margaret. And so on, and on—save for Pamela Gillespie, who found the idea of sex with anyone distasteful, and Roger Tesdale, for whom it appeared to be impossible. The rest may sound to modern ears like a small circle engaged by mutual consent in wife-swapping, but no—these were secret adulteries, fraught with pain and danger for all concerned. And the greatest danger? Love. Men and woman alike will die, in *The White Thorntree*, and worms presumably devour them, for love.

It is, after all, with romantic love, not just sex (although we find plenty of both) that the book concerns itself. Ten years before it was published, Frank had written to Vance of his project (p. 155) that it would be called *Land of Blue Horses*, "symbolizing the world of the emotions as against that of hard fact. There is an incident fairly early in the book which will make the reference unmistakable."[35] What it was we do not know, since the name itself was later lost in combination. The title *The White Thorntree* is of course symbolic, too, and predictably with the same meaning, although the explanation does not appear until almost the end and in connection with a relatively minor character, Jeff's last love, Lyn Sheridan. Earlier, at the end of a second unhappy affair, Lyn had read a translation of a Norwegian novel. In it "romantic love was likened to a white thorn-tree on cliffs of obsidian. Her wounded spirit had settled for the image at once. She could see those sky-tall cliffs as if she were actually at the foot of them; black as midnight, they were, and as slippery as glass. She could see that white thorntree on its high niche, miraculously clad with blossom, almost luminous in its enticement but only to be reached by perilous ways, difficult to pluck, and prone to wilt in human hands. She knew all about it, for she had twice got a hand among those scented flowers, and had almost died in the long, helpless, endless, bumbling fall that followed."[36]

It is this devastating power of sexual love as portrayed in *The White Thorntree* that is particularly difficult to credit in its Sydney setting. Australia of all nations has a reputation as a man's country. There the West was won not by families making their way into the wilderness in covered wagons, as in America, but by horsemen—explorers, then drovers, who set up cattle and sheep stations far from home and womenfolk. As a result this young country has long been the land of "mateship," celebrated alike in Australian song and story, a dependence not upon women but upon one's fellowmen. Woman's place was definitely in the home; if she emerged, she was poorly paid, and usually retreated to it upon marriage. In years considerably more recent than the setting of *The White Thorntree*, the sexes at middle-class Australian social gatherings have tended to drift to opposite ends of the room to indulge in man-talk and woman-talk. National literature by writers of both sexes, as well as reports of observant visitors from abroad, abound in references to the Australian man as an unromantic, even an inept lover: he continued to be a man's man, who drank in pubs which only men might enter rather than at cocktail parties, talked of horses rather than women, and devoted himself to sports—rugby, swimming, sailing, manning a lifeboat. Sex has of course not been neglected by these manly men (though the birthrate has long been disconcertingly low), but it has not been anything to make much of a fuss about, either.

In *The White Thorntree*, however, it is the *only* thing. Many a novel has attained popularity through the subject of sex—sex in-

troduced naturally, as part of many-faceted life, or pornographical-
ly, to stimulate. Here it is treated comprehensively, to instruct. The
author's purpose being what it is, his subject is inevitably the
aberrations, physical as well as social, resulting from the frustration
of the natural sex drive by the culture of the time and place. Well
and good, but the reader comes to wonder if fiction is the proper
vehicle for such a limited intention. The author's technique, one
suspects, was to make an outline of all possible types of sex experience, normal and otherwise (he had read Kinsey), and then to
create—or recall—persons and situations to illustrate each. There is
nothing wrong in such a method if the results truly reflect life. But
The White Thorntree becomes a monochrome of sex, more tedious
than titillating, and the reader is left unconvinced, needing less,
wishing more.

Frank pleads "the interests of fictional freedom" as his excuse for
ignoring public events and giving little attention in the book to
"period fixings."[37] Well and good but what of other components of
life that we have come to expect, in fiction, to enrich the bare bones
of event? Where, for instance, are hints, at least, of the Sydney
scene, to give us a sense of place? Once, when Tom Gillespie is
brooding on the beach at Manly—about sex; again, when Diana
Moorshead is leaving the Harbour on a ship—because of sex.

Where too are those visually distinguishing features that serve to
imprint a character sharply on the reader's mind? Jeff Mitchell is
the "leading man" throughout, but not until well along in the book
do we so much as know that he is dark-haired—and then only
because his wife Norma, on a tram, becomes interested, by contrast,
in the blond body hair of a young male passenger clad only in
shorts. Tom Gillespie, the number two male, comes to be
recognizable without his clothes, but not by them. Several of the
main women characters, despite wifehood, motherhood (for some),
and approaching middle-age, are, we are given to understand, fatally attractive; but it is a generic appeal of breasts and bottoms and
crotches; we don't know one from another in personal appearance,
dressed or undressed.

The reader needs tangible specifics to give him a sense of belonging. One of Frank's close literary contemporaries who read the book
early pronounced it privately "a crashing bore," an opinion easy to
support with still other evidence. Its size alone is a serious flaw, not
that length is objectionable in itself (*War and Peace* is somewhat
longer) but that it should be compatible with the material. The

points Frank is trying to make here are often valid, but he makes them and makes them, over and over again, in what often becomes a monumental verbosity.[38] This is a strange comment to be called forth by the work of a writer trained in the short story and capable of masterly small works like *Man-Shy* and *The Wells of Beersheba*. It is easy to believe that *The White Thorntree* was twenty years in the writing, and a pity that a few more—months, at least—were not spent in excising and tightening.

The author's obsession with sex (and it is admittedly no less) is clear in his choice of incident. In these post-Freudian days other human drives are accepted as ranking with sex: the need for personality fulfillment, for example, and greed, and the passion for power. For married couples, other preoccupations than sex include building up their homes and fortunes, raising their children, participating in the life of their communities. But Frank has little or no room for such. Even his child characters must conform. We hear little about the Mitchells' four offspring, but volume two opens with three pages devoted to them, as follows: Jennifer, the eldest daughter, is caught looking through the dressing-table drawer in which her mother keeps her contraceptives; Beverly confesses, blushing, to having talked intimately with an older schoolmate about babies; Eric is found drawing in the garden soil that 'short, unspeakable, unprintable word; and to cap all this dubious behavior, Gordon, only eight, is discovered by his mother (not the only mother in the book to do such spying) in an ecstasy of masturbation which frightened her so that she sent out a hurry call to his father to come home from work. In another novel, the three little neighborhood boys who discovered Roger Tesdale's body (a suicide, appropriately, as the result of frustrated sex) might reasonably have been playing ball or maybe cops and robbers at the time. But not here. Inspired by the discovery of a used "french letter" in the bushes, they were diligently comparing the size and power of their penises.

The Publisher's Note at the beginning of the second volume of *The White Thorntree* explains the necessity for producing the book in two volumes, because of its size, but the reason for their being released several months apart was not mentioned. This delay caused difficulties for readers of volume one. As Frank had realized when he decided to wait and combine his proposed *Land of Blue Horses* with *The White Thorntree*, he did not have two books, only one, and there was no logical place to divide it. Of the four sections of which the entire book is composed, the third, occupying some three-quarters of the whole, is overwhelmingly the longest and is inevitably split by the volume break. As the two volumes are almost identical in size (578 and 571 pages), one might assume that the division was made arbitrarily as a matter of publishing convenience. According to the publisher, however, Frank himself carefully determined where the break should be made, "ending volume one 'at a point where the reader would have strong motives for continuing, and beginning volume two at a point where he would have little difficulty in picking up the thread of the narrative even after a lapse of time.' "[39] This is accepted practice, of course, in magazine serials, but it failed to work well here, despite the appearance in each volume of the author's important Foreword. There was not only an awkwardly long pause for any early reader of volume one, but when volume two did appear, many buyers undoubtedly started with it, since the first was by that time frequently unavailable. This was unfortunate, the first being very much needed for a full understanding of the second.[40]

IV   *Melodrama*

In another way, however, he who started with volume two was blessed, for at this point the tiresomely detailed anatomizing of sex is pretty well out of the way, and the narrative begins to move much more vigorously. To the reader of the whole, however, there is a new element in this second volume that is both surprising and disappointing. Let us assume him to be an admirer of Frank's earlier works, not only of the economy of their telling but of their quiet truthfulness to life. He will consequently be unprepared for the strong element of melodrama that the author allows himself here.

Before we examine this contention, let us note that this novel is not set in the loneliness of the outback nor in the brutal ignorance of a Sydney slum nor even in the nonconformist atmosphere of King's Cross, but in urban and suburban Sydney in the 1920s and 1930s in a small circle of middle-class Australians whose business and social lives impinge in one way or another upon that central and most normal couple, Jeff and Norma Mitchell. In the span of the roughly two decades covered by the action, it is to be expected that some deaths would occur, and some do. But save for one of Norma's brothers, who expires toward the end of the book (previously unknown to us and of causes presumably natural), no one dies of accident, disease, or age. No, all are in the prime of life, and come to violent ends by their own hands, or those of others, or an avenging law. The tally includes three suicides, three murders (complete with murderers known to the victims and to us), and one hanging. Furthermore, these deaths are remarkable not only for their numbers, in the small world in which the story moves, but also for the shocking fact that every one of them was motivated by sex.

I have already mentioned my doubts about Australia's being a credible setting for *The White Thorntree's* concentration on sex, but my question is based on only a superficial comparison of cultures; for all I know, even Macquarie Street may lead straight to Peyton Place, as the book suggests. But I have personally observed from a close reading of Australia's newspapers that crimes of passion do not appear to be in the ascendant there, or if they are, they certainly yield place to more urgent national concerns such as sports. Yet the *Thorntree's* list of major events provides us not only with the fatalities just mentioned but with several rapes. All of these justify us, surely, in accusing Frank Dalby Davison of having surrendered, in this late book, to the coarse delights of melodrama.

In an excerpt from a review of the book that the publishers included on the dust jacket of volume one, critic Geoffrey Dutton states: "Everything that happens is only too credible. . . . One believes the whole appalling lot, because Frank Davison is obviously such a thoroughly honest, decent bloke." But surely these personal qualities in an author, admirable as they may be, do not assure us, *per se*, of credibility in his fiction. To weigh this judgment with any accuracy we need to examine the story in its specifics.

Sex is understandably the chief business of sensual men like Leo Taunton and Guy Moorshead, their many early indulgences in women having led to sex only, not love. Yet for the two leading male characters, Jeff Mitchell and Tom Gillespie, love (necessarily illicit, since both are now married men) becomes ALL, superseding wife, children, and yet more unbelievably, business. Even their sanity is close to being sacrificed.

Granted, both are ripe for it, in years. They are approaching that period of middle-age when Sinclair Lewis's American George F. Babbitt threw over the traces to become a classic victim of the male menopause. But neither Jeff nor Tom falls, as might have been expected, for a fresh young thing with whom he might hope to renew his passing youth, or for a siren experienced in seduction, or for any new piece on the feminine landscape. Both become the just-short-of-babbling slaves of married women of their own age, wives of friends and neighbors, near whom they have lived for some time in sexual peace and quiet.

Of the two (and two would not seem necessary, to illustrate this particular facet of sex life), Tom is the more convincing victim. With his record of a thwarted first love and a less-than-satisfactory marriage bed, it is understandable that he should become a candidate for an extramarital affair; inevitable, even, when Norma Mitchell, long contentedly married to Jeff but approaching a middle-aged longing for youthful romance, modestly encourages him. The dancing skill they share throws them together, there is a stolen kiss—and they are off on a voyage promising all the ecstasies and miseries that are the inevitable lot of those who find nature and society at odds. The extent to which Tom is affected by what should reasonably have been a passing romance is hard to accept. With little immediate reward he reaches the point where the sun rises and sets in Norma; so does his business and his life. His devotion leads her to take him far too much for granted, but no matter how often she uses him for whipping boy or floor mat, he remains faithful—to the point of giving up not only his home and family but his very good position as sales manager in an automobile agency, to drive a cab. And he is destroyed personally to the point that he sinks for a time into unspecified but darkly hinted-at perversions. Credible?

Even harder to accept is the sad tale of protagonist Jeff Mitchell. He is the typical boy with whose conventional romance and marriage the book opens, the always understanding husband who looks on indulgently when he thinks his wife is having an innocent fling with neighbor Tom. He is the contented family man who overlooked for a year the fact that neighbor Margaret Tesdale, Roger's unfulfilled wife, had enticed him to bed during that fateful party. And he is the man who later suddenly finds himself as slavishly devoted to Margaret as Tom to Norma; who is separated from any joy in her upon learning that another man's affair with her had overlapped his own; and who nonetheless gives up his cherished family business as craftsman printer to start selling real estate, and allows himself to become utterly estranged from his wife, banishing himself from his home and children, because his mind and his heart are elsewhere. Credible?

Curiously, Frank's most convincing characters and certainly the most appealing are those who are least able to lead normal lives, perhaps because they make the heaviest demands on our sympathies. As a result of Roger's continued impotence, he could not keep his mind on his work as a research chemist and had to settle for a minor clerkship—a more reasonable circumstance than Tom's and Jeff's self-demotions for love. But he is not embittered. At that general take-off point, the party at which his long-deprived wife Margaret seduced Jeff, Roger chanced to be a witness to their coupling, but not as a dog in the manger; his observations fascinated him and left him with no jealousy of Jeff, only admiration.

The novel finally takes off, near the close of volume one, with Roger's grievous attempt to restore his own powers through rape. From a tedious recounting of sex, it turns to a concentration on character and event that often moves rapidly and dramatically. Roger continues to engage the reader's sympathetic understanding whenever he appears. Always his efforts toward normality are made with Margaret in mind. Hope that was dashed after the rape is revived when he at length succeeds with a girl who resists him just enough to restore his manhood. But his triumphant return home is ruined by finding that Margaret (now engrossed, Jeff having abandoned her, with another familiar figure, Guy Moorshead) is no longer either sympathetic or welcoming. Roger's contrived witnessing of one of Guy's subsequent couplings with her thus arouses in him none of the admiration that Jeff's had done, but (understandably) murderous hate, and murder Guy he does, committing suicide thereafter "not only because he had killed a man and would be answerable to the police, but because he had come to the end of himself."[41]

An even worse end awaited young David Munster as the result of his sadly maladjusted sexuality. Released from his jail sentence for a homosexually related offence, David turned devoutly to religion and resolutely from sex, only to find himself so fearful in the presence of young girls that he had himself castrated. This act gratified his conscience but, as the doctor had warned him, did not for long end his sexual desire. He found his first heterosexual satisfaction in an attack on a young lady entrusted to his care—for which he was shortly hanged. David, like Roger, is a character who moves us by his credible if unsuccessful struggle against the manifold difficulties imposed by society to defeat man's basic urge.

Frank makes clear in his Foreword that his exploration into the ways and byways of sex will include no advice, no moral, and he is almost as good as his word. In a moral world, Allan Kimpton, the young man responsible for David's first brush with the law, would have come to a bad end. Instead, he finds himself yearning for a normal life, shortly marries, and possibly lives happily ever after, since he altered his direction in youth. Less convincing is the reverse change in the life of middle-aged Leo Taunton. Bachelor Leo had been sure of his manhood since his nursemaid first fondled his genitals. As a man he devoted himself to seduction and the law, achieving considerable success in both. Incapable of love, however, he hungered, as time went by, for undemanding companionship and found it for a while (small world again, in a large city) in the intellectually stimulating Shirley Beighton, that young woman of many parts indeed. But she wanted sex and permanent love, too. Leo, having found her friendship a gratifyingly new experience, yielded reluctantly to the first demand, vanished before the second.

This is the Leo who in middle life suddenly turned homosexually to young Allan Kimpton. With all the sexologists tell us of the effects of early experience on the direction of one's sex life, this is a change far harder to accept than Allan's later marriage. Still more difficult to comprehend is the depth of real love for Allan that is pictured as accompanying Leo's physical yearning. When the boy, shortly wearying, left him without a word, Leo nearly lost his mind. This successful head of a successful law firm followed in the footsteps of Frank's other middle-aged lovers by neglecting his career. More, he took to drink, and his steady excessive drinking, we are given to understand, was responsible for his fatally strangling Phyllis Gurney for merely mocking his inquiry about Allan's whereabouts. This is more believable, however, than that an intelligent, cultured, experienced adult would so quickly have become, under the circumstances recounted, a mindless sot, prey to frustrated emotions. Unlike David Munster, hanged though his rape victim lived, Leo got only life imprisonment for murder—perhaps a reflection on the paramount importance of sex control, in society's canon.

It is Phyllis who represents the lesbian in the author's catalog of sex types, and it was her current love who ran away with Allan Kimpton (if marriage doesn't work out well for that pair, it won't be because they don't understand each other's problems). We first heard of Phyllis in her unsuccessful attempt to interest Norma Sherwood in lesbianism while they were girls; later, in her successful if passing relationship with Shirley Beighton. With all of Phyllis's inevitable difficulties in adjusting to an off-beat life, she never did anything, least of all to Leo, to merit death. But the author did not promise a moral book.

V   *Realism and Its Limits*

Toward so complicated an emotion and activity as sex, several attitudes can be taken. There is the romantic view of its intensity, its raptures; this sees it as the Great Experience of Life, and that is one truth. And there is, inevitably, the view that sees rational mankind as the victim of a most irrational compulsion; this finds sex to be the Great Joke of Life, and that is another truth. Then there is the scientific view, marked by an interest in techniques and results physical rather than spiritual, which is truth of yet another kind. Frank lacked the poetry to share with us much of sex's ecstasies. And if he had, as one suspects from occasional remarks, the irony to let us in on the great cosmic joke, he rarely exercised it; rapture and amusement alike have little place in his matter-of-fact reporting. Instead, he was primarily concerned with a factual presentation of the urge, the outlets, the consequences of sex. Someone has credited *The White Thorntree* with having avoided the pornographic; great sections of it read with all the titillation of a how-to-do pamphlet, and its people often seem less characters in a novel than case histories out of Kraft-Ebbing or Kinsey.

This is realism rather than romanticism or caricature, but it is a realism with curious limits. For instance, one of the major problems of sex for Western man since the Crusades has been the venereal diseases, from which Australia is, unhappily, not free. Yet with all the promiscuity in the book, including a good deal of prostitution, not one case appears; the subject is never even mentioned.

Another problem of sex, far older and more universal than syphilis, springs from its basic purpose, reproduction. This, too, Davison almost completely ignores. Children are born occasionally to the married, and not always by intention: of the Mitchells' four, the first two were planned, the second two just happened. But for the unwed, conception is a matter of little concern here. True, fringe-dweller Shirley once found herself in need of an abortion (and this, after she knew better), but the problem was readily taken care of—during a lunch hour, for her, and in less than a paragraph, for us. Another extramarital pregnancy resulting from the book's many copulations is suffered by the Taunton's eighteen-year-old maid as a result of the adolescent efforts of young Leo, but this is mentioned with no concern for the maid or the offspring, only as evidence of Leo's precociousness. A maturer Leo assures virginal Norma Sherwood that there will be no undesirable consequences of his introducing her to sex, but throughout their holiday week of frequent intimacies no hint of the source of his assurances is given. Nor do we know the kinds of "preventatives against misadventure" that young Jeff finds indiscriminate young ladies carrying in their handbags, nor what Norma's growing daughter discovers by snooping in her mother's private drawer. Only once, after a union between herself and Tom Gillespie, Norma was moved to preventive action (nature undisclosed—again our sex manual is incomplete) by the thought of the thousands of little Toms struggling to reach their destination. For the rest of the innumerable couplings in the book—many of them unpremeditated and under the most unhygienic conditions of automobile, beach, or hedgerow—none is described as being accompanied by any concern for possible consequences, nor do consequences occur. And this, be it noted, is in the pre-pill era. We scarcely remember, amidst all this happy infertility, to be grateful that Madelaine Curnell, violated by David Munster, was saved by his earlier self-elected emasculation from a fate worse than rape. One might call *The White Thorntree* an idyll of constant but disease-free, virtually pregnancy-free, sex.

But if its characters suffer no physical consequences from sexual love, their mental and emotional scars are innumerable. The list of broken hearts runs higher than that of violent deaths, even, since hearts do mend for further breaking. Jeff Mitchell's was broken only once, by Margaret Tesdale, but he broke hers, in turn, not to mention his wife Norma's and Diana Moorshead's. Presumably he even chipped Vivienne Thurgood's a little or she would not have shot him when he announced that he was leaving her, and his death broke Lyn Sheridan's to the point of suicide, as it did Diana's (already broken once by his desertion). Tom Gillespie's heart had been broken early by Sylvia Cullen, the fact of whose existence half-broke his later wife Pamela's, and he had his own badly shattered by Norma. Even Roger Tesdale's broke when he found that his sought-after gift of potency for Margaret had arrived too late, but he did away with himself before he had suffered long. Only Guy Moorshead stayed heart-whole through all his vast sex experience until he met Margaret, and Roger killed him, happily, before he could be disillusioned. Of the fringe-dwellers, only Leo Taunton's heart broke, and that, over Allan Kimpton, but he perhaps suffered the most serious case of all.

A quick count shows that despite Frank's clear and commendable effort to put men and women on an equal footing in the sex game, his females tend to come to more emotional grief, more often, perhaps because they suffer sex without love, that keynote of a promiscuous society, less gladly, and when off with an old love, are mostly slower at getting on with a new. They fare variously, Pamela taking to business, Diana to scholarship, Margaret to drink. The chief sacrifice of man for love is his career: Leo his law, Jeff his craft, Tom his business, Roger his research. Only Guy, professional lecher that he is, carries on serenely.

Of the many points that Frank had to make about sex in this prolonged study, one of the wisest is his concentration on its innate selfishness. This appears unwittingly in the copulative act itself, the author observing of Jeff and Norma in their youth that:

they were never further lost from each other than in yielding to the con-
vulsive seizure with which nature crowned their efforts—those few
moments of complete abandonment to erotic frenzy to which all earth's
creatures are so commandingly drawn—and were restored from the most
profound personal preoccupations to loving awareness of one another only
as spent flesh subsided and the consuming waves of pleasure ebbed away. [42]

From this physical fact we move to broader manifestations of sex only to find selfishness still, all too often, attendant. This might be expected in violent acts: Roger Tesdale and David Munster, both bent on their own deep inner purposes, certainly gave little thought, at least until afterward, to the victims of their rapes. But the same self-centeredness is true in normal relationships, too. Selfishness is present every time that one partner takes another for sexual satisfaction without due regard for the consequences to the other. With the possible physical results for the woman Frank does not concern himself here, as we have noticed, but equally selfish is the disregard by either partner of another's likely emotional in-volvement. Leo, an experienced philanderer, thoughtfully made clear to all his women, including Norma, the transitory quality of his sexual attentions. Even Roger, seducing Nola Burton in an effort to make a man of himself for his wife, felt some concern lest the girl's emotions become involved—but not enough to desist. Jeff, more typically, was conscious only of his own desire, with his first girl, Loma, and not until long afterward did memory bring twinges of guilt about her.

No one should read *The White Thorntree* without first looking at the poem that prefaces each volume as a kind of text—Australian

Kenneth Slessor's thought-provoking little "Cannibal Street." It is well worth returning to, to brood over as the reading progresses. There is hardly a character in the novel but what sometimes visited that street where such things as "skewered hearts" are for sale, and (God save them) "bargained there, / Paid my pennies and ate my share." Take Norma Mitchell, as an example, for the couples' group. Responding eagerly at first to the excitement of Tom Gillespie's attentions, she soon yielded to him, but once sure of him she treated him shamefully, not making a clean break, which would have been acceptable, but keeping him dangling. Much earlier Tom, able to see married Sylvia Cullen only irregularly, entertained himself in the lonely intervals by paying court to Pamela, with no thought for what it might make the girl suffer later. His insistence on a prenuptial weekend was equally selfish, on a smaller scale.

Allan Kimpton of the fringe-dwellers was the prime Cannibal Street customer. He took joy in flaunting before passionately devoted David Munster the fact that he himself was having other homosexual affairs with older men. When Leo Taunton, one of them, succumbed to love for Allan rather than mere lust, the boy drew him on heartlessly, then, having decided on marriage himself, abandoned him without a word of farewell.

The theme of *The White Thorntree,* the pull of sex between nature and culture, is no new one, of course. One is reminded of Thomas Hardy's reflection, at the time of Tess of the D'Urberville's unwed pregnancy, that if she had been on a desert island, she would have experienced to the full the joys of motherhood; only the social pressures deprived her of them. Frank, however, strikes this note not once but dozens of times. His greatest contributions to the subject besides his thoroughness (which unfortunately has the weakness of its strength) are two: first, his sympathetic understanding that perversion is not the result of a monstrous love of degradation but devious paths into which society's pressures encourage the weak or the maladjusted; second, his recognition that sex is almost equally a problem for girls and for boys, for women and for men. This awareness leads him to do justice to an aspect of his subject that too many writers, from ignorance or tradition, have neglected.

VI   *Style*

It also leads him to a curiously excessive trick of balance. We first become conscious of it early in the book in his tracing of the cradle-to-altar sexual experiences of Jeff and Norma, particularly in a chapter called "Dreams Before Waking." To show that adolescent sex problems exist for girls and boys alike, every aspect of sex experience for the growing Jeff is matched in the growing Norma and presented with great richness of incident for each: narcissism, with hours before the looking-glass; tender but undeclared feelings for a schoolmate of the opposite sex; desires to be a member of the opposite sex, with a period of aping its life-style; adoration for a young but older relative of the same sex; violent attachment for one of the same sex and age; romantic awareness of an older person of the opposite sex; brief experiments with fetishism, voyeurism, and pygmalionism; narrow escapes from being drawn into homosexuality; pursuit by a considerably older person of the opposite sex; and an interest in a person of the opposite sex and the same age. Balancing Jeff's premarital experience with Beryl Sinclair is Norma's with Leo Taunton. David Munster's boyish adoration of Norma is balanced by Shirley Beighton's girlish worship of Jeff.

The wedding with which the book opens ends their sex problems for some time. But in later years both Norma and Jeff experience a reawakening to attractive persons of the opposite sex. Shortly (and simultaneously) each is unfaithful, shortly becoming seriously involved with a neighbor's spouse. Ultimately we find them separated, each enjoying—or trying to enjoy—a series of purely physical relationships with a miscellany of men and women. All of this goes to substantiate the author's contention that sex, youthful and mature alike, is equally a temptation, equally a joy, even equally a disillusionment, and a source of pain and grief for both sexes—a point well worth making after the imbalance of the past.

But the author falls in love with his own device and tends to overuse it. In even so mundane a matter as taking sleeping pills the Mitchells march to the same drummer: Norma no sooner finds herself dependent on them than she discovers a phial of them in Jeff's drawer, regularly diminishing. The trick reaches the height of the ridiculous, surely, when Tom, about to couple illicitly with Norma under the inconveniences of evening and the out-of-doors, finds himself somewhat put off by an uncontrollable fart on her part—only to yield to one of his own a moment later. The only excuse for this incident would seem to be to indulge in a moment of high humor over the comic side of sex, but the author failed to take advantage of the opportunity. This is not the only time that his style suffered from the seriousness of his purpose, presumably, and his effort to remain a reporter, not an entertainer.

By the time *The White Thorntree* was published it was a less daring book than it must have seemed during the earlier years of its writing; Frank's concern about its publication was caused increasingly by its size, not its contents. Certainly accounts of intercourse, with anatomical details, were appearing more and more frequently as the century ground on. Yet, though the book still ranks as daring, its author seems curiously torn between the pruderies of his youth and the freedom—and convictions—of his age. Sometimes he writes with all the scientifically objective details of a treatise on sex, as when he concludes his account of Roger Tesdale's first ill-fated effort to consummate his marriage to Margaret with "there were emissions and an orgasm of sorts, but without erection or intromission."[43] He seldom uses any of the vulgar words descriptive of sex; one (presumably *fuck*) is frequently in the offing, but he does a kind of ceremonial dance around it. Disillusioned Pamela Gillespie "found herself increasingly disposed to think of what she and Tom did by its vulgar name"[44] (left unnamed). Still more elaborately, as a young woman passes by in a park, "In three single-syllabled words—a verb, a pronoun, and another verb—Kevin inquired whether it was the young woman's habit to copulate."[45] The characters may occasionally refer to the penis slangily as a "jigger," but long and lovingly as the author hymns its beauties, its potentials, and its accomplishments, he himself never calls this particular spade a spade. It is always an "organ"—a "sexual" or a "male" organ—or a "masculine member." These constant euphemisms come to seem curiously Victorian, even coy, as when Norma's inconvenient menstruation the day before her wedding is explained as a "periodic visitation," and at their first attempted union, Jeff's "body took charge of events disappointingly soon."[46]

The reader of *The White Thorntree*, packed with sex though it is, may nonetheless agree with Frank's remark on the subject back in 1942: "I am disgustingly normal, Mr. Meacham."[47] Although his interest here extends to sexuality in all its manifestations, his narrations of the sex act are confined almost entirely to the simplest sort of normal heterosexual intercourse. His sympathy for the pervert of all stripes is constant, but the techniques of perversion he almost completely avoids, and there is only a hint of procedures toward homosexual satisfaction, male or female. Between the reader and the perhaps unspeakable (at least unspoken) goings on in the strange circle of Belle Carruthers, in which good family man Tom

Gillespie loses himself for a time when desperate with longing for
that good family woman Norma Mitchell—between those goings on
and the reader a black curtain is drawn. It seems fair to add to Geoffrey Dutton's description of the author as an "honest, decent bloke"
this further adjective, "normal," which may suggest limits to
Frank's experience for some, but which probably adds validity to it
for the average reader.

Whatever one may think of *The White Thorntree*—and the book
is certain to be debated, pro and con, for as long as it is read—its
style marks a notable improvement over much of its author's earlier
writing. While the book was still in process Frank was priding
himself that he had never written better (p. 155), and it is true that
his style had matured to the point that it is fluent and altogether
serviceable. Gone are the clumsy constructions so prevalent in *Blue
Coast Caravan* and occasional in most of his early work, creative as
well as critical. But missing too is the lyricism of much of *Man-Shy*
and *The Wells of Beersheba*, denied to the *Thorntree*, no doubt, by
both subject and purpose. Still, if the heights to which inspiration
had carried him in those small works are missing here, a more than
satisfactory middle level is remarkably well sustained, for a book
that occupied so many years, so many pages.

VII   *Critical Opinion*

Style alone, however, neither sells books nor holds readers. How
many copies of *The White Thorntree* have been bought I do not
know, beyond the original Cugley five hundred. But since the later
and larger Ure Smith edition, the book has at last come home to
Angus & Roberton, publishers of all of Frank's previous works, as a
paperback in their A & R Classics series (1975)—two fat volumes
again. How many people have read the book in any form is still
another question, and unanswerable, save to surmise that so large a
novel is hardly compatible, for the general public, with the televi-
sion age and outdoor Australia. Yet the author has been quoted as
saying, "It is a book for rereading."[48]

It has been widely read by Frank's friends, of course, and in
Australian literary circles generally. Some praised it no doubt
sincerely; others, in memory of its author; others, perhaps, because
it would be unthinkable to belittle so vast an enterprise. Still others
frankly deplored it. Perhaps the wisest were those who admitted
that time would be required to determine its place among
Australian novels.

Its advertised subject matter alone would inevitably have drawn some readers, but whether it was able to hold them to the end is another question. For Australia's literary critics it was of course required reading, and it elicited a variety of opinions. Even these professionals were confused, however, having no precedent for coping with such a book as *The White Thorntree*, whose initial reception was once described as ranging from "the dismissively hostile to the respectfully perplexed."[49] Reviews continued to appear over an almost two-year period, owing to the spread of publication dates. One of the earliest, published shortly after the original edition, was entitled "Bizarre Novel as a Curiosity."[50] In it Maurice Vintner enumerated three problems: one, whether to take the book seriously or as a "gigantic send-up"; two, how to relate it to its author, to whom it did not seem to belong; three, how to uncover the ore beneath "the mass of trite and clumsy verbiage." Vintner gave Frank credit for his industry, his integrity, and his sincerity, but concluded: "The thing just does not come off. . . . All one can predict for it is that, like one of those strange houses to be found in every city, loaded with rococo stonework, embellished with towers, spires, and blind attics, riddled with passageways and stairs, it will stand in the Australian landscape as a curiosity for sightseers."

Maurice Dunlevy was one of those who read the later Ure Smith volumes as they came off the press several months apart. Reviewing the first under the title "No Ordinary Novel,"[51] he objected strongly to its narrow perspective, life outside sexuality being nonexistent in it and its characters not real people but sex types. Besides, "It combines the pseudo-scientific prose of an Ellis or Freud with polysyllabic effusions and circumlocutions reminiscent of the worst bureaucratese" and the "decorous verbiage of cheap Victorian novelettes." His conclusion: "Structurally and aesthetically, this half of the book seems to me to be a failure." He admitted, however, that toward the end of the volume, the characters began to take over from the amateur sociologist and psychologist who created them, so that the story started to come to life, leaving the reviewer eager for the second. When it arrived several months later, however, he completed his judgment under the title "An Ambitious Failure,"[52] for he found the language still cliché-ridden, the dialogue stagey, the action lacking in grandeur, the characters in distinction. His conclusion: Davison wanted it to be a tract for the times, but he was too late. "If Australian sex mores still need more permissiveness, it won't come through his decorous language or bowdlerized psychology."

Others withheld final judgment. In the quarterly *Southerly*, which he edited, G. A. Wilkes concluded, after criticizing the book in detail as a "laboratory study" but crediting its author for his consistent patience and sympathy: "*The White Thorntree* is a large, challenging, awkward book that demands to be reckoned with. It may be some time before it settles into place in twentieth century Australian fiction."[53] This judgment was rendered only a few months after the book's first appearance. A. A. Phillips, speaking at a memorial ceremony shortly after Frank's death, was similarly cautious. Although by that time *The White Thorntree* had been available for a year and a half, he could only say, "We stand too close to that book to judge its literary worth—that we must leave to the verdict of time."[54]

Australian critics were inevitably confused not just by the book itself but by its having come from the same hand as *Man-Shy* and *Dusty*. Here Owen Webster, a relative newcomer to Australia from England, had an advantage, in that *The White Thorntree* was his first encounter with Frank's writing. He did not hesitate to make favorable judgments. His first conclusion was that "In the canon of Australian literature, [it] is a maverick. To instance only one if its characteristics, few writers since Lawrence, and none of them Australian, have shown such insight into the private nature of women. Undeniably, it is a remarkable book. Among traditional novels, it may be a minor masterpiece"[55] (later amended to a "flawed one").[56] After a second reading such as Frank had recommended, and a year more of reflection, reading, and living, Webster found the *Thorntree* even greater and wiser than he had first thought. He became aware of the slow accumulation of minutiae that allows no one to escape: "at first one recognizes oneself and finds an excuse to differ. Then one recognizes somebody one knows, then somebody one has heard about, then somebody one has read about. At last, by extrapolation, one acknowledges that it is all there, which inexorably includes oneself."[57] The title of this review was "Preparing for Permissiveness," indicating Webster's interest in *what* Frank said, rather than, like so many reviewers, in *how* he said it. In fact, Webster felt that an understanding of the book would promote tolerance and good will, and give us hope for a permissive society. But even he, reviewing the second volume, recognized the difficulties ahead in his title "Thorny Path."[58]

In letters to the author, which may not be quite as impartial as published reviews, poet-and-critic Dorothy Green, Australian

National University, wrote, "I have just finished reading *The White Thorntree* and wanted to tell you how deeply moving I found it." Fiction-writer Peter Cowan, University of Western Australia, went farther: "It seems to me one of the most important novels we've ever had—for itself, and for the issues it raises."[59]

Strangely, the longest and most profound study of this final novel and of Frank's earlier work as well appeared before *The White Thorntree* was officially available even in its first limited edition. It is H. P. Heseltine's "The Fellowship of All Flesh: The Fiction of Frank Dalby Davison,"[60] published in *Meanjin* more than a year before Frank's death. This thoughtful essay not only does a credible job of relating the author's first period to his second, but at this early date arrives at a reasoned, and reasonable, conclusion about the future. "How, in the end, will *The White Thorntree* affect Davison's standing in our literature? I cannot, in honesty, forsee large-scale popular or critical success for the book. It is sufficiently in harmony with the prevailing temper of criticism to recommend itself to significant numbers of the *cognoscenti*. The long-term destiny of *The White Thorntree*, I will hazard the guess, is to become one of the 'sports' of Australian literature—a huge troubling lump on its otherwise coherent surface."

Some literary people simply overlooked the book, apparently from choice, preferring to remember Frank for his first period only. John Morrison, for instance, was a frequent visitor at Folding Hills during the many years that Frank was absorbed in the *Thorntree* project, but in a recent article on Frank in those days, he never mentions it, neither the writing of it nor the publishing, which had taken place eight years before his recollections appeared. Morrison's subject is "Frank Davison the country man who gave us *Man-Shy* and *Dusty*,"[61] whom he finds "at his literary best when he is contemplating with the same warm objectivity those so-much-more complicated animals, men and women, as in his short story collection *The Road to Yesterday*"[62]—but not, it appears by omission, in his study of human sexuality.

Angus & Robertson, who not only had published all of Frank's previous works but had kept his major books continuously in print, always followed publishing custom by including in the fore matter of each a list of "other books by this author," kept up to date so that editions of *Man-Shy* after 1946, for instance, include *Dusty*, and editions of both after 1964, *The Road to Yesterday*. But in reprints of the earlier books following the appearance of *The White Thorn-*

tree, the list has not been expanded to include that new novel, though several of them have been listed in it. Possibly Angus & Robertson were deliberately ignoring it because they had not been publishers of either the first or second edition. In 1975, however, they gained the right to an edition of their own; yet in subsequent reprints of Frank's earlier books, they still have not added *The White Thorntree* to the list of his previous works. This may be an oversight—or a feeling that the author would be better advertised by the tried and true output of his first period than by this unprecedented behemoth.

CHAPTER 15

Conclusion

TEMPERAMENTALLY as well as physically, Frank Dalby Davison was a man of ups and downs—"melancholy-happy," as Marjorie Barnard once described him, and prone to "oscillate between high spirits and the dumps."[1] As to his character, she early found him to be "above everything generous,"[2] a quality that those who knew him well were to name repeatedly. John Morrison's fine reminiscent article on him in a recent *Overland* is a good a summing up of other aspects of Frank's character as we have. He remembers him as "one of the best listeners I ever met,"[3] and as being "always forthright" but "fundamentally kind and tolerant," compassionate, and "more indulgent than censorious," a critic whose avowed attitude toward reviewing was "Be as gentle as you can."[4]

On the other hand, Frank could be irascible. He was known for having exploded at public meetings, on occasion, and in later years confessed himself pleased with the memory of having twice assisted in throwing someone objectionable out of a meeting by kicking him downstairs. Marie, who described Frank as kind and gentle, also spoke of him as "magnificent in wrath," and Morrison recalled one evening at Folding Hills when, Marie having reported at bedtime that one of their cows in difficult labor might ruin their night, "Frank startled me by letting himself go in an outburst that consigned cows and all their accursed progeny to a blistering, everlasting, and decidedly obscene hell."[5]

It is Morrison who felt that Frank's personality was reflected in his work: "There aren't any all-black scoundrels in it; at the worst only a few weaklings in an interesting variety of shapes and sizes."[6] There might be some disagreement with this, though not much: Frimwade, the station agent in "A Letter to Colleen," may be a rare Davison character, but he exists—no weakling but snobbish and downright mean. Bill Connolly, in "Nobody's Kelpie" was quite gratuitously cruel. And it has been remarked that despite Frank's effort to deal evenhandedly with his sex-disturbed people in *The White Thorntree,* he conspicuously withheld all sympathy from David Munster's unsympathetic mother.

Frank once remarked to Morrison: "I've been very well treated on the strength of a very small body of work."[7] Let's look briefly at the record. He started off his career at the top, one might say, with the A.L.S. award for the best novel of the year, a thing of bits and pieces patched up by an amateur from writing he had done long before. His arrival into literary circles was sudden, but his ability and his charm soon won him many friends there, notably the Palmers, Barnard, Eldershaw, and Leonard Mann. His popularity as a person as well as his reputation as a writer put him into the president's chair of the esteemed F.A.W. for two consecutive years and for yet another term four years later. Literary friends and his own steady output got him work as a reviewer for the Sydney *Morning Herald* and later a place with the much-admired *Bulletin.* With only four slight books that could be called novels, he was given a long and appreciative treatment in M. Barnard Eldershaw's *Essays in Australian Fiction* (1938), in company with such long-established notables as Henry Handel Richardson, Katharine Susannah Prichard, Vance Palmer.[8] That same year he was accorded the right to have M.B.E. after his name for his services to literature.

The C.L.F. Fellowship for 1940 was an honor as well as a financial aid, as was the *Argus* award for *Dusty* in 1946. His later application for a fellowship in 1951 "to write a novel of life in Sydney" was refused, but a lifetime literary pension beginning at age seventy greatly eased his final years of work on that book.

Frank had the pleasure, and profit, of seeing three of his early books (*Man-Shy, Children of the Dark People,* and *Dusty*) continually in print throughout his life, and there has been no dropping off since his death; new editions of all three have appeared in the mid-1970s, *Man-Shy* and *Dusty* in the new A & R Classics series. When a couple of dozen books of all types were published during the second world war in the paperback Australian Pocket Library to make Australia's classics available, in that period of shortages, to allied service men as well as home folks, *Man-Shy* was understandably one of the nine novels chosen. Selections from several of his early novels as well as numbers of his short stories have been extensively anthologized from the 1940s to the present.

The dinner at the Union Club at the University of Melbourne at which Frank read his notable address "Testimony of a Veteran" was in a sense the climax of his long career. He was seventy-five, and he had known a lifetime (an especially long one, since his boyhood had been cut so short) of steady hard work, first physically, in Victoria, on the battlefield, and in Queensland; then mentally, in Sydney and Melbourne; and finally, at Folding Hills, both physically and mentally mingled with intervals of ill health. But he had persevered, and at this dinner he was celebrating, and being celebrated for, two outcomes that he must often have despaired of: first, the completion of the enormous novel that he had been "wanting to write since he was a young fellow" and that had gone so far past his original expectations in size; second, its actual publication.

After the appearance of the Cugley edition of *The White Thorntree* in 1968, Frank lovingly revised it in preparation for the two Ure Smith volumes. The first of these appeared in April, 1970, to his infinite delight and satisfaction, and he may have settled right down to yet another stint of revision, for a Publisher's Note in the A & R Classics edition of 1975 mentions that it incorporates all of the author's corrections to *both* of the earlier editions. But he did not live to have volume two, published in September, in his hands. Consequently he never knew, but would surely have been touched had he known, that to his own dedication of the first volume "to the reader," the publisher had added one in the posthumous second volume "to the author."

Frank once said, "I am a writer; therefore I write."[9] He was not only revising but writing, almost to the end. He may have paused briefly, after *Thorntree* was complete, to receive the congratulations of his friends, but he was not long idle. He began work on a typescript "The Folding Hills," which was to recount in detail his life there with Marie. It was never finished. His health, which had been steadily declining, grew worse; he had developed lung cancer, but having always lived in harmony with nature, he would tolerate no extraordinary medical means to prolong existence. He died in Diamond Valley Hospital, Victoria, May 24, 1970, a month before his seventy-seventh birthday.

His funeral was as he would have wished it, with old friends, his favorite flowers (always yellow), music, and a copy of the private edition of *The White Thorntree* (in a new cover) in the casket beside his body. Later, cremation, and under a full moon at midnight on June 22, a month after his death, Marie faithfully carried out his last instructions: she went down to the box tree in a field not far from their house, and there, where together they had earlier buried their beloved dog Sheila, she scattered Frank's ashes.

It was no accident that all of Fred Davison's magazines and half his books had "Australia" in the title, in some form, and this devotion to his native land certainly rubbed off on his son. We have seen how as man and critic Frank worked throughout his first period to further the cause of Australian letters, and how as writer he limited himself almost entirely to Australian subjects. He never travelled abroad after his return from the war; when the Palmers were going to Europe in 1935, he expressed a fervent wish that he himself could spend a year there—but his objective was not to learn of Europe but to be helped in getting Australia into perspective!

Scarcely a word in all his writing of those five impressionable years in the United States; the only thing he "published" while he was there was a long poem about Australia. England and Europe fared little better from his pen, appearing only in wartime, and then, in "Fathers and Sons," surrounded by an Australian frame; and Palestine, in *The Wells of Beersheba*, is only a backdrop against which we watch the heroism of Australian horses and men. All of the rest of Frank's early writing is not only written by a native son but is itself pure dyed-in-the-merino Australian, in settings, in characters, and most of all, in spirit.

This is why, quite apart from the subject matter of *The White Thorntree*, the Davison devotee may find himself ill at ease with this late novel. Set in Sydney, yes, with a long character list of Australians, but there is nothing to identify them as such; the entire book could just as well have been written of a big city in, say, the United States—maybe better. It is as though one must balance the land, the animals, the people—the very soul of Australia—in Frank's first period against this monumental aberration of his second.

Time, as the critics unwilling to commit themselves concluded of *The White Thorntree*, will tell. But the odds seem at the moment to be heavy on the side of Frank Dalby Davison's continuing to be known as a writer for his first period rather than his second—on the power of that red heifer and that half-dingo dog (not to mention those cavalry horses and even the dark people's children) to outweigh in reader affection and esteem all the sex in Sydney. Some part of his public will think all the more highly of him for that last twenty years' work; and those who do not will forgive him for it, in view of his notable earlier contributions to his country's literature.

Notes and References

Chapter One

1. Walter Murdock, *Alfred Deakin: A Sketch* (London, 1923).
2. *The Advance Australia*, vol. 1, no. 1 (January 26, 1897), p. 13.
3. Ibid. As late as August 1, 1898, there still appears a complaint that this "boasted literary association" is offering prizes of £750 cycling, only £100 for art and literature.
4. Ibid., p. 6.
5. P. 1.
6. Webster interview, March 18 - 19, 1967, Archival Transcript, Tape 1.
7. Quoted from a letter from Frank by his friend, critic T. Inglis Moore, in his *Social Patterns in Australian Literature* (Sydney, 1971), p. 85.
8. Barnes interview, *Westerly*, no. 3, 1967, p. 19.
9. Webster interview, March 18 - 19, 1967, Archival Transcript, Tape 1, p. 7.
10. FDD to D. C. Meacham, September 5, 1942.
11. Webster interview, March 18 - 19, 1967, Archival Transcript, Tape 2, p. 8.
12. Ibid., p. 4.
13. Ibid., p. 9.

Chapter Two

1. *Australian Post*, September 1, 1920, p. 32.
2. Ibid., December 7, 1920, p. 36.
3. Ibid., January 7, 1921, p. 14.
4. Ibid., October 1, 1920, p. 17.
5. Ibid., January 7, 1921, pp. 17 - 20.
6. Ibid., December 7, 1920, pp. 1 - 4, 44 - 45.
7. Ibid., October 1, 1920, pp. 1 - 2, 43 - 44. This title continues for the November 7 installment, pp. 33 - 37. The third is "T. Bone's Horse Deal," December 7, 15 - 16, 34 - 35; the fourth, "In South-West Queensland," January 7, 1921, pp. 25 - 29; the fifth and last, "Corned Beef and—Goannas," February 7, pp. 21 - 24.
8. A "new chum" was a newcomer to Australia, an amateur, at this period usually English.
9. *Australian Post*, December 7, 1920, p. 16.
10. Ibid., February 7, 1921, p. 22.

11. Ibid., p. 1.

12. Owen Webster, "The Crown Lands Ranger, Jack Cumming and Frank Dalby Davison," *Overland*, no. 61, 1975, p. 12.

13. Webster interview, March 18 - 19, 1967, Archival Transcript, Tape 3, p. 4.

14. Ibid., p. 1.

15. Ibid., p. 5.

16. FDD to D. C. Meacham, August 22, 1942.

Chapter Three

1. *Australian*, March, 1923, pp. 11 - 16. The "laughing jackass" here is the kookaburra, an Australian kingfisher.

2. Ibid., pp. 54 - 55.

3. Ibid., pp. 23 - 26.

4. Ibid., May, 1923, pp. 18 - 19.

5. Ibid., June, 1923, pp. 31 - 36.

6. *Australia*, August, 1923, pp. 6 - 24. The change of magazine title from the *Australian* to *Australia* began with the July, 1923 issue.

7. Ibid., July, 1923, pp. 5 - 21.

8. Ibid., September, 1923, pp. 5 - 14.

9. Ibid., March, 1924, pp. 3 - 12.

10. Ibid., October, 1923, pp. 7 - 13.

11. Ibid., April, 1923, p. 24.

12. Ibid., March, 1923, pp. 41 - 49.

13. Ibid., April, 1924, pp. 5 - 14.

14. Ibid., June, 1923, pp. 7 - 17.

15. Ibid., September, 1924, pp. 52 - 72.

16. FDD to D. C. Meacham, October 20, 1942.

Chapter Four

1. FDD to D. C. Meacham, October 20, 1942.

2. Webster interview, March 18 - 19, 1967, Archival Transcript, Tape 3, p. 13.

3. MB to NP, July 19, 1932.

4. MB to NP, September 16, 1932.

5. M. Barnard Eldershaw (Melbourne), p. 52.

6. *Man-Shy* (Sydney, 1933), p. 1.

7. Ibid., p. 2.

8. Ibid., p. 4.

9. Ibid., p. 5.

10. Ibid., p. 11.

11. Ibid.

12. Ibid., p. 12.

13. Ibid., p. 19.

14. Ibid., p. 48.
15. Ibid., p. 53.
16. Ibid., p. 32.
17. Ibid., pp. 28 - 29.
18. Ibid., p. 59.
19. Ibid., p. 61.
20. Ibid., pp. 74 - 75.
21. Ibid., p. 85.
22. Ibid., p. 89.
23. Ibid., p. 94.
24. Ibid., p. 100.
25. Ibid., p. 102.
26. Ibid., p. 104.
27. Ibid., p. 114.
28. Ibid., p. 115.
29. Ibid., p. 122.
30. Ibid., p. 124.
31. Ibid., p. 135.
32. Ibid., pp. 143 - 44.
33. MB to NP, September 16, 1932.
34. FDD to D. C. Meacham, August 22, 1942.
35. Ibid.
36. Webster interview, March 18 - 19, 1967, Archival Transcript, Tape 3, p. 11.
37. "One in Ten Thousand," *Australia*, November, 1923, pp. 16 - 22.
38. FDD to D. C. Meacham, October 10, 1942.
39. Ibid.
40. She was created D.B.E. (Dame of the Order of the British Empire) in 1936 for her contribution to literature.
41. Pp. 167 - 68.

Chapter Five

1. "Testimony of a Veteran," *Southerly*, no. 2, 1969, p. 85.
2. *Forever Morning* (Sydney, 1931), p. 97.
3. Ibid., p. 103.
4. *Australia*, December, 1924, p. 56.

Chapter Six

1. "Dalby" is furthermore the name of a fishing village on the Isle of Man, where Frank's mother's people, who came out to Australia at the time of the gold rush there, had originated.
2. Author's Note, *The Road to Yesterday* (Sydney, 1964).
3. FDD to D. C. Meacham, September 5, 1942.

4. FDD to NP (for V&N), February 25, 1933.

5. Ibid.

6. *The Wells of Beersheba* (Sydney, 1947), p. 3.

7. Ibid., p. 6. These four words gain strength as a single paragraph.

8. Ibid., p. 9.

9. Ibid., pp. 9 - 10. This five-word paragraph gains further emphasis by ending a section.

10. Ibid., p. 12.

11. Ibid., pp. 18 - 19.

12. Ibid., p. 22.

13. Ibid., p. 30.

14. Ibid., p. 31.

15. Ibid., pp. 31 - 32.

16. Ibid., p. 41.

17. Ibid., p. 42.

18. Ibid., p. 45. A "township" is a town, in Australia; the "bush," its back country.

19. Ibid., p. 48. This last paragraph marks the first statement of what is recognized as the unifying theme throughout Frank's writing. See "Conclusion" to M. Barnard Eldershaw's essay on him *(Essays in Australian Fiction*, Melbourne, 1938, pp. 77 - 80) for an early view, and H. P. Heseltine's "The Fellowship of All Flesh: The Fiction of Frank Dalby Davison," *Meanjin*, no. 3, 1968, pp. 275 - 290, for an extensive late one.

20. Ibid., p. 53.

21. Ibid., p. 54.

22. Ibid., p. 57.

23. Ibid., p. 61.

24. Ibid., p. 64.

25. Ibid., p. 65.

26. FDD to D. C. Meacham, September 5, 1942.

Chapter Seven

1. FDD to D. C. Meacham, August 22, 1942.

2. *Blue Coast Caravan* (Sydney, 1935).

3. FDD to VP, August 12, 1934.

4. FDD to VP, n.d., pencilled "December 1934."

5. MB to VP, March 4, 1935. "Snakes and Ladders" is an English game popular among children in Australia at this time, a game of "ups and downs" in which a throw of the dice may send one's counter to a square from which it is permitted to be moved the length of a ladder toward victory or down the length of a snake toward defeat.

6. *Blue Coast Caravan*, p. 179.

7. Ibid., p. 166.

8. Ibid., p. 40.

9. Ibid., p. 215.

10. Ibid., p. 63.
11. Ibid., p. 204.
12. Ibid., p. 8.
13. Ibid., pp. 8 - 9.
14. FDD to VP, August 12, 1934.
15. *Blue Coast Caravan*, p. 52.
16. FDD to VP, August 12, 1934.
17. FDD to D. C. Meacham, August 22, 1942.
18. MB to VP, February 14, 1938.

Chapter Eight

1. MB to VP, October 8, 1935.
2. *Caribbean Interlude* (Sydney, 1936), p. 27.
3. Ibid., pp. 35 - 36.
4. Ibid., p. 116.
5. Ibid., p. 214.
6. Ibid., p. 30 - 31.
7. Ibid., p. 34.
8. Ibid., p. 109.
9. Ibid., pp. 83 - 84.
10. A wallaby is a small kangaroo. "Nuggety" is strong, tough. A dingo is a wild native dog of Australia. To "fossick" is to rummage about. Bush is the interior of the country, the backwoods.
11. *Caribbean Interlude*, p. 23.
12. Ibid., p. 22.
13. Ibid., p. 149.
14. Ibid., pp. 158 - 59.
15. Ibid., p. 99.
16. Ibid., p. 94.
17. Ibid., p. 152. The discovery by George Bass in 1798 of the strait that now bears his name proved that Tasmania was an island, not part of the Australian continent.
18. Ibid., p. 133.
19. Ibid., p. 247.
20. Ibid., p. 104. "Swot" is British slang for "cram."
21. Ibid., p. 33.
22. Ibid., p. 231.
23. FDD to D. C. Meacham, August 22, 1942.
24. Ibid., September 5, 1942.
25. Webster interview, March 18 - 19, 1967, Archival Transcript, Tape 1, p. 8.

Chapter Nine

1. FDD to N & VP, June 1, 1936.

2. MB to NP, July 13, 1936.

3. *Children of the Dark People* (Sydney, 1950), "Acknowledgments" in front matter.

4. Ibid., p. 1.

5. Ibid., p. 11.

6. Ibid., p. 22.

7. Ibid.

8. Ibid., p. 218.

9. Ibid., p. 187.

10. FDD to D. C. Meacham, August 22, 1942.

Chapter Ten

1. FDD to VP, December 28, 1932.

2. FDD to V and NP, November (no day), 1932.

3. FDD to VP, December 28, 1932.

4. Ibid. "Plurry" is a euphemism for the adjective that the Australians, like the English, regard as the height of vulgar sacrilege—"bloody."

5. FDD to NP, March 2, 1934.

6. FDD to NP, April 8, 1934.

7. FDD to VP, September 14, 1934.

8. FDD to NP, October 26, 1932.

9. FDD to NP, February 25, 1933.

10. FDD to NP, November 2, 1933.

11. FDD to NP, February 25, 1933.

12. FDD to NP, May 10, 1939.

13. FDD to NP, November 2, 1933.

14. FDD to NP, April 8, 1934.

15. HHR to NP, October 30, 1932.

16. FDD to NP, September 4, 1933.

17. Ibid.

18. FDD to NP, November 2, 1933.

19. FDD to V and NP, June 1, 1936.

20. *Bulletin*, January 6, 1937, pp. 2, 9.

21. Ibid., June 9, 1937, p. 2.

22. FDD to VP, August 7, 1937.

23. *Bulletin*, January 20, 1937, p. 2.

24. Ibid., March 24, 1937, p. 8.

25. Ibid., April 14, 1937, p. 8.

26. Ibid., November 11, 1936, p. 2.

27. Ibid., October 27, 1937, p. 2. Paterson's early ballads appeared in the *Bulletin* signed "The Banjo."

28. "Australian Writers Come to Maturity," *Australia, National Journal*, No. 2, 1939, pp. 68 - 69.

29. "Australian Fiction Today," *Australian Mercury*, July 1935, pp. 57 - 61.

30. "What Is Literature?" *Australian Writers Speak* (Sydney, 1942), pp. 11 - 20.

31. Ibid., p. 20.

32. "Some Aspects of Australian Literary Criticism," in Clement Semmler & Derek Whitelock, eds., *Literary Australia* (Melbourne, 1966), pp. 51 - 68.

33. "Salute to the Beast," *Home Annual*, October 16, 1939, p. 34.

34. Ibid., p. 35.

35. Ibid.

36. Ibid., p. 82.

37. "Still Waters of the West," *Home Annual*, October 15, 1940, p. 45.

38. Ibid., p. 46.

39. Ibid.

40. Ibid., p. 47.

41. *While Freedom Lives*, p. 1b.

42. Ibid., p. 21b.

43. Ibid., p. 4.

44. Ibid., p. 22b.

45. Ibid., p. 24b.

46. An M.B.E. is a Member (the fifth and lowest rank) of the Excellent Order of the British Empire, one of the awards instituted a generation earlier by George V in recognition of important services to the British Empire. Some of Frank's friends expected him, as a vociferously independent Australian, to refuse this honor, but he later claimed to have been persuaded to accept lest a refusal stand in the way of further awards to other authors. (Webster interview, March 18 - 19, 1967, Archival Transcript, Tape 4, p. 5.) At the time, however, he was reported as "immensely pleased" (MB to VP, February 14, 1938).

47. FDD to D. C. Meacham, August 22, 1942.

48. Webster interview, March 18 - 19, 1967, Archival Transcript, Tape 4, p. 9.

49. "Australian Writers Come to Maturity," *Australia, National Journal*, No. 2, 1939, pp. 68 - 69.

50. FDD to VP, August 7, 1939.

51. FDD to VP, February 11, 1940.

52. FDD to VP, October 23, 1940.

53. *Soviet Culture*, N.S.W. Aid Russia Committee (Sydney, 1942), pp. 73 - 77.

54. Ibid., pp. 78 - 85.

55. Ibid., pp. 86 - 89.

Chapter Eleven

1. *The Road to Yesterday* (Sydney, 1968), Author's Note.

2. (Melbourne), p. 41.

3. Five successive monthly installments, October 1, 1920, to February 7, 1921.

4. "Pommy" is short for "pomegranate," a nickname given to the Englishmen who came to try their luck in Australia, because of their typically pink cheeks.

5. *The Woman at the Mill* (Sydney, 1940), p. 241.

6. Ibid., p. 243. "Cockatoo" implies the ineptness of a small farmer.

7. Ibid., p. 246.

8. Ibid., p. 251.

9. "Graft" being Australian slang for manual labor, these characters are "genuine Australian hard workers."

10. *The Woman at the Mill*, p. 220.

11. FDD to D. C. Meacham, October 20, 1942.

12. Ibid.

13. *The Woman at the Mill*, p. 3.

14. Ibid., p. 16.

15. Ibid., pp. 17 - 18.

16. Ibid., p. 65.

17. Ibid., p. 195.

18. Ibid., p. 212.

19. Ibid., pp. 212 - 13.

20. Ibid., p. 227.

21. Ibid., p. 231.

22. Ibid., p. 236.

23. Ibid., p. 232.

24. Ibid., p. 233.

25. Ibid., p. 234.

26. Ibid., p. 236.

27. Ibid., p. 237.

28. Ibid., p. 239.

29. "The Night Watch," *Australian Writers' Annual*, p. 16.

30. Ibid., p. 21.

31. Ibid.

32. *The Woman at the Mill*, p. 97.

33. Ibid., p. 84.

34. Ibid., p. 90.

35. (Sydney), p. 262.

36. *The Woman at the Mill*, p. 39.

37. Ibid., p. 41. "Gin" is the Australian word for an aboriginal woman.

38. Ibid., p. 45.

39. Ibid., p. 48. A goanna is a large Australian lizard.

40. Ibid.

41. Ibid., pp. 191 - 92.

42. Ibid., p. 119.

43. Ibid., pp. 118 - 19.

44. Ibid., p. 137.
45. Ibid., p. 138.
46. Ibid., pp. 138 - 39.
47. Ibid., p. 139.
48. Ibid., p. 104.
49. Ibid., p. 112.
50. Ibid., p. 113.
51. Ibid., p. 140.
52. Ibid., p. 142.
53. Ibid., p. 143.
54. Ibid., p. 144.
55. Ibid., p. 155.
56. FDD to D. C. Meacham, August 22, 1942.
57. FDD to D. C. Meacham, October 20, 1942.
58. FDD to NP, October 26, 1932.
59. Frank also included something virtually unknown in the history of *Coast to Coast*—several pages of introduction to the volume, deplored by his friend Marjorie Bernard as a mistake, being both "pedagogic and apologetic" (MB to NP, August 23, 1944).
60. FDD, ed., *Coast to Coast 1943* (Sydney, 1944), p. 241.
61. *The Road to Yesterday* (Sydney, 1968), p. 129.
62. Ibid., p. 52.
63. Ibid. pp. 95 - 96. (*The Woman at the Mill*, p. 51.)
64. *The Woman at the Mill*, Author's Note. See p. 000 here.
65. *The Road to Yesterday*, Author's Note.
66. Ibid., p. 241.
67. Ibid., p. 244.
68. Ibid., pp. 244 - 45.
69. Ibid., p. 240.
70. Ibid.
71. Ibid., p. 249.
72. Ibid., p. 248.
73. Ibid., p. 262.
74. Ibid., p. 256.
75. Ibid., p. 254.
76. Ibid., pp. 264 - 65.
77. Ibid., p. 265

Chapter Twelve

1. FDD to VP, February 11, 1940.
2. Ibid.
3. FDD to NP, February 16, 1941.
4. *Public Enemy No. 1*, p. 18.
5. Typescript (1969) toward projected work to be entitled *The Folding Hills*. Marie was indeed an "accomplished dancer," having done a good

deal of exhibition ballroom dancing.

6. Ibid.
7. FDD to NP, April 13, 1944.
8. FDD to VP, n.d., pencilled "1944."
9. "Testimony of a Veteran," *Southerly*, no. 2, 1969, p. 86.
10. *Dusty* (Sydney, 1954), p. 46.
11. Ibid., p. 63.
12. Ibid., p. 65.
13. Ibid., p. 72.
14. Ibid., pp. 76 - 77.
15. Ibid., p. 104.
16. Ibid., p. 164.
17. Ibid., p. 170.
18. Ibid., p. 210.
19. Ibid., p. 212.
20. Ibid., p. 240.
21. Ibid., p. 242.
22. "The Killer," *Australia*, June 1923, p. 17.
23. Ibid.
24. Ibid.
25. *Meanjin*, no. 4, 1946, p. 325.
26. *Meanjin*, no. 3, 1946, p. 245.
27. *Meanjin*, no. 4, 1947, p. 250.
28. *Meanjin*, no. 1, 1947, p. 37.
29. "Vance Palmer and His Writing," *Meanjin*, no. 1, 1948, pp. 10 - 27.
30. "Vance Palmer," *Walkabout*, August 1, 1950, p. 36.

Chapter Thirteen

1. Typescript (1969) for projected book *The Folding Hills*, lent by Marie Davison.
2. Ibid.
3. Ibid.
4. Ibid. A "hatter" is Australian for one who becomes eccentric from living alone in a remote area.
5. Ibid.
6. Ibid.
7. Ibid.
8. FDD to VP, August 17 (1949 in pencil).
9. *Argus*, Melbourne, July 22, 1950, p. 2.
10. "Bush Diary," *Argus*, July 24, 1950, p. 2.
11. Ibid., July 26, 1950, p. 2.
12. Ibid., August 8, 1950, p. 2.
13. *Argus*, October 18, 1950, p. 2.
14. Typescript for *The Folding Hills*. The feature ran for a 75-day

period, but only 67 installments appeared, as Frank missed a scattering of days throughout.

15. *Westerly*, no. 3, 1967, p. 24.

16. Ibid., p. 25.

17. Typescript for *The Folding Hills*.

18. Ibid.

19. Ibid.

20. "Frank Davison," *Overland*, no. 65, 1976, p. 24.

21. FDD to NP, February 19, 1951.

22. FDD to NP, July 8, 1951.

23. FDD to NP, October 22, 1951.

24. FDD to VP, August 29, 1958.

25. FDD to VP, May 24, 1959.

26. FDD to NP, April 20, 1960.

27. FDD to NP, March 7, 1961.

28. FDD to NP, November 13, 1961.

29. The rejection would have come as no surprise to Frank, as he had added to Nettie on November 13: "I don't expect it will be considered suitable for local publication." After the word arrived, he wrote her further on November 30 that he "gathered" that editor George Ferguson regarded it as "a most regrettable piece of literature." Yet a year and a half later, he reported that Ferguson wanted to see the whole thing when it was finished, on the grounds of having been too involved to give it proper attention before (he had had it three months) (FDD to NP, July 7, 1963). But nothing came of this, either.

30. Melbourne, p. 36.

31. FDD to NP, November 13, 1961.

32. "Testimony of a Veteran," *Southerly*, no. 2, 1969, p. 87.

33. FDD to NP, July 7, 1963.

34. FDD to NP, June 27, 1964.

35. "Testimony of a Veteran," *Southerly*, no. 2, 1969, pp. 88 - 89.

36. Ibid., pp. 89 - 90.

37. *The White Thorntree* (Sydney, 1970), Publisher's Note in front matter, vol. 1, p. vii.

Chapter Fourteen

1. "Testimony of a Veteran," *Southerly*, no. 2, 1969, p. 86.

2. Ibid., p. 85.

3. Ibid., p. 86.

4. Ibid., p. 88.

5. Ibid., p. 83.

6. Ibid., p. 88.

7. *Forever Morning* (Sydney, 1931), p. 309.

8. *Caribbean Interlude* (Sydney, 1936), p. 31.

9. *The Road to Yesterday* (Sydney, 1968), p. 245.

10. *The Woman at the Mill* (Sydney, 1940), p. 26.
11. Ibid., pp. 26 - 27.
12. Ibid., p. 30.
13. Ibid., p. 150.
14. Ibid., pp. 153 - 54.
15. Ibid., pp. 128 - 29.
16. Ibid., p. 137.
17. Ibid., p. 128.
18. Ibid., p. 211.
19. Ibid.
20. Ibid., p. 212.
21. Ibid., p. 213.
22. *The Road to Yesterday*, p. 119.
23. *The Woman at the Mill*, p. 39.
24. Ibid., p. 45.
25. Ibid., p. 232.
26. Ibid., p. 235.
27. "Testimony of a Veteran," *Southerly*, no. 2, 1969, p. 91.
28. *The White Thorntree* (Sydney, 1970), "Foreword," vols. 1 & 2, p. xi.
29. Ibid., vol. 1, p. xiii.
30. Ibid., p. 228.
31. Ibid., p. 255.
32. Ibid., p. 303.
33. Ibid., p. 306.
34. Ibid., vol. 2, p. 98.
35. FDD to VP, August 29, 1958.
36. *The White Thorntree*, vol. 2, pp. 535 - 36. Frank could not recall later where he had come across this pregnant comparison.
37. Ibid., "Foreword," vols. 1 and 2, p. xiii.
38. Vivian Smith feels that *The White Thorntree* is one of the long Australian novels of this century which by excessive documentation is almost aesthetically nullified. He has a point. (*Vance and Nettie Palmer*, Boston, 1975, p. 113.)
39. *The White Thorntree*, Publisher's Note, vol. 1, p. vii.
40. As a case in point, I recently discovered that one of the largest collections of Australiana in the United States contains all of Frank's books, even the pamphlet *While Freedom Lives*—except for the first volume of *The White Thorntree*, which was probably unavailable by the time the second was obtained. I myself owned volume 2 long before I could locate a copy of volume 1 and start reading.
41. *The White Thorntree*, vol. 2, p. 392.
42. Ibid., vol. 1, pp. 7 - 8.
43. Ibid., p. 314.
44. Ibid., vol. 2, p. 28.
45. Ibid., vol. 1, p. 174.
46. Ibid., p. 5.

47. FDD to D. C. Meacham, August 22, 1942.
48. Stuart Sayers, "Making Two from One," *Age*, April 25, 1970, p. 15.
49. Owen Webster, *Bulletin*, May 2, 1970, p. 54.
50. Sydney *Morning Herald*, January 11, 1969, p. 19.
51. Canberra *Times*, May 2, 1970.
52. Ibid., October 3, 1970, p. 12.
53. "Writer and Reader," *Southerly*, no. 2, 1969, p. 156.
54. *Meanjin*, no. 2, 1970, p. 252.
55. "Frank Davison's Magnum Opus Has a Soft Sell-out," *Bulletin*, July 5, 1969, p. 44.
56. "Preparing for Permissiveness," *Bulletin*, May 2, 1950, p. 54.
57. Ibid., p. 55.
58. *Bulletin*, October 10, 1970, pp. 53 - 54.
59. Both quoted on the dust covers of both volumes of the Ure Smith edition of *The White Thorntree* (1970).
60. *Meanjin*, no. 3, 1968, pp. 275 - 290.
61. "Frank Davison," *Overland*, no. 65, 1976, p. 24. Morrison had earlier written an acount of the writing and publishing of *The White Thorntree* for Melbourne's *Age*, but gave no account of its contents, as it had already been reviewed in that paper ("So Worth Saying," May 9, 1970).
62. Ibid., p. 25.

Chapter Fifteen

1. MB to NP, April 29, 1940.
2. MB to NP, April 26, 1934. Marie was proud that toward the end of his life Frank *gave* his papers to the National Library, whereas the Palmers had *sold* it his letters!
3. John Morrison, "Frank Davison," *Overland*, no. 64, 1976, p. 24.
4. Ibid., p. 23.
5. Ibid.
6. Ibid.
7. Ibid., p. 25. This was before *The White Thorntree* doubled his output.
8. On the question of whether or not he deserved this distinction, see my comment on two of the perils besetting Australian criticism (p. 95). Before the book was published by Frank's good friends, Marjorie wrote Vance, "Sorry Frank is the bare spot in the essays. He doesn't offer much foothold to the essayist" (February 2, 1937). Recognizing this, the writers concluded that his significance was to be found "both in achievement and in promise." Up to that time his achievement had been small and uneven, compared to that of the other authors treated, and the extent to which he later fulfilled his promise, and their hopes, is debatable.
9. "Testimony of a Veteran," *Southerly*, no. 2, 1969, p. 83.

Selected Bibliography

(chronologically arranged)

PRIMARY SOURCES

1. Novels

Man-Shy. Sydney: Australian Authors Publishing Co., 1931. 2nd ed., Sydney: Angus & Robertson, 1932. Many subsequent editions at home and abroad (in England and the United States, *Red Heifer*) to this date, including Sydney: Australian Pocket Library, 1945.

Forever Morning. Sydney: Australian Authors Publishing Co., 1931. 2nd and 3rd eds. Sydney: Angus & Robertson, 1932.

The Wells of Beersheba. Sydney: Angus & Robertson, 1933. Rev. ed., Sydney: Angus & Robertson, 1947. Reprinted, again revised, in *The Road to Yesterday*. Sydney: Angus & Robertson, 1964.

Children of the Dark People. Sydney: Angus & Robertson, 1936. Numerous reissues to this date.

Dusty. Sydney, Angus & Robertson, 1946. Numerous reissues to this date.

The White Thorntree. Melbourne: The National Press, 1968, limited ed. Sydney: Ure Smith, 1970. 2 vols.

2. Collected short stories

The Woman at the Mill. Sydney: Angus & Robertson, 1940.

The Road to Yesterday. Sydney: Angus & Robertson, 1964. Pacific Books paperback no. 93, 1968; reprinted with new cover, 1970.

3. Travel

Blue Coast Caravan, with Brooke Nicholls. Sydney: Angus & Robertson, 1935.

Caribbean Interlude. Sydney: Angus & Robertson, 1936.

4. Criticism

"Australian Fiction Today" (radio talk). *Australian Mercury*, July, 1935, pp. 57 - 60.

Articles on Red Page of *Bulletin:* "Censor and Syndicate," November 12, 1963. "A New Australian Writer" (Dal Stivens), January 6, 1937. "Australian Writers: M. Barnard Eldershaw," March 24, 1937. "Australian Writers: Norman Lindsay," April 14, 1937. "A New Barnard Eldershaw" *(Plaque with Laurel)*, April 28, 1937. "Tom Collins and His Books," June 9, 1937. "Australian Literary Currents," October 27, 1937. "Deputation to Canberra," June 29, 1938.

"Australian Writers Come to Maturity." *Australia: National Journal*, no. 2, 1939, pp. 68 - 69.

"What Is Literature?" (radio talk). *Australian Writers Speak*, pp. 11 - 20. Sydney: Angus & Robertson, 1942.

"*Tomorrow and Tomorrow*" (M. Barnard Eldershaw). *Meanjin* 6:4, Summer 1947, 249 - 50.

"Vance Palmer and His Writings." Commonwealth Literary Fund lecture, University of Melbourne, July, 1947. *Meanjin* 7:1, Autumn 1948, 10 - 27.

"Vance Palmer." *Walkabout*, August 1, 1950, Our Authors' Page, p. 36.

5. Editing and prefaces

Coast to Coast 1943. Ed., with extensive preface, by FDD. Sydney: Angus & Robertson, 1944. Of all its editors, only FDD and Vance Palmer (1944) provided prefaces.

"Foreword," new issue of Mary E. Fullerton's *Bark House Days* (1921). Melbourne: Melbourne University Press (Melbourne Paperback), 1964. Appreciation of her contribution to knowledge of pioneer days.

6. Reflective essays

"Salute to the Beast." *Home Annual* (Sydney), October 16, 1939, pp. 34 - 35, 82.

"Still Waters of the West." *Home Annual* (Sydney), October 15, 1940, pp. 45 - 47.

"Bush Diary." *Argus* (Melbourne), July 22 - October 17, 1950.

"Vignettes from 'The Folding Hills.'" *Westerly*, no. 3, 1967, pp. 24 - 26.

7. Autobiographical sources

Letters to Vance and Nettie Palmer, 1932 - 1964. National Library's Palmer Collection, no. 1174.

Letters to D. C. Meacham, August - October, 1942. Library, University of Melbourne.

John Barnes's interview with FDD for the Australian Broadcasting Commission, February, 1967. *Westerly*, no. 3, 1967, pp. 16 - 20. Photographs.

Owen Webster's interview with FDD for the Australian Broadcasting Commission, March 18 - 19, 1967. Archival Transcript in Library, University of Melbourne.

Address at University of Melbourne, "Testimony of a Veteran," November 12, 1968. *Southerly*, no. 2, 1969, pp. 83 - 92.

Unfinished ms. (1969) for projected book "The Folding Hills" (courtesy of Marie Davison).

Recording of "Our First Meeting" (his and Marie's) on Gwen Dow's machine, March, 1970 (transcript courtesy of Marie Davison).

SECONDARY SOURCES

1. Books

M. BARNARD ELDERSHAW. "Frank Dalby Davison," *Essays in Australian Fiction*, pp. 41 - 80. Melbourne: Melbourne University Press, 1938. An over-generous first study of FDD's work.

E. MORRIS MILLER. *Australian Literature from Its Beginnings to 1935* (subsidiary entries to 1938). 2 vols. Vol. 1, pp. 585 - 86. Melbourne: Melbourne University Press, 1940.

COLIN RODERICK. *The Australian Novel*, pp. 251 - 252. Sydney: Wm. Brooks & Co., 1945.

NETTIE PALMER. *Fourteen Years: Extracts from a Private Journal, 1925 - 1939*, pp. 111 - 12, 126, 134, 250. Melbourne: Meanjin Press, 1948. Impressions of FDD from correspondence and conversations, 1933 - 39.

COLIN RODERICK. *An Introduction to Australian Fiction*, pp. 73 - 74, 158, 164, 177. Sydney: Angus & Robertson, 1950.

H. M. GREEN. *Australian Literature 1900 - 1950*, pp. 25 - 26, 33, 52, 54. Melbourne: Melbourne University Press, 1951.

MILES FRANKLIN. *Laughter, Not for a Cage*, p. 168. Sydney: Angus & Robertson, 1956. On *Man-Shy*.

E. MORRIS MILLER & FREDERICK T. MACARTNEY. *Australian Literature* (A Bibliography to 1938 extended to 1950), pp. 13, 15 - 16, 139 - 41. Sydney: Angus & Robertson, 1956. Includes FDD and father Fred.

FREDERICK T. MACARTNEY. *A Historical Outline of Australian Literature*, pp. 39, 43. Sydney: Angus & Robertson, 1957.

A. A. PHILLIPS. "The Family Relationship." *The Australian Tradition*, pp. 83 - 84. Melbourne: F. W. Cheshire, 1958.

CECIL HADGRAFT. *Australian Literature*, pp. 266 - 67. Melbourne: Heinemann, 1960.

H. M. GREEN. *A History of Australian Literature*, 2 vol. Vol. 2, pp. 851, 1034 - 36, 1039 - 41, 1145, 1160 - 2. Sydney: Angus & Robertson, 1961.

JOHN HETHERINGTON. "Frank Dalby Davison, A Seat in the Kitchen," *Forty-Two Faces*, pp. 36 - 41. Melbourne: F. W. Cheshire, 1962. Photograph of FDD with books and dog.

HARRY HESELTINE. "Australian Fiction since 1920," *The Literature of Australia*, ed. Geoffrey Dutton, pp. 193 - 94, 200 - 7. Penguin Books, 1964.

IAN TURNER. "The Social Setting," *The Literature of Australia*, ed. Geoffrey Dutton, p. 46. Penguin Books, 1964.

JOHN K. EWERS. *Creative Writing in Australia*, pp. 79 - 80, 157 - 58, 190. Melbourne: Georgian House, rev. ed., 1966.

L. J. Blake. *Australian Writers*, p. 143. Adelaide: Rigby, 1968.

Encyclopaedia of Australia. A. T. A. and A. M. Learmonth, comps. "Literature," vol. 5, pp. 335a, 336b, 339a, 340a. London: Frederick Warner & Co., 1968.

G. A. Wilkes. *Australian Literature: A Conspectus*, pp. 66, 71. Foundation for Australian Literary Studies, Townsville; Monograph No. 2. Sydney: Angus & Robertson, 1969.

Harry Heseltine. *Vance Palmer*, pp. 198 - 202. St. Lucia: University of Queensland Press, 1970. FDD's opinions on Palmer's work.

Hume Dow, *Frank Dalby Davison*. Pamphlet series *Australian Writers and their Work*, ed. Grahame Johnston. Melbourne: Oxford University Press, 1971. Small but thorough study.

T. Inglis Moore, *Social Patterns of Australian Literature*, pp. 2, 15, 80 - 81, 85, 135, 162, 244 - 45, 262. Sydney: Angus & Robertson, 1971.

Louise E. Rorabacher. *Marjorie Barnard and M. Barnard Eldershaw*, pp. 67, 81, 89, 113, 143 - 45, 148, 152 - 55, 165. New York: Twayne Publishers, 1973.

Vivian Smith. *Vance and Nettie Palmer*, pp. 29, 91 - 92, 101, 112 - 13. Boston: Twayne Publishers, 1975.

2. Articles on First Period

M. Barnard Eldershaw. "Australian Writers no. 3: Frank Dalby Davison." *Bulletin*, November 10, 1937, p. 50.

H. M. Green. "Australian Literature, 1936 - 40." *Southerly*, vol. 2 (April 1941), p. 17. FDD's *The Woman at the Mill* establishes him as among the two or three leading Australian short story writers today.

A. J. A. Waldock. "Our Island Story" (review of *Coast to Coast 1941*). *Southerly*, vol. 2 (November 1941). Examines FDD's subtle "Return of the Hunter" with its interesting time shifts.

W. Mulgate. Review of *Australian Writers Speak. Southerly*, vol. 4 (April 1943), p. 30. Finds FDD's answer to "What Is Literature?" personal and stimulating.

H. J. Olivers. Review of *Coast to Coast 1942. Southerly*, vol. 4 (September 1943), p. 28. Objects to length of time FDD takes to sketch the character of Con in "Transition."

Marjorie Barnard. "*Coast to Coast 1943*," ed. FDD. *Australian Women's Digest*, September 1944, pp. 12 - 13. Finds his own story, "The Good Herdsman," best.

R. G. Howarth. Reviews of ten Australian Pocket Library Books. *Southerly*, vol. 6, no. 2 (1945), pp. 11 - 12. Rare adverse criticism of *Man-Shy* and "The Road to Yesterday."

John Reed. "*Man-Shy*, A Criticism - Mainly Destructive." *Angry Penguins*, ed. Reed and Harris, 1945, pp. 167 - 68.

R. H. Morrison. "Stories of 1944" (review of *Coast to Coast 1944*). *Southerly*, vol. 7, no. 1 (1946), p. 50. Finds FDD's "The Road to Yesterday" the major story and "a little masterpiece."

O. N. BURGESS. "Human Dog." *Southerly,* vol. 8 (1947), pp. 117 - 19. Review of *Dusty.*

H. M. GREEN. "Australian Literature 1950." *Southerly,* vol. 12 (1951), p. 187. Review of *Dusty.*

KATHLEEN BARNES. Review of *The Tracks We Travel* (short story anthology ed. S. Murray Smith). *Southerly,* vol. 16 (1955), p. 39. Discussion of FDD's "Transition."

JOHN BARNES. "Lawson and the Short Story in Australia." *Westerly,* no. 2 · (July 1968), pp. 83 - 87. Finds FDD closest in manner to Lawson.

OWEN WEBSTER. "The Crown Lands Ranger, Jack Cumming and Frank Dalby Davison." *Overland,* no. 61, 1975, pp. 7 - 13. Account of this "biographer tracing the steps of Davison" in Queensland, published after Webster's death.

3. Articles on Second Period

H. P. HESELTINE. "The Fellowship of All Flesh: The Fiction of Frank Dalby Davison." *Meanjin,* no. 3, 1968, pp. 275 - 90 (with Louis Kahan sketch of FDD's head, p. 274). First serious study attempting to reconcile FDD's two periods.

MAURICE VINTNER. "Bizarre Novel as a Curiosity." Sydney *Morning Herald,* January 11, 1969, p. 19. Review of 1st ed. of *The White Thorntree.*

G. A. WILKES. "*The White Thorntree.*" *Southerly,* no. 2, 1969, pp. 153 - 56. Review of 1st ed.

OWEN WEBSTER. "Frank Davison's Magnum Opus Has a Soft Sell-out." *Bulletin,* July 5, 1969, pp. 43 - 44. Account of writing, publication, and reception of 1st ed. of *The White Thorntree.*

OWEN WEBSTER. "Frank Dalby Davison." *Overland,* no. 44, 1970, pp. 35 - 37.

JOHN McLAREN. "Harvest of Stories." *Overland,* no. 44, 1970, pp. 52 - 53. Finds *The Road to Yesterday* stories the "missing link" between the animal novels and *The White Thorntree.*

MAURICE DUNLEVY. "No Ordinary Novel." Canberra *Times,* May 2, 1970. Review of 2nd ed. of *The White Thorntree,* vol. 1.

OWEN WEBSTER. "Preparing for Permissiveness." *Bulletin,* May 2, 1970, pp. 54 - 55. Review of 2nd ed. of *The White Thorntree,* vol. 1.

JOHN MORRISON. "So Worth Saying." *Age* (Melbourne), May 9, 1970, Saturday Review, Books. Account of writing and publishing of *The White Thorntree* (no review). Picture of FDD at typewriter.

ALAN BRISSENDEN. "Sex in the Sinny Suburbs." *Advertiser* (Adelaide), May 23, 1970, p. 22. Review of 2nd ed. of *The White Thorntree,* vol. 1.

BRIAN KIERNAN. "Frank Dalby Davison, Author of *Man-Shy,* Dies at 77." *Australian,* May 25, 1970, p. 3. Obituary.

ARTHUR PHILLIPS. "Frank Dalby Davison, M.B.E.," valediction at ceremony at Ivanhoe, Melbourne, May 28, 1970. *Meanjin,* no. 2, 1970, pp. 251 - 52.

BRIAN KIERNAN. "Destroyed through Sexuality." *Australian*, June 13, 1970. Review of *The White Thorntree*.

MAURICE DUNLEVY. "An Ambitious Failure." Canberra *Times*, October 3, 1970. Review of 2nd ed. of *The White Thorntree*, vol. 2.

OWEN WEBSTER. "Thorny Path," *Bulletin*, October 10, 1970, pp. 53 - 54. Review of 2nd ed. of *The White Thorntree*, vol. 2.

JOHN MORRISON. "Frank Davison." *Overland* no. 65, 1976, pp. 23 - 25. Warm intimate tribute, but no mention, despite date, of *The White Thorntree*.

Index